YOUTH IN EUROPEAN LABOR CAMPS

Youth in European Labor Camps

A report based on an inquiry conducted for the American Youth Commission. The membership of the Commission is as follows:

POLISH LABOR SERVICE BOY BEING INTERVIEWED

Youth in European Labor Camps

By

KENNETH HOLLAND

A Report to the American Youth Commission

AMERICAN COUNCIL ON EDUCATION
WASHINGTON, D. C.
1939

Preface

WHEN the American Youth Commission was formed by the American Council of Education in September 1935 it was asked by the Council:

(a) to consider all the needs of youth and appraise the existing facilities and resources for serving those needs;
(b) to plan experiments and programs which seem to be most effective in meeting the needs; and finally
(c) to popularize and promote desirable plans of action through conferences, publications, and demonstrations, with the objective of getting something done about its findings and recommendations.

From the beginning the Commission has recognized that modern life has brought many problems in the care and education of youth that the traditional agencies are not meeting. Consequently it has been very much interested in the contributions of the Civilian Conservation Corps camps not only to the economic welfare of young people, but also to their social and educational life. Quite early in its program the Commission, with the whole-hearted support of federal officials, authorized a comprehensive study of the camps to ascertain whether their program would merit continuance, modification, or enlargement.

Since several European nations had had experience with the labor camps for youth prior to the establishment of the CCC, the Commission felt that an inquiry into foreign programs would be a valuable supplement to the study of the camps in the United States. Therefore, the Director of the Commission's CCC study, Mr. Kenneth Holland, was asked to visit the European camps and report his findings and observations. Earlier, in 1933, Mr. Holland had spent several months working alongside the youth of other countries in the labor camps of Europe. He returned to this country to become the First Corps Area Educational Adviser in the CCC, then went back to Europe in 1936 to gather material for this report. Since then Mr. Holland has received up-to-date information from many sources in regard to the camp situation abroad.

Youth in European Labor Camps takes its place in the series of studies made by the staff members of the American Youth Commission. It is not published as a statement of the attitude of the Commission toward the various systems of labor camps but as a report to the Commission and the public on the labor camps in Europe. A companion volume on the CCC camps and NYA resident centers will be published as soon as the current study of these organizations is completed.

HOMER P. RAINEY,
Director

May 1939

Foreword

SINCE the beginning of recorded history, nations have realized the importance of the welfare of their youth. Down through the ages people have recognized that the future of a nation depended on the rising generations who were eventually to take their place. Here in the United States special emphasis has long been placed on the importance of youth. Young men and women were numerous among those who first came to our shores; they founded and helped to build this country. We are characterized as a young nation.

Because of the tremendous riches with which nature has endowed the United States, it has been a land of opportunity for youth. The conquest of the vast area between the Atlantic and the Pacific challenged and gave opportunity to American youth. If work opportunities were limited in one area by crop failures or industrial depressions, the youth could always go to the frontier where land was cheap and it was possible to wrest from a bountiful nature the basic necessities of life. The frontier, however, has disappeared and when the economic depression came in 1929 the youth of the United States were affected seriously. Many were unable to find jobs, or to attend school because of the limited incomes of their parents. Some young boys became transients; others remained in their home communities to deteriorate mentally and physically, if not morally.

When Franklin D. Roosevelt was inaugurated president in 1933 the nation was confronted with the most serious unemployment problem in its history. Millions of highly skilled men with years of experience, many of them heads of families, were seeking work. It was inevitable that these men would be the first to be re-employed when job opportunities became available. Even if business should improve materially and men with families were re-established in work, there was little hope that many of the unemployed youth could obtain jobs, for young men of working age leaving school were without work experience and employers were unwilling to take inexperienced young people. A "vicious circle" was the result—youth could not obtain jobs to get work experience and without work experience employers were unwilling to hire them.

During the years immediately following the World War, several of the European nations faced conditions similar to those in the United States.

As a result, work camps for youth were developed largely under private auspices between 1920 and 1931. With the exception of the compulsory labor service of Bulgaria, which still exists, projects were conducted for only short periods during the summer and received very little if any government support. Then as the depression made the conditions of these young people even worse, the government assisted in financing some of the projects and in a few instances took over the systems and developed them for unemployed young people.

Another step in the development of the labor camps in Europe was taken as the possibility of war became more imminent and some of the systems of camps were militarized. National Socialist Germany is the outstanding example of a nation which took over a system of camps established by a republican government to care for unemployed workers, peasants, and students and incorporated them in its intensive military program. The Polish camps have also become part of the military training system of that country. In the more democratic countries of Europe, however, the emphasis has been placed on vocational and citizenship training.

As early as 1930 the attention of the Congress of the United States was called to the problem of the youth of working age, whom industry could not absorb. Various proposals to assist them were made. The late United States Senator James Couzens from Michigan proposed that the War Department be authorized to take care of the young men in existing CMTC and other army camps. These young men were not to receive military training but, under the supervision of army officers, were to work on projects which would benefit the whole of the United States.

While Franklin D. Roosevelt was still governor of the state of New York, he was well acquainted with the urgent needs of idle youth. Then, during his campaign for president he announced his intention, if elected, to meet this problem by employing young men to conserve and to restore the natural resources of this country.

As soon as President Roosevelt assumed office in 1933 he launched his plan for the Civilian Conservation Corps. At this time available information about the various systems of camps in Europe was meager and general. As the Civilian Conservation Corps developed, those in charge became increasingly interested in the camps of other countries. It was with the idea of providing the CCC officials and the general public with information on these camps that the American Youth Commission gathered the important data presented in this volume on European youth camps. By doing so the Commission has rendered a valuable service.

In America the purpose of the work camps has been definitely to carry out a peace-time program. In his message to Congress on March 21, 1933 the President said:

> I propose to create a Civilian Conservation Corps to be used in simple work, not interfering with normal employment, and confining itself to forestry, the prevention of soil erosion, flood control, and similar projects. I call your attention to the fact that this type of work is of definite, practical value, not only through the prevention of great present financial loss, but also as a means of creating future national wealth.

In the development of the Corps the importance of education and religion has been recognized, and instruction in both has been given without weakening the work program. The CCC camps are *work* camps and the value of manual labor and the work accomplished are never forgotten. Youth from the cities and industrial centers quickly adjust themselves to entirely new surroundings and learn the importance of what they are doing and what its place is in the program for the conservation of natural resources.

After six years of continuous operation of CCC camps I believe that the plan used in this country has met with general approval from the public. No opposition has arisen from either political or religious groups. No fear that the camps will become part of the military force of the nation or a powerful propaganda agency for any group has developed to any extent. The Civilian Conservation Corps has fully justified the vision of the President and the approval of the public.

Because an unlimited amount of work needs to be done in the field in which the CCC operates, I believe that as long as there is a substantial number of unemployed youth for whom private industry cannot provide employment, the federal government should assist in providing healthful and constructive work through the CCC. The thoughtful study of similar organizations in other countries presented here should be read by everyone interested in a carefully planned national program for the conservation and development of youth and natural resources in the United States.

ROBERT FECHNER,
Director, Civilian Conservation Corps

May 1939

Acknowledgment

THE material in *Youth in European Labor Camps* is based largely on the experiences of the author during the last seven years visiting, and in some cases working in, labor camps in the United States, Germany (both before Hitler and after), Denmark, Sweden, England, Wales, Switzerland, Austria, Czechoslovakia, and Holland. In the course of these visits to the camps notes on conversations, impressions, and experiences were kept. Supplementary materials have been collected from both governmental and private agencies engaged in this type of activity.

This book is not a scientific treatise on the labor camps in the various countries of Europe and is not as complete as the study of social and educational aspects of the CCC camps which the American Youth Commission has been making during the past three years. It is hoped, however, that this general description of the camps in the various foreign countries will be helpful in developing a sound labor camp program in the United States.

Assistance has been received from the diplomatic and consular representatives, and labor camp officials of the countries whose camps are considered in this volume, in collecting information on the various systems of camps and in obtaining translators of the materials in Danish, Norwegian, Finnish, Polish, Swedish, Czech, and Dutch. While this reliance on translators was necessary it has made it difficult to check the accuracy of all of the details on these countries.

International Student Service and the International Labor Office in Geneva, Switzerland, and the branch International Labor Office in Washington have helped greatly in the preparation of this volume. However, the assistance received from both the International Labor Office and International Student Service was of a purely factual nature and involved no criticism of the systems of camps in any country. Special credit should be given to Miss Hazel C. Benjamin for the service she rendered as research assistant. The staff members of the American Council on Education and the American Youth Commission also gave invaluable assistance to the author. In spite of all these able collaborators errors have probably been made in this book by the author and he takes full responsibility for them.

MAY 1939 KENNETH HOLLAND

Contents

	PAGE
Preface	vii
Foreword by Robert Fechner	ix
Acknowledgment	xii
Introduction	1
The International Voluntary Service Camps	20
The Bulgarian Labor Service	39
Work Camps in Switzerland	51
German Camps Before Hitler	70
The National Socialist Labor Service	92
The Austrian Labor Service	130
Projects for the Unemployed in Great Britain	147
The Scandinavian Countries	181
The Polish Labor Camps	206
The Czechoslovakian Labor Service	223
Work Camps in the Netherlands	234
Labor Service for Women	243
Camps in Other Countries	269
Summary and Conclusion	288
Acknowledgment for Illustrations	301

CAMP ENROLLEES

e: CCC enrollees in Pennsylvania. *Right:* unemployed in a camp near Zürich. v: California CCC enrollee

CAMP ENROLLEES

Upper left: Englishman, Ge
man, and Frenchman workin
together in an IVS camp
Rhos, Wales

Upper right: Leader of a Na
German girls camp

Left: Students in a Frienc
service camp

Below: CCC enrollees in Penn
sylvania

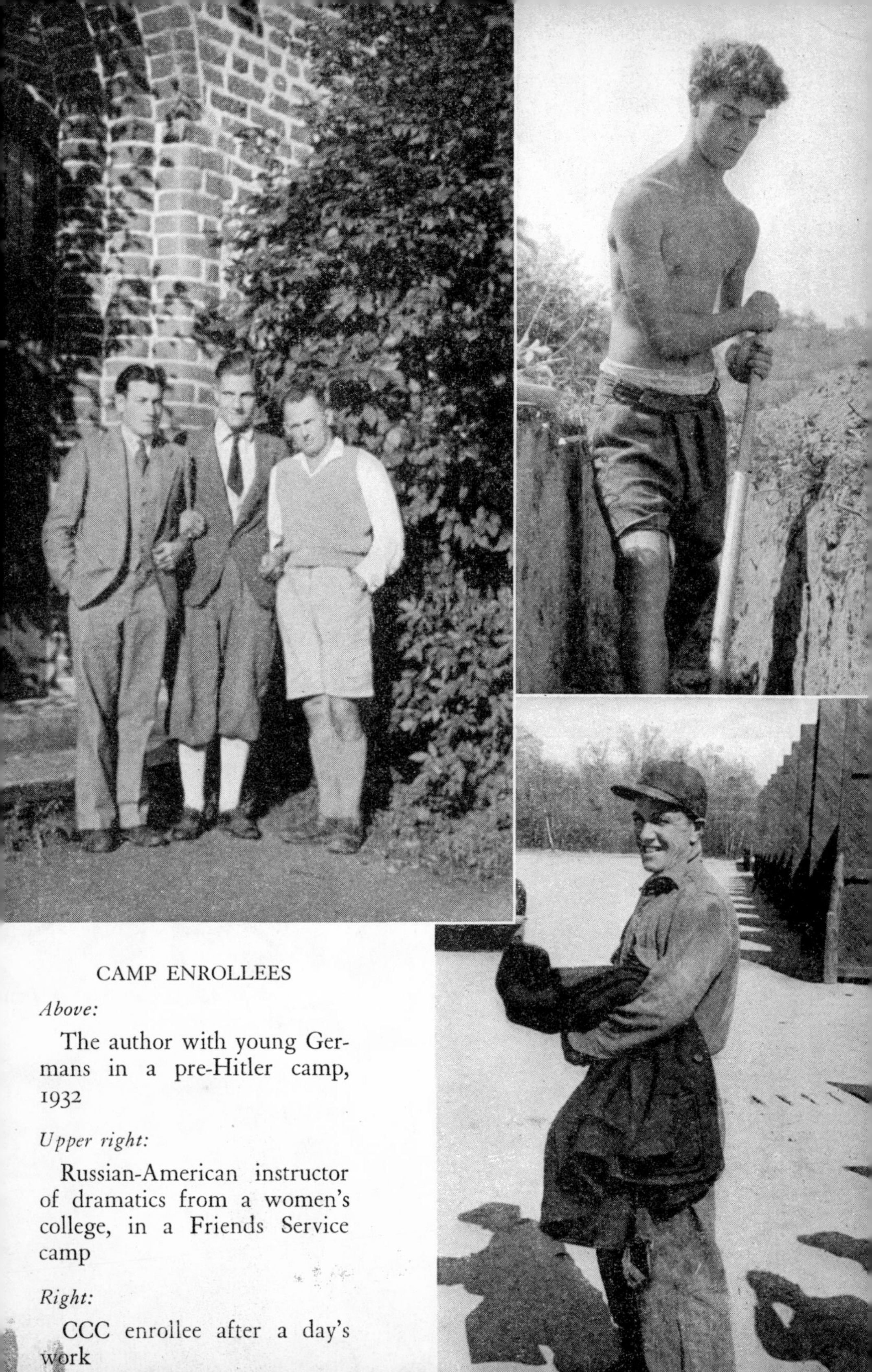

CAMP ENROLLEES

Above:

The author with young Germans in a pre-Hitler camp, 1932

Upper right:

Russian-American instructor of dramatics from a women's college, in a Friends Service camp

Right:

CCC enrollee after a day's work

SHOVELS IN THREE COUNTRIES

Left: Nazi Germany. *Above:* Unit-
States. *Below:* Poland

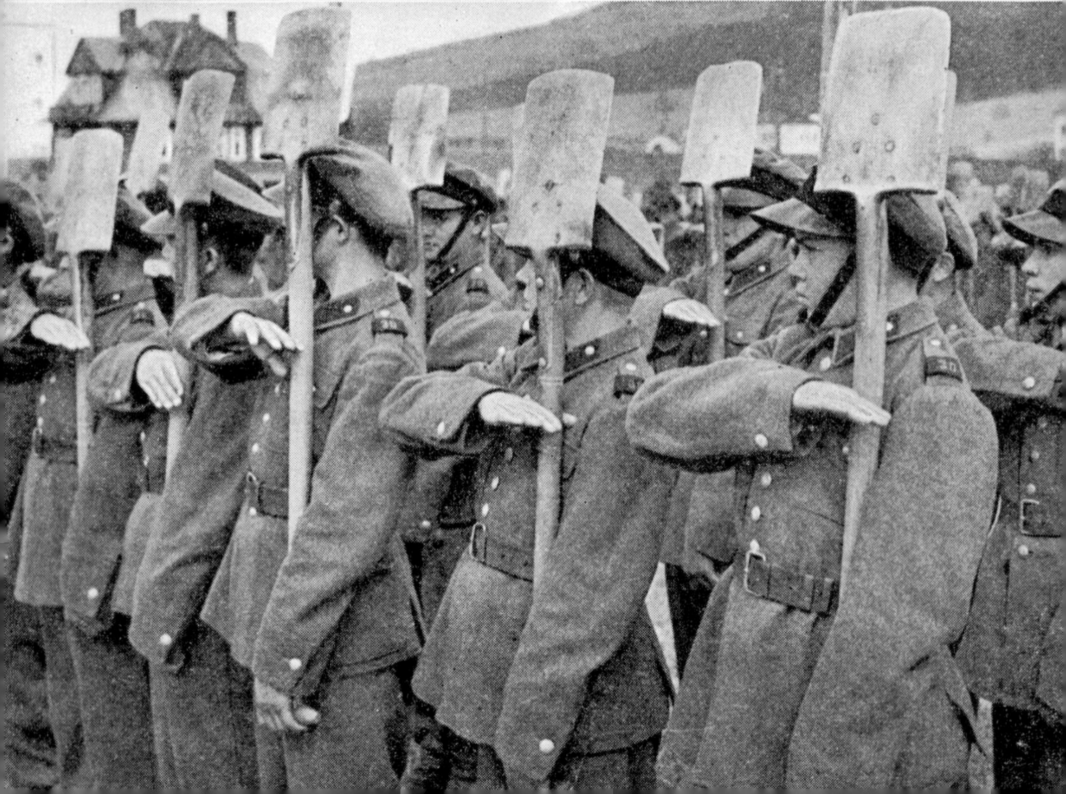

:AMP ENROLLEES

'bove and below:

Vhite and colored
oys in the CCC

ight:

re-Hitler Austrian
amp participants
loing construction
vork near Vienna

Introduction

A GROUP of barracks stands in the gray dawn, scarcely discernible through a heavy mist. Lights burn feebly yellow in the officers' quarters and from the mess hall comes the rattle of dishes and pans, barely audible through the cold damp blanket covering the camp. Suddenly a uniformed figure stalks from a door and blows furiously on a whistle. He moves from building to building, and following the shrill of his whistle are heard the sounds of creaking beds, the yawning and swearing of sleepy men, the scraping of shoes.

Fifteen minutes elapse; then a small group of figures emerge from the officers' quarters. They confer with the "top kick"; the whistle sounds again. This time the barracks pour out disheveled and unshaven men to wash and then to assemble before the mess hall for breakfast. Half an hour later the eastern sky grows lighter as the men answer to their names, and silently watch the flag raised to the top of the pole.

Duplicate this fifteen hundred times in the United States and you have seen 250,000 young men begin a working day in the Civilian Conservation Corps. Shift the scene to Germany, modify the surroundings, and substitute awakening German youth for American, and you have added nearly 300,000 more. Move on that same morning to still other countries—more than twenty in Europe—to Japan, to Australia, modifying the scenes, and you will have witnessed the start of a day for nearly three quarters of a million of the youth of the world.

Importance of Work Camp Movement

The importance of the work camp movement is better understood when it is realized that already during the past decade more than four million young men and women have spent from a few weeks to two or three years in labor camps. If the same number of young men and women remain in work camps, in ten more years about fourteen million of the youth of the world will have participated in various types of labor camp service.

While there are, of course, many other influences in the lives of these youth, the camps are an important factor. Schools and similar institutions usually occupy young people only during certain hours on weekdays, but youth in camps are influenced by one environment night and day, with the exception of a few week ends. Thus the camps are a great potential force for good or bad, depending on the way they are administered.

Labor Service in the United States

On June 28, 1937 the President of the United States approved a bill passed by Congress to extend the Civilian Conservation Corps three years "for the purpose of providing employment, as well as vocational training, for youthful citizens of the United States who are unemployed and in need of employment."[1] Thus CCC camps lost their strictly relief character and became a part of the educational and vocational program of this country. During January 1939 bills designed to establish the Corps on a permanent basis were introduced in both houses of Congress. At the present writing no action has yet been taken on these proposals. Since serious consideration is being given to the camps as permanent institutions for young men it might be valuable to know something of the experience of other nations with labor camps. How did such camps begin? What has been their development? What dangers are inherent in a system of camps? What are their constructive possibilities? These are a few of the questions that should be answered before the advantages and disadvantages of a permanent labor service in the United States can be properly weighed.

Predecessors of the CCC

The Civilian Conservation Corps was established in the United States in 1933. From eight to thirteen years prior to this date, however, work camps had existed in half a dozen European countries. Considerable thought had also been given to the camp idea by writers and thinkers of both the nineteenth century and of the pre-World War years of the twentieth.

In the works of Thomas Carlyle and John Ruskin there are passages suggestive of the idea of a labor service in the modern sense of the term. Both men sought to dignify labor and to improve the conditions under

[1] Public No. 163, Seventy-fifth Congress.

which it was performed. Living in an age faced with a serious unemployment problem, Carlyle believed that the first step of the state in assisting the workers should be the organization of the paupers, the idlers, and the unemployed. These should be provided with work by the state, and only in return for work should they receive food, clothing, and shelter. He advocated "Industrial Regiments . . . regiments not to fight the French or others, who are peaceable enough toward us, but to fight the Bogs and Wildernesses at home and abroad. . . ."[2]

Ruskin would have had the regular army, when not employed in warfare, occupied in works of peace side by side with civilians. Addressing a group of military students he once asked:

> Suppose, instead of this volunteer marching and countermarching, you were to do a little volunteer ploughing and counterploughing? It is more difficult to do it straight; the dust of the earth, so disturbed, is more grateful than for merely rhythmic footsteps. Golden cups, also, given for good ploughing, would be more suitable in color. . . . Or, conceive a little volunteer exercise with the spade, other than such as is needed for moat and breastwork, or even for the burial of the fruit of the leaden avena-seed. . . . If you were to embank Lincolnshire more stoutly against the sea? or strip the peat of Solway, or plant Plinlimmon moors with larch—then, in due season, some amateur reaping and threshing?[3]

On at least one occasion Ruskin's ideas inspired an attempt at a labor service for youth. While he was Slade Professor of Art at Oxford, he remarked on the great waste of time he had noticed in athletics. He believed that the same training of muscles could be turned to better account if the young men would combine physical training with helping a neighboring village. He also expressed the wish that Oxford young men, most of whom came from sheltered homes, might learn the meaning of a life of hard physical labor.

The suggestion was taken up by twelve Balliol men, and Ruskin obtained permission for them to build a road through a green which was much damaged by cart ruts two miles from Oxford, at Ferry Hinksey. There in the first summer term of 1874 sixty men in relays of twenty worked two days each week with pick, spade, and barrow. Later Ruskin himself often joined them, directing and encouraging their efforts. The

[2] Thomas Carlyle, *Latter-Day Pamphlets* (New York: Harper, 1850), pp. 42-43.

[3] *Nunera Pulveris* (New York: Wiley, 1872), pp. 142-43.

experiment of the "Hinksey Diggers" became the butt of jokes and cartoons. It was scoffed at by college dons and jeered at by villagers. As a matter of fact the effort was not successful. A mile or two of the road was laid out, but it led nowhere, and soon fell into disrepair. Though Ruskin himself called it the worst road in three kingdoms, he did not lose faith in the idea. In a letter to one of the diggers, he expressed the hope that some of them might "band themselves together, one day, and go out in a kind of Benedictine brotherhood to cultivate waste places and make life tolerable in our great cities for the children of the poor."[4]

In 1912 three different proposals for the establishment of labor service appeared in print in three different countries—Austria, the United States, and Germany. Josef Popper-Lynkeus, an Austrian engineer and socialist, urged that the state introduce a universal compulsory labor service in order to insure a minimum subsistence to all its citizens.[5] In the same year, William James, of Harvard University, wrote an essay entitled, "The Moral Equivalent of War," in which he advocated "a conscription of the whole youthful population to form, for a certain number of years, a part of the great army enlisted against nature." As a result of such a plan, he believed that

> . . . injustice would tend to be evened out, and numerous other goods to the commonwealth would follow. The military ideals of hardihood and discipline would be wrought into the growing fiber of the people; no one would remain blind, as the luxurious classes now are blind, to man's real relations to the globe he lives on . . . our gilded youth would be drafted off, according to their choice, to get the childishness knocked out of them and to come back into society with healthier sympathies and soberer ideas . . . they would tread the earth more proudly . . . they would be better fathers and teachers of the following generation.[6]

At about the time of the proposals of James and Popper-Lynkeus, a memorandum was prepared by a group of professors at Heidelberg College and sent to the German Minister of War suggesting an "army

[4] Frederich W. Roe, *The Social Philosophy of Carlyle and Ruskin* (New York: Harcourt, 1921), pp. 262-64.

[5] *Die allgemeine Nährpflicht als Lösung der sozialen Frage* (Dresden: Reissner, 1912). See also Fritz Wittels, *An End to Poverty* (London: Allen and Unwin, 1925).

[6] William James, *Memories and Studies* (New York: Longmans, 1912), pp. 290-91.

CAMPS IN DIFFERENT
COUNTRIES

bove:

CCC camp in California

ght:

A Swiss camp near Zür-
h

low:

British camp, Fermyn
oods

CAMPS IN DIFFERENT COUNTRIES

Above:

Camp quarters near Stockholm, Sweden

Left:

Pre-Hitler labor camp housed in an o
monastery near the Baltic

Below:

Camp Kemleten, Switzerland

of public peace" which would bring together for constructive work the different classes of German youth. Eugen Rosenstock, whose ideas were incorporated in the memorandum, believed that class divisions could be overcome by stimulating the development of a voluntary institution which, like universal military service, would bring together youth of all economic levels, but would be free from the iron discipline and social inequalities characteristic of the German army. He proposed an experimental camp of from eighty to ninety men, with about ten leaders, which would undertake some project of public benefit, and declared his belief that out of this work together would come a feeling of unity. Such a project, he said, "must create the benediction of a meaningful form, not an empty possibility like war."[7]

None of these proposals, however, resulted in the establishment of labor services such as we have today. It took the World War and its aftermath of disillusionment and unemployment of youth to launch the work camp movement. At first its program tended to realize the ideals of James, Ruskin, and Rosenstock, although the Europeans who led the movement had never read the essay of the Harvard philosopher and were not familiar with the ideas of the English writers or the Heidelberg professors.

In 1920, Pierre Ceresole, a Swiss pacifist, with the assistance of the Fellowship of Reconciliation and the Society of Friends, organized a group of young men, some of whom had fought on opposite sides during the war, and assisted in rebuilding the devastated areas of northern France. With the continued backing of the Fellowship of Reconciliation and the Society of Friends, the International Voluntary Service for Peace, as it is now called, has spread to other countries. It provides a way for conscientious objectors to demonstrate their willingness to perform constructive services in time of peace and to undergo the rigors of battle, not with other human beings, but with the forces of nature. These camps also give volunteers an opportunity to study social and economic conditions in depressed areas, and the international volunteers stand ready to assist in time of disaster or to help to complete worthy projects for the underprivileged.

---

[7] Werner Picht and Eugen Rosenstock, "Ein Landfrieden," *Im Kampf um die Erwachsenenbildung, 1912-26* (Leipzig: Quelle & Meyer, 1926), S. 2-9.

The work of the volunteer is somewhat different in each country. In Wales, volunteers have worked with picks and shovels eight hours a day to convert areas of slag heaps and mine tips into recreation centers for poor mining communities. In Switzerland, France, and Liechtenstein they have built roads, cleaned up after avalanches and floods, and helped reconstruct villages that have been burned. In India new villages are being erected on better sites in an area subject to floods. In the United States volunteers have built dams and roads, cleared lands, installed water systems, and constructed or repaired buildings in several areas of economic distress.

The youth who participate in these camps receive only their board and room for the work. In some instances volunteers have actually paid to take part in the camps. Straw ticks placed along the floor of an old school or public building serve as beds. Usually the food is plain. Those who sponsor these voluntary projects feel that they require sacrifice and toil comparable to military service, and that this work is a "moral equivalent of war" in the fullest sense of the word.

About the time the International Voluntary Service was established, Bulgaria, impoverished by the World War and disrupted because of the modification of boundaries by the Treaty of Neuilly, also began to organize a system of work camps to help extend her roads into isolated areas. These camps were also to teach voluntary group living and cooperation to young men accustomed to military training before and during the war, but for whom it was forbidden by the Treaty of Neuilly. The Bulgarian labor service attracted considerable attention, especially from German youth, and experiments with systems of camps soon began in other countries.

Like Bulgaria, Germany had been left impoverished by the World War, and needed some type of project or form of institution to provide the different classes of German youth with a common objective, and to unite them in constructive work for the state. Work camps seemed to offer these opportunities.

The German camp system, which began in 1925, developed largely because university students and professors wanted to teach the different classes of youth, who were tending toward the extremes of communism and fascism, how to live and work together. Another aim of the German movement was to give the youth who were overcrowding the universities an opportunity to work with their hands, lose their impractical tendencies, study the requirements of various types of jobs, and perhaps be guided into nonacademic and nonprofessional pursuits. In Switzerland and other countries, also in 1925, students organized summer work camps.

The succeeding trend in the labor camp movement began as the world depression deepened, and unemployment among young men and women increased. Before 1931 only a relatively small number of youth, most of them students, participated in the camps; then, as the crisis continued, private organizations, and later governments, came to look upon camps as a means of providing jobs and decent living conditions for unemployed young people.

In 1931 the Brüning government was faced with an unprecedented unemployment problem among German youth. Camps which had been developed by students, Christian organizations, and sport associations over a period of seven years were expanded and subsidized by the government on a national scale. After a few months, however, the primary purpose of providing food, shelter, and work began to give way to emphasis on the educational aspects of the program.

These camps were both successful and popular, and though the National Socialists opposed their control by the Republican government, they saw their possibilities as propaganda and training centers. In 1933, soon after Hitler became Chancellor, all existing camps were coordinated under Konstantin Hierl, the National Leader of the Labor Service. It was then only a matter of time before participation in the German labor service became an obligation of youth to the state and a regular part of training for life in the so-called "New Germany." Since July 1, 1935 all German young men of Aryan blood have been required, if physically able, to give six months of unpaid labor to public work projects and are subjected, during this time, to the full force of the remarkably efficient, though unscrupulous, propaganda machine.

Some of the smaller democratic countries—for example, Norway, Sweden, Denmark, and Switzerland—organized camps for their unemployed in 1932 and 1933. The leaders soon realized, as had those in Republican Germany, that work, food, and shelter did not fully meet the needs of the youth. They therefore began to develop camps which provided for more than the physical necessities of the participants—camps which at the same time afforded opportunity for increasing general knowledge and trained the young people for such jobs as unemployment studies revealed to be available.

The experience of the United States with the Civilian Conservation Corps, established to provide relief for unemployed young men on an emergency basis, has been similar to that of the democratic countries of Europe. Nine months after the establishment of the CCC in March of 1933, educational advisers were appointed to assist with the recreational and educational program. As the years have passed, greater emphasis has been placed on the training and educational aspects of the camps until, as we have seen, when the Seventy-fifth Congress extended them for a three-year period, it was specified that the camps were to provide general education and vocational training opportunities as well as work for youthful unemployed citizens.

Attitudes of the Public Toward the Camps

In almost every country in which labor camps have been introduced, they have been popular and have attracted considerable public attention. Although its general attitude is favorable, the public is often inadequately informed about its camps and lacks direction in planning for them. Certain groups within each nation have rather definite ideas as to the possibilities of labor camps, and these ideas are often colored by their own ideals or interests. Most important among these groups are: the pacifists, the militarists, the "emergencyists," the conservationists, and the educators.

The pacifists look upon the camps as substitutes, in the form of constructive civil service, for what they consider destructive military service. This is the attitude taken by the members of the International Voluntary Service for Peace.

The militarists see the labor camps as semimilitary or military in their functions, and usually favor camps of this type, considering them contributory to the military strength of the nation. In discussing the

CAMPS IN DIFFERENT COUNTRIES

ve:

oman Catholic labor camp boys, "Vredesteijn," Egnd, Netherlands

ht:

CC camp radio shack, Masusetts

ow:

tudent camp quarters near Furka Pass, Switzerland

CAMPS IN DIFFEREN
COUNTRIES

Above:

Side camp in pre-Hi
Austria at Nasswald

Left:

Flag salute in a CCC ca
in Ohio

Below:

A Danish castle used
camp site

enrollment of men they generally refer to it as "a test in mobilization." They compare the physical condition of the members of the camp with that of recruits of the army, and advocate a program similar to that in army camps.

In some countries the labor service, in spite of official denials, is a substitute for or supplements compulsory military training. This is true in Germany, where the compulsory labor service requires that all eighteen-year-old German youth spend six months in work camps. Two years of compulsory military service immediately follows this period. Even in the United States, where the camps are not set up as military training centers, the young men of the nation are better prepared for war service, because of the training given in these camps. Much of the routine is similar to that of a regular army camp. The men live in barracks under the supervision of army officers, are equipped with uniforms, are disciplined to camp routine, and are kept in good physical condition. The CCC camps also offer the army an opportunity to try out and train reserve officers.

In 1933 one subcommission of the League of Nations' Permanent Disarmament Commission gave considerable attention to the military aspects of labor services in different countries, especially to those of Germany and Bulgaria. With reference to the military games *(Wehrsport)* which the government representatives admitted was part of the camp program, the subcommission voted that the training given in the German labor service in question was military in character. It was pointed out that in Bulgaria institutions such as the labor service afforded an excellent opportunity to develop a spirit of discipline among the young men, to build them up physically, and to give them a feeling of unity. The subcommission, while it decided not to regard the compulsory labor service in Bulgaria as having a military character, did call attention to the general importance of this question in connection with the proposed standardization of armies.[8]

Another group looks upon the establishment of the camps as an emergency measure to assist only unemployed young people whom

[8] League of Nations, Conference for the Reduction and Limitation of Armaments, *Report of the Special Committee on Effectives to the General Commission* (Conf. D. 162. 1933. IX. 8.), Annex 1, Part III, pp. 8-15.

the economic system cannot absorb during times of depression. This group feels that the camps are merely temporary expedients, to be continued only so long as economic conditions necessitate, and that they ought not to be made so attractive to the young people that they prefer to stay in the camps rather than return to private industry. Some industrialists in the United States feel that when the depression has passed the camps should be closed, thus forcing the young men back into private industry. Before the "recession" of 1938 one American industrialist stated: "I personally think the camps are not needed today. They are not training the boys for skilled labor or semiskilled, and jobs are available for those who want to work. Private industry could absorb all of these boys."

The conservationists emphasize the work performed by the enrollees. Individuals advocating this type of camp would see the youth of the various countries, who are idle because of the scarcity of jobs, working at reforestation or building firebreaks, roads, trails, game refuges, recreation grounds, and the like. Robert Fechner, director of the CCC camps in the United States, seemed to agree with this point of view when, in his annual report for the fiscal year 1936, he stated:

> As long as there are young men, eager to work, yet idle through no fault of their own, the CCC can continue to be an effective part of our national policy, because the work in conservation which needs doing is so great as to be able to use, for many years, the services of many men.[9]

Some individuals among the conservationists feel that the preservation of natural resources should be the sole aim of any such organization as the CCC camps, and that if the program is to include more than the conservation of natural resources, it should not be in the hands of foresters. D. S. Jeffers, dean of the School of Forestry, University of Idaho, stated at a meeting of the Society of American Foresters in 1936:

> If we are to consider the CCC first, as a social program, if it is to be one of the great youth movements of this generation and this century, then, by all means, gentlemen, foresters in the Forest Service and out of the Forest Service, let's wash our hands of the CCC. . . .

---

[9] *Annual Report of the Director of Emergency Conservation Work, Fiscal Year Ending June 30, 1936*, p. 6.

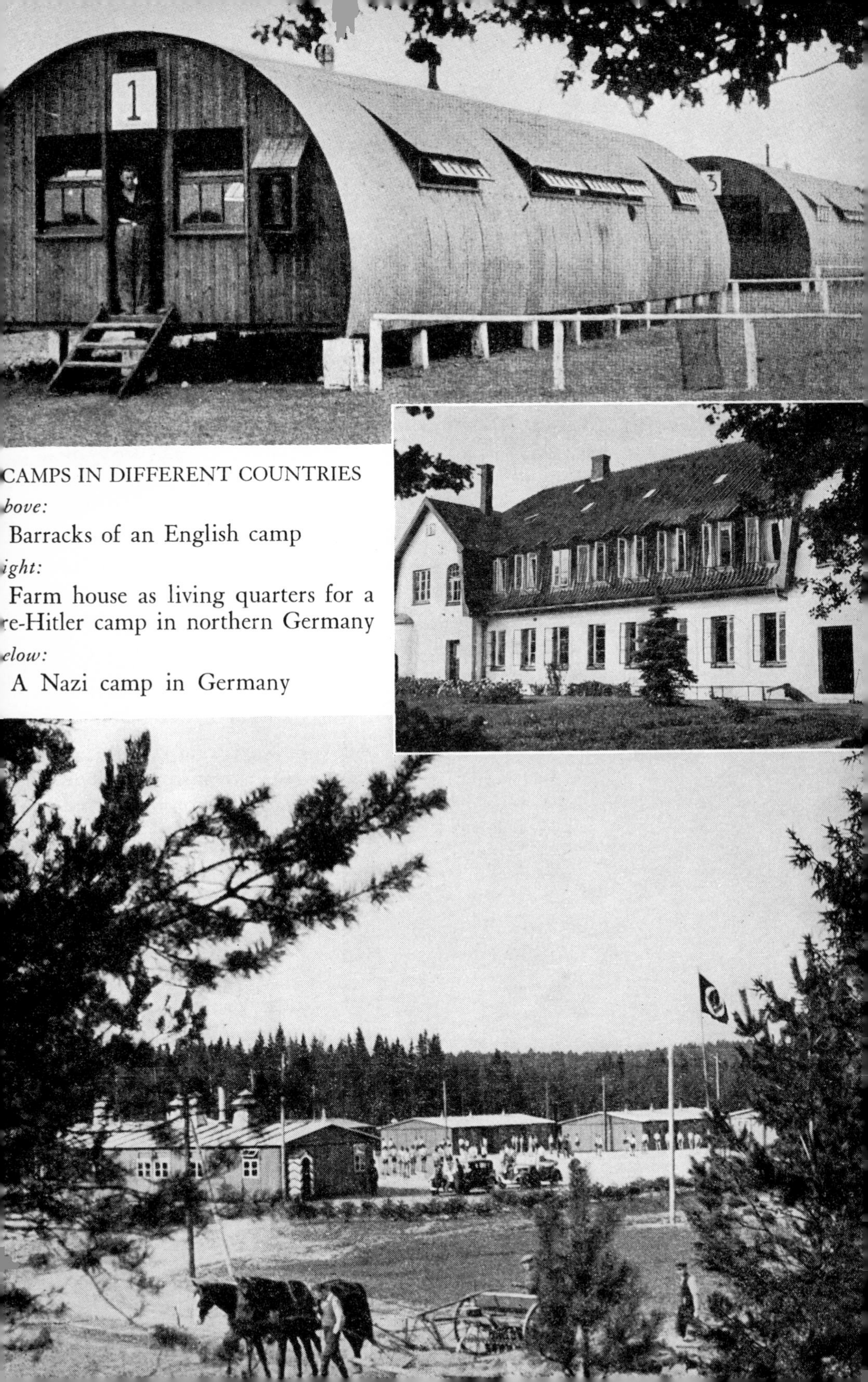

CAMPS IN DIFFERENT COUNTRIES

bove:

Barracks of an English camp

ight:

Farm house as living quarters for a re-Hitler camp in northern Germany

elow:

A Nazi camp in Germany

CAMPS IN DIFFERENT COUNTRIES

Above:

Nazi camp south of Mun (the slogan reads: "Remember ways and constantly that you a German.")

Left:

CCC boys building a side ca at Eveleth, Minnesota

Below:

A pre-Hitler Austrian ca near Vienna

> Ours is another problem. We are trained to grow trees, and harvest trees and manage lands, and to economically place upon the markets of our country, and the world, products manufactured from timber, suitable for human use and consumption. We are not, let me say emphatically, leaders in youth movements, nor trained in social work.[10]

Finally, there are the educators, who see the camps essentially as places to train and educate young people. Frequently systems of camps have been set up as emergency measures to take care of the unemployed youth physically, and then later, as possibilities have been realized, they have been developed into educational and vocational training centers. German educators convinced the Republican government, soon after the camps had begun to receive official support, that they were excellent places for young people to spend several months, to work with their hands, to lose some of their academic characteristics, and to consider the requirements of various types of jobs. The camps were also intended to break down class feeling and to give youth a desire to cooperate in making Republican Germany function efficiently. It was at this point in the development of the camps that the *Arbeitsdienst* began to be thought of as a permanent part of the training program for German youth.

Some educators feel that the camps in the United States should be integrated with the educational systems of the various states, so that when it is found that the standard school curriculum does not fit certain young men and women, they can go into camps to participate in a training program better suited to their needs and interests.

In this connection Charles H. Judd, when chairman of the Department of Education of the University of Chicago, said:

> . . . If the present secondary schools could have access to well-equipped institutions of the camp type, to which they could assign cases of the kind not suited to the ordinary secondary school organization, there would be great gain for society.
>
> The camps will be looked upon, when the social history of this country is written, as important experiments in the adjustment of industry and education to the young people of the country. It is a fundamental mistake

---

[10] *The Forestry News Digest,* March 1936, p. 3.

for educators to overlook the suggestions for enlargement of the secondary education program which these camps have brought to light.[11]

If the camps could become part of a coordinated and integrated youth program, combining work and education, they would be better adapted to many individuals than are the programs of the present educational institutions.

Bibliography

G. D. H. Cole. *The Next Ten Years in British Social and Economic Policy.* London: Macmillan, 1929. Chap. III, "The Unemployed," pp. 48-67.

Kingsley Davis. *Youth in the Depression.* Chicago: University of Chicago Press, 1935. 47 pp.

Die Deutsche Studentenschaft. *Der Arbeitsdienst in der Welt und die Studentische Jugend.* Hamburg: Hanseatische Verlagsanstalt, 1935. 123 S.

Karl Epting and Rena Datta, (editors). *Work Camps and Voluntary Work Service in Germany, Switzerland, Holland, Wales.* Geneva: International Student Service, 1933. 55 pp.

"Farewell to Youth; Regimentation of European Youth," *School and Society,* XLIV (Nov. 14, 1936), 650.

Henri Fuss. "Unemployment among Young People," *International Labor Review,* XXXI, 5 (May 1935), 649-69.

Kenneth Holland. "The American Work Camp Movement," *International Education Review,* VI, 4-5 (1937), 249-69.

——— "Education in C C C and European Camps," *The Phi Delta Kappan,* XIX, 9 (May 1937), 317-22.

——— "The European Labor Service." *The Annals of the American Academy of Political and Social Science,* CXCIV (November 1937), 152-64.

——— "The European Work Camp Movement," *Junior-Senior High School Clearing House,* X, 3 (November 1935), 145-51.

International Labor Office. International Labor Conference, 19th Session, Geneva, 1935. Report III: *Unemployment among Young Persons.* Geneva, 1935. 189 pp.

——— International Labor Conference, 19th session, Geneva, 1935. Report III (supplement): *Unemployment among Young Persons* (supplementary report). Geneva, 1935. 26 pp.

——— International Labor Conference, 23d session, Geneva, 1937. Report III: *Planning of Public Works in Relation to Employment.* Geneva, 1937. Chapter X, "Public Works for Young Persons," pp. 163-74.

Inter-Parliamentary Union. *Inter-Parliamentary Bulletin,* XIV, 9-10 (September-October 1934), 194.

Walter M. Kotschnig. *Unemployment in the Learned Professions; An International Study of Occupational and Educational Planning.* London: Oxford Press, 1937. 347 pp.

League of Nations. *Official Journal,* Special Supplement No. 142. Records of the 16th Ordinary Session of the Assembly, Minutes of the Fifth Committee, p. 74.

---

[11] "Educational Activities in the CCC," *The Phi Delta Kappan,* XIX (May 1937), 300.

League of Nations. Child Welfare Committee. *Report on the Work of the Tenth Session, April 12-17, 1934.* C. 149. M. 62. 1934. IV. 5. (C. P. E. 476 (1)). Geneva, 1934. pp. 21-24.

——— Child Welfare Committee. *Report on the Work of the Eleventh Session, April 25-May 3, 1935.* C. 187. M. 104. 1935. IV. 2. (C. P. E. 513). Geneva, 1935. pp. 14-16.

——— Conference for the Reduction and Limitation of Armaments. *Preliminary Report on the Work of the Conference,* by Arthur Henderson. (Conf. D. 171 (1). 1936. IX, 3), pp. 47-48.

——— Conference for the Reduction and Limitation of Armaments. *Report of the Special Committee on Effectives to the General Commission* (Conf. D. 162: Conf. D., C. S. E. 37-1933. IX. 8). Geneva, 1933, Annex 1, Part III, pp. 8-15.

Liaison Committee of Major International Associations. *Unemployment among Young Persons.* Paris: Institut International de Coopération Intellectuelle, n.d. 24 pp.

Müller-Brandenburg. "Der Arbeitsdienst in der Welt: ein Vergleich," *International Education Review,* VI, 4-5 (1937), 282-84.

Werner Picht and Eugen Rosenstock. *Im Kampf um die Erwachsenenbildung, 1912-1926.* Leipzig: Quelle & Meyer, 1926. 240 S.

Josef Popper-Lynkeus. *Die allgemeine Nähr pflicht als Lösung der socialen Frage; Eingehend bearbeitet und statistisch durchgerechnet; mit einem Nachweis der theoretischen und praktischen Wertlosigkeit der Wirtschaftslehre.* Dresden: Reissner, 1912. 813 S.

Frederich W. Roe. *The Social Philosophy of Carlyle and Ruskin.* New York: Harcourt, Brace, 1921, pp. 262-64.

Eugen Rosenstock. *Arbeitsdienst-Heeresdienst?* Jena:Diederichs, 1932. 80 pp.

——— "The Army Enlisted against Nature," *Journal of Adult Education,* VI, 3 (June 1934), 271.

Save the Children Union. *Children, Young People and Unemployment; A Series of Inquiries into the Effects of Unemployment on Children and Young People.* Geneva, 1934. 322 pp.

Second International Work Camp Conference, Seelisberg, September 5-12, 1937. *National Reports.* Preliminary edition. Zürich: Secretariat, 1937. Mimeographed.

State of New York. Temporary Emergency Relief Administration. *Aiding the Unemployed,* by Hertha Kraus. Albany: T. E. R. A., 1935. 104 pp.

J. R. Tunis. "Dictators Discover Sport," *Foreign Affairs,* XIV (July 1936) 606-17.

W. Thacher Winslow. *Youth, A World Problem; A Study in World Perspective of Youth Conditions, Movements, and Programs.* Washington: Government Printing Office, 1937. 138 pp.

Fritz Wittels. *An End to Poverty.* Translated from the German by Eden and Cedar Paul. London: Allen and Unwin, 1935. 224 pp.

Wladimir Woytinsky. "The Social Consequences of the Economic Depression," *Studies and Reports,* Series C, No. 21. Geneva: International Labor Office, 1936. 364 pp.

The International Voluntary Service Camps

As early as 1914 the World War forced men in many countries to face the deep contradiction between war and their Christian principles. Those who refused to fight were treated as "slackers" and in some instances as traitors; they were berated for unwillingness to serve their countries and were popularly depicted as weak and cowardly individuals. During the first year of the war, men and women from various classes of society, belonging to different churches, or to no church at all, met in England and found themselves united in the conviction that war was wrong and for them impossible.[1] They felt, moreover, that they must justify their refusal to take part in the war by presenting ways in which Christian service could be substituted for fighting. During the latter part of 1914, 130 persons having this point of view gathered at Cambridge, England, and founded the Fellowship of Reconciliation. Their attitude, however, brought opposition from both church and state, and they were regarded as bad citizens and bad churchmen.[2] But the members of the Fellowship wanted to do more than protest against war. Some of them joined in relief work, especially that carried on by the Society of Friends among the refugees and the civilian populations of devastated areas of France and Belgium. This Fellowship spread to the United States in 1915, and to Holland and Sweden in 1917.

In November 1918 the Armistice brought an end to the four years of tragic struggle. During the summer of 1920, the International Fellowship of Reconciliation held a congress at Bilthoven, Netherlands. At this conference a German proposed "the formation of an international group of volunteers who should offer their unpaid services to the task of reconstruction in the devastated areas of northern France."[3] This suggestion resulted in the formation of the International Volun-

[1] Lilian Stevenson, *Toward a Christian International* (Paris: International Fellowship of Reconciliation, 1936), p. 2.

[2] *Ibid.*, p. 3.

[3] *The International Voluntary Service Movement: A History*, p. 1.

tary Service,[4] "to create a spirit of friendship and a constructive attitude toward peace among all peoples by giving practical help on the occasion of natural catastrophes or in the carrying out of work of public utility, thus providing people of good will—both men and women—with a sound system of training in mutual help, voluntary discipline, and comradeship." At the same time support was given to "all efforts to replace military service in times of peace by an international constructive service which will foster greater confidence between the nations of the world." In carrying out these projects, care has always been taken not to perform work which competes with ordinary labor or in any way tends to break strikes.

In the development of the IVS during the last twenty years it has continued to bring together youth of different nationalities to work and live with each other. As a result of this policy a camp frequently contains thirteen or fourteen different nationalities. The majority of the volunteers have been Swiss, German, English, Scandinavian, and French, but almost all European countries have at one time or another sent volunteers. Youth from the United States, Mexico, India, and Iceland also have taken part in the camps, but to a lesser extent.

Projects of the Service

The place selected for the first project of this group was near Esnes-Verdun, France, a few miles from the devastated region of Hill 304 and Dead Man's Hill. In offering his services one of the German volunteers wrote: "For a long time I have hoped for a chance to go and repair in France a little of what my brother—killed at Verdun—and his comrades were forced, under military orders, to destroy."[5]

In 1920, under the leadership of Pierre Ceresole, a Swiss pacifist, a group of internationally-minded men built five temporary dwellings, repaired a road, cleared debris away from foundations of houses, filled mine and shell holes, and cleaned and prepared fields and kitchen gardens for cultivation. During the five months that the project lasted, Germans, Swiss, Dutch, Americans, English, and a Hungarian shared in the work. This first project was finally abandoned because it was

[4] In September 1934, the name of the organization was changed to International Voluntary Service for Peace.

[5] *The International Voluntary Service Movement: A History*, p. 1.

felt that passions and hatreds still ran too high to permit the proper development of international service. A woman in charge of the local station for emergency relief, known as *Secours d'Urgence,* did more than anyone else to stop the work. She thought that the presence of Germans in those regions where such a large number of soldiers of the Allies had been killed was "an insult to the dead." However, the idea of constructive civil service in time of peace lived on and became more widely known and discussed.

The second service project was organized in 1924 at Vers l'Eglise, Switzerland, in the Diablerets, where thirty men worked for three weeks, clearing away remains of an avalanche that had spread over fields, restoring the stream to its original bed, and building a bridge. This IVS assistance given to the villagers developed a remarkably fine spirit of friendship and understanding. A festival was arranged for the volunteers the last night, and to show their appreciation these poverty-stricken people presented the group with 250 Swiss francs ($57.50) to make similar work possible in other villages.

That same autumn of 1924, a landslide at Someo, Switzerland, in the Canton of Ticino, caused considerably more damage than that of the previous fall at Vers l'Eglise. An appeal was made, through the Swiss press, not only to those who opposed war, but also to other people who might be willing to assist their countrymen in time of need. More than 300 volunteers responded, and the work was successfully carried out in a spirit of real devotion and unselfish service.

In the summer of 1926 some seventy volunteers, all pacifists, including teachers, ministers, officials, businessmen, and artisans, worked at Almens, in the Engadine, Switzerland. Working in shifts of about twenty over a period of two weeks, they repaired the damage done by an avalanche of mud and stone which had blocked the bed of a stream.

In 1927 another project was organized, at Feldis, a village in the neighborhood of Almens, to clear away bushes from overgrown pastures. This type of work cannot be done in the winter because of the snow, and during the summer the peasants' time is fully occupied with planting, mowing, and harvesting.

In 1928 the principality of Liechtenstein suffered a serious flood when the Rhine River overflowed its banks and covered acres of land with stone, gravel, sand, and debris. Fifty-four well-known Swiss educators, government officials, and members of the professions, many of whom were pacifists, appealed for assistance. Their statement read in part:

> Across frontiers and barriers erected by man we wish to bring effective help to those in distress. Undeterred by divergencies of opinion on the military question, we wish, by mutual assistance between the peoples, to help to create the new spirit which already makes the very thought of invading another country, weapon in hand, morally impossible. We would desire to pay our tribute to the Austrian and Swiss engineer corps who, in the hour of greatest need and danger, were the first to come and bring help to suffering inhabitants beyond their own frontiers. We wish to continue their work and we hope that the day is not far distant when the armed forces of all lands will know no other task than that of helping their neighbors.[6]

The International Fellowship of Reconciliation assisted in recruiting workers, and more than 700 volunteered, coming from Norway, Sweden, Denmark, Great Britain, France, Iceland, Yugoslavia, Mexico, Spain, Germany, Holland, Austria, Russia, Poland, Rumania, South Africa, India, Italy, the United States, Finland, and Czechoslovakia. The Liechtenstein commune provided buildings and supplied straw for bedding. Work clothes, tools, and equipment were loaned by the Swiss army, and the Swiss and Austrian railways gave reduced fares to workers traveling to and from the project.

The work began in April and, with each man serving an average of twenty-seven days, lasted six months. Seventy-eight women, called "sisters," mostly from Switzerland, did the cooking, cleaning, mending, and caring for the sick. Of the volunteers, 268 were students, 221 professional men, business men, and clerks, 143 manual workers, laborers, and artisans. Among the women, 22 were teachers, and 6 were nurses. None of the volunteers came with the idea of making his stay in Liechtenstein a vacation, but instead worked steadily eight and nine hours a day. The circular sent to the applicants includes the following statement:

> The week's work will be 48 hours, spread over five and a half days. It will be hard. No one should come who is not in thoroughly sound health or whose main idea is a holiday abroad. Those, however, who are

[6] Stevenson, *op. cit.*, pp. 31-32.

really anxious to come into contact with the peasant folk of other lands will find this a unique opportunity for real international friendship. . . . Volunteers will be lodged in tents, barns, and empty buildings. Work will have to be done in the rain. . . . This enterprise represents hard work and willingness to cooperate with people of all views, classes, and nations. We believe that the work, if done in the right spirit, has a real moral and spiritual value, and only ask for offers of service from those who are prepared to look upon it in that light.[7]

Probably the results of this project are best illustrated by a letter written by one of the volunteers, which reads in part as follows:

Our field of work is immense. The best fields and lands of Liechtenstein have been turned into a dreary desert of sands and stones. . . . A day's work of nine hours brings us together as friends. The work consists chiefly in carting off rubbish till good soil is reached; then the peasants can begin to plough so that there may still be a harvest for this year. . . . Our dining room is the village hall. We sleep on straw sacks on the floor and in the gallery, also in the school house. . . . Every room is a little League of Nations. . . . Hardly anywhere else could there be such a good opportunity of talking with people from different parts of the world of all that lies in one's heart. But still better and more satisfying is the working together, which not only forges links among the volunteers and between these and the people of Liechtenstein, but will eventually do so between the nations. . . .

We have all come here to help, whether intellectuals, clerks, or artisans. This Civilian Service is to show that we must, and can, all work together in the disinterested service of a small people.[7]

In 1930 serious floods occurred in southern France, and 250 volunteers from sixteen countries went to help the village of Lagarde. Then, in 1931, at the request of Peter Scott, the leader of a Quaker reconstruction center at Brynmawr, South Wales, a camp was set up to assist in building a swimming pool, a wading pool, and gardens, where there had been an ugly pit dump. In succeeding years similar help was given at Rhos, in North Wales, and at Oakengates, in Shropshire (1933-37), while the work of assisting the Swiss mountain villages continued in 1931 at Klingnau, in 1932 at Safien Platz, and in 1934 in the Jura.

A new field of work was added in January 1934, when an earthquake devastated a large area of Bihar, India. Pierre Ceresole, who has been

---

[7] Stevenson, *op. cit.*, pp. 33-34.

STUDENT CAMPS

Above: Work started, and, *ow:* near completion—swimng pool and park, IVS camp, ynmawr, Wales

ght:

Laying cement floor, Delta operative Farm, Friends serv- camp, Mississippi

AMERICAN FRIEND
SERVICE CAMPS

Left:

Folk dancing in th
Highlander Folk Scho
camp

Below:

Campers laying drai
for small dam in th
Tennessee Valley

the moving spirit of the whole International Voluntary Service, went to India to consult with relief workers about the possibility of developing a service there. On his return to Europe he interested several volunteers, and they spent six months in India, working with the peasants and reconstructing their villages on a higher level, where they were removed from the floods which had followed the earthquakes. During the winters of 1935-36 and 1936-37 Pierre Ceresole was again at work in Bihar.

Since January 1937 the International Voluntary Service, through co-operation with the Neutral Committee for Assisting Spanish Children, has been helping to alleviate the suffering in Spain. The Service was specially charged by the committee with the organization of an evacuation service for Spanish children. This evacuation was accomplished by the use of motor trucks, which left Madrid and other centers of population each day, carrying persons to less dangerous territory, and were driven back loaded with food and supplies.[8]

The majority of work projects of the IVS involve repairing of damage done by floods, landslides, and avalanches, clearing and repairing of roads and trails, digging ditches, preparing land for planting, clearing pastures of brush, constructing swimming pools and recreation centers, leveling ground, planting gardens, and whitewashing residences.

Administration and Finance

The service projects are administered by the five members of the executive committee of the IVS, who, with the president and secretary, are elected at annual meetings from the membership. The camps are financed by contributions from individuals and from organizations interested in peace and better international understanding. Each camp is directed by a service leader, who is selected because of his experience and his ability to organize and carry on the camp program. Neither leaders nor workers receive compensation for their labors, and the volunteers frequently pay their own traveling expenses. If, however, they are unable to pay for their transportation, this is furnished by the IVS. Sometimes the volunteers also make a contribution to the camp, which

[8] *Le Service Civil*, VII-VIII, 5 mars 1935; IX, 24 juillet 1937.

covers their expenses while living there. Usually the camps are open only during the summer from six weeks to two months.

The costs of the voluntary service camps are kept to the minimum, since the tools are for the most part picks and shovels, and the food and accommodations are the simplest. A volunteer is usually fed at a cost of 7 shillings 6 pence, or at about $1.75 a week.[9] This simple plan of living corresponds with the ideology of the whole service camp program, which holds that people opposed to war should, in rendering service to the state in time of peace, undergo somewhat the same hardships and discipline to which soldiers submit under military training.

Volunteers for the Service

The volunteers for the service are selected without regard to nationality, color, religion, or political opinion. They must be physically fit, however, and willing to obey camp regulations. Every volunteer must provide his own personal linen, work clothes, and a pair of strong boots. Ordinarily, young people must be at least eighteen years old to take part in the work. Volunteers are generally not accepted at a camp unless they agree to remain for twelve working days, but the average length of service per person has been about thirty-nine days. The volunteers work eight hours a day, and from forty-four to forty-eight hours a week.

The women volunteers, or "sisters," usually prepare the food and do the washing and cleaning. They are also required to know how to give first aid and to care for the sick. During the period covering 1920 to 1934, 315 women, or 13 per cent of the total number of volunteers, took part in the camps. The women have separate living quarters from the men, but are active in all camp games, discussion groups, and parties. Sometimes they assist with the lighter manual work connected with the

---

[9] Costs of services have been as follows: Total cost at Almens (1926), 2,093.70 Swiss francs ($481.55); at Rhos (1932) £54 ($270).

Cost per working day:

Almens	2.607 Swiss francs	(60 cents)
Liechtenstein	2.42 Swiss francs	(56 cents)
Albefeuille-Lagarde	11.21 French francs	(45 cents)
Safien-Platz	2.40 Swiss francs	(55 cents)

projects, or help in the homes of ill, disabled, or unemployed people in the surrounding community. In Wales they have helped to beautify the dingy brick houses of the miners by whitewashing them and making small flower gardens. Sometimes they have helped needy families in the vicinity of the camp by doing general housework, or by taking care of the children and teaching them how to play.

Camp Facilities

The type of housing provided for the workers depends on the facilities available locally, since no funds are spent to build special quarters. Tents, barracks, club buildings, and schools have been used in various places. Sometimes the camp members live in the homes of the people residing near the work projects. When workers are quartered in old schools or other buildings, they are supplied with straw pallets, blankets, and sleeping bags.

An attempt is made to develop a community spirit within the camp. Even if the youth live in scattered places, a common room is provided where meals are eaten and discussions are held. The camps also try to develop friendly relations with the surrounding communities by having entertainments, song fests, folk dances, sight-seeing trips, and discussion groups with the people. Sometimes when the campers first appear in a small village, the country folk are afraid they are to be patronized or investigated by "outsiders," but usually a friendly relationship soon grows up between the camp and the community.

Education in the Camps

The camps are educational in the broadest sense of the word. They teach the discipline of labor, respect for manual work, and they give youth an insight into conditions in "areas of social and economic tension." Since the workers are of different nationalities, an opportunity is given for exchange of ideas concerning the problems of different countries. Frequently members of the near-by communities also work on the projects, and students from universities use picks and shovels alongside unemployed Welsh miners, Swiss or French villagers, or Liechtenstein farmers. Friendships develop, and the students return to their universities or colleges with a new understanding of the problems of less fortunate classes.

Evening discussion groups are frequently arranged, in which both campers and members of the community participate. In 1934, in addition to the time used for this purpose during the evenings and on week ends, an extra hour was given each day to a talk or discussion group.

Work Camp at Rhos

During the summer of 1933, the writer traveled to Wales to visit and work in the camp at Rhos, near Wrexham and Oakengates in Shropshire, England. Rhos is a village with a population of 11,000. For generations, the people have been dependent upon the collieries in the vicinity, but today many of the coal veins can no longer be worked on a paying basis, and most of the mines are closed. Many of the villagers now exist on unemployment insurance, or are helped by their neighbors, if employment or savings have placed the latter in a more fortunate position.

On my arrival in Rhos I walked to the Miners' Institute, which was also the headquarters of the IVS camp and the place where meals were served. A young English student, clad in shorts, greeted me and acted as my guide to the small brick house of Mrs. Roberts, where I was to live during my stay in Rhos. My hostess proved to be a pleasant white-haired woman, who made me welcome, and installed me in a bedroom that occupied the whole second floor of her home. The room was plainly furnished, but spotlessly clean. I learned later that Mrs. Roberts' husband had been killed in a mine disaster and her brother was dying of tuberculosis in a small matchbox of a cottage on a hill about five miles from Rhos.

I breakfasted the next morning at the Miners' Institute, where I met the other workers, about twenty in all, four young women and sixteen young men—all university students, and representing seven nationalities —English, German, French, Danish, Swedish, Dutch, and American.

At seven we were on the work project, making a park and recreation center for the villagers of Rhos, which was to be developed out of eighteen acres of wasteland, an area known as Ponkey Banks, in the center of the village. For years this spot had been a dumping-ground, and during strikes the men of Rhos had dug coal there, leaving the shallow pits to cave in, or fill up with debris. Already in 1933 there were small areas of gardens and grass, and some children's playground equipment. The recreation area has since been completed and contains a bandstand, a wading or "paddling pool" for children, sand piles, playground apparatus, cricket and football fields, gardens and paths.

Groups of three young men worked on different parts of the area. Some leveled the ground by filling in holes and low places with earth; others cut sod to hold the earth in place, while still another group laid out walks and paths. In all these activities, youth of different nationalities worked side by side. The sod-cutting crew, for instance, was made up of an Englishman, a Frenchman, and a German. As the morning wore on, some of the villagers of Rhos joined the volunteers and worked with students of economics, sociology, and government from different countries.

At eleven o'clock the campers were given a rest period of fifteen minutes. Conversation at such times was often an interchange of ideas on problems of unemployment and relief. We then worked until noon, when we returned our tools to the shed and walked to the Miners' Institute for lunch.

At one o'clock we were back on the project, and worked until five. Then we returned to our quarters, washed and changed clothes, and ate dinner in the Miners' Institute at six. One evening several foremen and miners from the village related their experiences, and discussed the problems of the people of Rhos. The miners were an independent group, proud to be Welshmen and critical of the "Britishers" who owned the mines and exploited both the human and the natural resources of the area. On other evenings discussions were led by members of the volunteers, who described conditions in their own countries.

Oakengates Work Camp

On that same trip I visited a second camp, established during the summer of 1933 at Oakengates, Shropshire, England. Like most mining villages, Oakengates stood dingy and dirty among the hills, its houses clustered among the piles of debris from the coal mines. Its great welts of slag and dirt made it singularly ugly in comparison with the surrounding countryside. Labor in the mines once supported 95 per cent of the working population, but in 1933 employment was available to only about 10 per cent. As a result of competition and private exploitation, the place was replete with castoff and wornout humanity.

Into this village of the living dead had come thirty-five young college and university men and women from fifteen European countries and the United States, to level some of the great welts, fill the deep gashes, and develop a park and recreation center. The vicar of a tiny brick church was the inspiration of this project, and he spent many hours assisting or watching the workers. It was in his parish house that the volunteers were fed, and it was he who obtained the old schoolhouse down beyond the railroad tracks as a dormitory for the young men, who slept on straw ticks on the floor. It was he, too, who helped to dissipate the skepticism of the villagers who wondered why these "outsiders" had come there.

Volunteer workers with their picks and shovels stayed on through the summer, walking through the streets to their work each morning with the first rays of the sun. Many of the villagers caught the spirit of the enterprise and joined in the work, and, as at Rhos, university students and villagers toiled side by side. Even the town "rowdies," who at first threatened to "pinch" the tools of the workers, shadowed the men from the "universities" to carry those same tools to the shed, there cleaning them until they shone. To the students, the unemployment problem became understandable in terms of human suffering. To the miners, the students became friendly young fellows, with more than an academic interest in social justice.

In the evening, miners, broken physically at forty-five, came to the parish house to talk about their experiences: when the cable broke and their partners were dropped to death, or of the cave-ins when men labored thirty hours without food or rest to clear the debris and bring the few remaining lives back to the light. Less dramatic but more typical of their lives were the facts concerning the depletion of the mines and the resulting periods of unemployment, when whole families were reduced to despair. On some evenings they sang their beautiful old songs, or told their folk tales. In return they heard the "foreigners" tell of conditions in their own countries. Common toil and common experiences brought students and miners into closer understanding. Students of different nationalities talked of, and planned for, a new world in which there would be no wars and no unemployed.

Beginning of American Camps

Americans frequently participated in these International Voluntary Service camps in Europe, and came back to the United States to relate their experiences. The American Friends Service Committee organized a camp along somewhat similar lines in the United States. From 1934 to 1938 the number of projects increased from the one original camp to six.

Penn-Craft

During the summer of 1937 a camp was established near Uniontown, Pennsylvania, an area with long lines of abandoned coke ovens, a few mine buildings, great piles of rock and cinders, and dingy, dust-laden villages, telling a mute story of exploitation of the coal and abandonment of the mines, with consequent ruin for many of the families that were dependent on these industries for a livelihood. The camp was located in a saucer-like valley of about two hundred acres, purchased by the American Friends Service Committee, for the purpose of rehabilitating about fifty of the miners and their families.

In the very center of the area stands a large red-brick farmhouse, originally known as Craft Farm. This, together with a smokehouse and an old brick barn across a road, now make up the headquarters of the service project. Eventually these buildings, with playgrounds and recreational facilities, will be the community center for the homesteaders and their families. Already a cooperative dairy, several dwellings, and a dozen large chicken coops, used temporarily as houses, have been constructed.

The plan is that the rehabilitation project, to be known as Penn-Craft, shall eventually become a community of about 300 people, who will raise most of their food on two-acre plots of land. It is hoped that some of them will be employed in steel mills or coal mines within commuting distance, so as to provide the families with a cash income. Those in charge of the project also plan to develop some small industry which will provide employment for the members of the rehabilitation project who are not employed in private industry.

Thirty-five young men and women, with the director, spent the summer of 1937 assisting in the construction of houses, chicken coops, and barns, laying water mains, building roads, developing a quarry, and raising vegetables and chickens on an experimental basis to provide food for the camp as well as to determine what produce could be raised most easily on the soil and sold in near-by towns and villages.

While the camp assisted materially in starting the rehabilitation project, of more importance was the opportunity given to the students from some thirty different colleges and universities in fifteen different states to participate in the life and work of this project and at the same time to study the problems of the soft-coal industry by discussing the problems of that area with the people themselves.

Among the topics given special consideration were regulation of labor relations, mechanization of industry, and labor displacement, and the problems and possibilities of rehabilitation and resettlement by government and private agencies. Throughout all these discussions the use of nonviolent techniques in the settlement of social and industrial conflicts, which have already involved violence, was emphasized.

The camp was directed by the members of the Society of Friends (Quakers), who had had experience during the previous summer directing a similar project in Ohio. The thirty-five volunteers were divided into crews of carpenters, painters, "kitchen police" and cooks, cement foundation workers, launderers, ditchdiggers, quarriers, truckmen, and pickup and toolroom men.

In the summer of 1937, the group of students attending the camp was made up largely of young men interested in the social sciences. There were in addition two or three divinity students and several men taking law courses. The participants were carefully selected for their leadership ability and for their pragmatic approach to social problems.

Usually no attempt is made to obtain a homogeneous group. Instead, an interesting and alert contingent of young people of sufficiently varied backgrounds and points of view is sought, to make the camp experience broadening. Thus Jews and Gentiles, Catholics—Greek Orthodox and Roman—and Protestants, Communists and Socialists, Democrats and

ɪERICAN FRIENDS SERVICE CAMPS

ve:

'ork in a quarry, Pennsylvania

er right and right:

ɪilding chicken coops at Penn-Craft Farm, ɪsylvania

w:

iscussion group at Highlander Folk School p

Republicans, of different social and economic backgrounds, are found among those participating in the camps. Foreign countries have been represented by students from Hungary, Mexico, and England. The majority of the campers were conscientious objectors and considered the constructive work which they were doing in time of peace a "moral equivalent of war." Since the students were quartered in the old farmhouse or in the chicken coops on army cots, the accommodations were not unlike those of an army in time of war.

The crew digging ditches and laying water mains was made up of a Harvard graduate student in government; a young White Russian of Greek Orthodox faith, who is an assistant in dramatics at a woman's college; a Princeton undergraduate, majoring in government; a graduate in government of the University of Michigan, who had taken a year out to work in the Resettlement Administration; and a Jewish boy who had completed three years at the College of the City of New York with interims of hitchhiking to the Pacific coast and the South and seven months' work in a transient camp in California. The crew in the quarry consisted of a mathematics professor from Purdue University, a girl undergraduate from Cornell, a student from Temple University, and a young physician from Edinburgh University.

The day began at half-past five, when the old farm bell was rung. At six o'clock breakfast was served in the farmhouse, and was followed by a fifteen-minute period of simple devotions or hymn singing. After cleaning their quarters and making their beds, the students started to the work projects at seven o'clock. Most of the young men wore only shorts and shoes, while the young women wore either overalls or shorts and halters.

At 9:30 sandwiches were distributed to the workers. At 11:30 the farm bell rang and the workers walked back to the farmhouse, leaving their tools on the project. Lunch was served at 11:45 and at 12:45 they were back on the job. At 3:15 the bell again rang, and the young people gathered up their tools and trudged back to camp to wash or take showers. Supper was served at 5:30 in the dining room of the old farmhouse.

The evenings were used chiefly for education and recreation. Sometimes after dinner a group of the campers played softball with young men from the mining community. During the late afternoon and on week ends, field trips were arranged to visit the mines or steel plants. The Friends Service Committee also arranged for special speakers and discussion leaders to travel from camp to camp during the course of the work period.

Camps Organized by Friends Service Committee

The American Friends Service Committee organized six camps during the summer of 1938: one in the coal-mining area near Uniontown, Pennsylvania, to assist with the Penn-Craft rehabilitation project; a second in the Tennessee Valley to assist the Tennessee Valley Authority in building a fish-rearing pool; a third in Flint, Michigan, to assist one of the city agencies in building a park; a fourth at Monteagle, Tennessee, to help the Highlander Folk School construct a storage cellar, an athletic field, and carry on a new forestry development; a fifth on the Delta Cooperative Farm in Mississippi, to construct buildings, make roads, clear lands on the Delta Farm, and conduct a progressive school for the children of the community; and a sixth in Los Angeles, to develop a playground and recreational facilities for underprivileged youth in an industrial area near San Pedro Harbor.

During the four years that the voluntary service camps have been in operation in the United States, 165 students and young professional people have participated in them. The students in the six camps have come from seventy-four different colleges and universities. Four of the camps organized during the summer of 1938 will be continued in the summer of 1939 and two new camps will be started. While the voluntary service camps in the United States have been organized for only four years, they have already demonstrated that such projects attract American youth and provide them with valuable educational experiences.

Conclusion

The International Voluntary Service camps have now been organized in various countries of the world over a period of eighteen years. Undoubtedly they will continue indefinitely and will expand to still other countries.

This peace-time service has grown and developed in a time of intense international rivalry. However limited in scope, it has provided a positive program for persons interested in breaking down barriers of race, creed, and culture by substituting constructive service in time of peace for military service. The camps have also provided an opportunity for youth of various nationalities to live and work as volunteers in areas of social need or economic tension.

Besides completing many needed work projects in depressed or damaged regions, the camps have often given people in backward areas their first opportunity to associate with students, and thus have provided a means for increasing their understanding of the attitudes of other classes. Finally, the example of men from colleges and universities at work with picks and shovels has given both the students and the residents of depressed areas a new respect for manual labor, and a realization that with only the simplest of tools and hard labor it is possible to accomplish public works of real value to the community.

Bibliography

HENRY BRINTON. *The Peace Army.* London: Williams & Norgate, 1932. 88 pp.

ALEXIS DANAN. *L'armée des hommes sans haine.* Paris: Attinger, 1929. 99 pp.

INTERNATIONAL VOLUNTARY SERVICE. *The International Voluntary Service Movement, A History,* London, n.d. 11 pp.

——— *Report, 1933-34.* London, n.d. 22 pp.

INTERNATIONAL VOLUNTARY SERVICE FOR PEACE. *Pick and Shovel Peacemaking; A Story of an Adventure in International Amity.* London, n.d. 4 pp.

INTERNATIONALE ZIVILDIENST. *Internationale Zivildienst, 1930 und 1931: Lagarde, Unter-Aargau, Brynmawr.* La Chaux-de-Fonds, n.d. 20 S.

KOMITEE FÜR DEN FREIWILLIGEN HÜLFSDIENST. *Der freiwillige Hülfsdienst in den wassergeschädigten Gebieten Liechtensteins und der Schweiz, 2. April bis 5. Oktober 1928.* Geneva, n.d. 72 pp.

Le Service Civil; bulletin de l'Association du Service civil international. Berne, 15 April 1935.

SERVICE CIVIL INTERNATIONAL. *Albefeuille-Lagarde, 1er mai au 27 septembre, 1930; annexes: Brynmawr, Basse-Argovie, été 1931.* La Chaux-de-Fonds, n.d. 30 pp.

——— *Exposé des motifs de la pétition en faveur du service civil.* Lausanne, n.d. 16 pp.

——— *1934; Jura, Vaudois, Sta. Maria, Hütten, Oakengates, B'aenavon, Bihar.* Berne, 1935. 20 pp.

——— *Service Civil International, 1932: Safiens, Brynmawr & Rhos.* La Chaux-de-Fonds: Secrétariat, n.d. 8 pp.

——— *Service civil pour les réfractaires.* Vienne: Société anonyme, n.d. 12 pp.

——— *Les soeurs du service civil.* Berne, 1935. 32 pp.

SERVICE CIVIL VOLONTAIRE. *Almens, 1926.* Zürich: Centre suisse d'action pour la paix, n.d. 44 pp.

LILIAN STEVENSON. *Towards a Christian International; The Story of the International Fellowship of Reconciliation.* London, 1936. 98 pp.

The Bulgarian Labor Service

FOLLOWING the World War, Bulgaria was near economic and political chaos. For nearly seven consecutive years 25 per cent of her man power had been under arms; for the two Balkan Wars, which lasted about three years, had almost immediately preceded the World War. Public services were disorganized, the food shortage was desperate, and there was widespread discontent and a very real movement toward communism. Strikes broke out. Without the strong military rule under which they had been trained and guided prior to and during the World War, without jobs, and in many cases without food and clothing, the youth of the country frequently participated in street rioting. The Bulgarian government had to conjure up the specter of a Greco-Servian invasion to maintain order.[1]

The Bulgarian youth needed projects to provide them with constructive activities and at the same time their country needed work done on their roads. During the five hundred years that Bulgaria had been dominated by Turkey little had been done to develop roads. The Turks had contented themselves for the most part with the old Roman roads on the Balkan Peninsula.[2] Since during the Balkan Wars and the World War the man power of the country had been engaged in fighting or in producing war materials, all means of transportation, except those necessary to the conduct of the war, had been neglected. Also, modification of frontiers as a result of the Treaty of Neuilly required complete reorganization of railroad and highway networks.[3]

Compulsory Labor Service Established

Bulgaria needed means of transportation and communication, and the youth of that small country needed work, food, shelter, and lessons in

[1] *Bulgaria and Romania* (Boston: Houghton Mifflin, 1924), p. 149.

[2] K. D. Spissarevski, *La Bulgarie au travail; cinquante ans après* (Marseille: Société anonyme du sémaphore, 1929), p. 224.

[3] G. T. Danailov, *Les effets de la guerre en Bulgarie* (New Haven: Yale University Press, 1932), pp. 413-14, 605.

cooperative living and discipline. It was because of these conditions that the labor service was established.

In June 1920 Bulgaria passed a Compulsory Labor Service Law which required every young man twenty years of age to spend one year, and every unmarried girl of sixteen to spend six months, in service to the state without compensation. The law also provided that in case of a national disaster all male Bulgarians under fifty years of age were liable to be called for compulsory service to the state for a period not exceeding four weeks.[4]

Opposition of the Allied Powers

In this form the law seemed to the Allies to restore under a new name the compulsory military service which had been forbidden by the Treaty of Neuilly. They protested against the act, and though the Bulgarian government denied their charges, it adopted an amendment in October 1921 which reduced the period of service to eight months for men and four months for girls, permitted a certain percentage of those liable for service to purchase exemption, provided that only 30 per cent of the given age group were to work at any one time, and made all persons up to fifty years of age liable for service for not more than twenty-one days in any one year when the welfare of the community absolutely necessitated it.[5] These amendments satisfied the Inter-Allied Commission of Military Control, and so the modified Compulsory Labor Service Law went into force.[6]

Survey of Bulgarian Camps

In 1922 Max Lazard was sent to Bulgaria by the International Labor Office to make a study of the compulsory labor service.[7] He reported that the Bulgarian government did not seem to be violating the spirit of the Treaty of Neuilly. Bulgaria was, and is, an agricultural country of limited resources and isolated and extremely backward areas. It there-

[4] International Labor Office, *Legislative Series,* 1920 (Bulgaria 1).

[5] In 1923 this temporary service was decreased from twenty-one to ten days a year, except that twenty might be required "if desired by the population."

[6] International Labor Office, *Legislative Series,* 1922 (Bulgaria 1, Appendix).

[7] Max Lazard, *Compulsory Labor Service in Bulgaria* (Geneva, 1922).

fore appeared to Lazard that because of economic conditions, social customs, and the need for better means of communication, the Bulgarian government was merely trying to utilize man power which could not be otherwise obtained in order to perform much needed public work.

Compulsory work on the roads had been customary in Bulgaria since the days of Turkish rule, and in 1920, when the first compulsory labor act was passed, five days' work a year on roads was already required of all men from twenty-one to fifty-five years of age. Even before the World War, the Bulgarians had become accustomed to compulsory service for the state, since three to six years in some branch of military service had been required of every man. In addition the ancient Slavic custom of all inhabitants of a village voluntarily cooperating on some project of mutual interest was still occasionally put into practice.

It is evident, therefore, that the compulsory feature of the labor service law passed in 1920 was not a startling innovation. It was in harmony with the principles of the Agrarian Union, which at that time was in political control of the country. As its name indicates, this was a peasants' party, and sought to glorify manual labor, especially of the rural and agricultural type. It was not opposed to compulsory military service, but even before the World War it had advocated reforms in the service such as those proposed during the Balkan Wars by a member of the party who said:

> . . . I am not against the barracks. I would go even further; the barracks may develop all the civic and family virtues that the school endeavors to inculcate. They may even serve national economic and cultural ends, but reforms will be needed for this. I can find no reason for imposing a service of two or three years solely for learning military arts and developing warlike aptitudes. We already have these aptitudes, and for learning the arts of war seven months are quite enough . . . .
>
> The barracks, then, must be reformed. Let us reject everything that prevents them from being a center of civilization for developing civic and humanitarian virtues; seven months for studying the arts of war; seven months of practical training and education in citizenship; seven months for the study of organization; seven months in the town barracks; seven months in barracks in one's native village, and seven months at home; in the village barracks all the supplies, food, and equipment, needed by the conscripts; municipal and departmental manoeuvres. In this practical way personal profit and competition between the villagers will combine to create common

interests, a care for and devotion towards both individual and national work . . . .[8]

Need for restoring order and normal ways of life in Bulgaria, as well as of meeting the exacting terms of the Treaty of Neuilly, gave Agrarian Union leaders opportunity to put their theories into practice. In January 1920 Stamboliiski, premier and party leader, declared:

> They exact from us the payment of enormous reparations, they force us to dissolve our military forces. Very well! Bulgaria will be the first to give to the world a good example of replacing a military army which absorbs, without profit for anyone, the best years of youth, with a labor army developing the idea of brotherhood and solidarity of social classes and producing materially useful and tangible results for the country.[9]

Aims and Methods of the Labor Service

The aims of the Compulsory Labor Service Law, as stated in Section 2, were:

> (*a*) organizing and utilizing the labor power of the country on a social basis in the interests of production and the welfare of the country;
> (*b*) awakening in all citizens, irrespective of their social status and means, a love of work in the service of the community and of manual labor;
> (*c*) improving the moral and economic condition of the people; fostering in all citizens a consciousness of their duties toward themselves and toward society, and instructing them in rational methods of work in all branches of economic activity.[10]

The original plan for the labor service had provided that the young men should devote the first three or four months of their year's service to improving their educational and vocational training. Shortening the enrollment period by four months, however, made it necessary to modify this plan in order not to reduce the economic effectiveness of the labor service.

The first ten days of each enrollment period are devoted to education, and during this time the meaning and the significance of the service

[8] Extract from the personal diary of T. Bakaloff, kept during the Balkan War, and published in the *Semledelska Misl,* under the heading "Anxious Days"; quoted at greater length in Max Lazard, *op. cit.,* Appendix III, pp. 123-24.

[9] Quoted by N. P. Nicolaev, "Le travail obligatoire en Bulgarie," *Revue politique et parlementaire,* XXX, 338 (10 janvier 1923), 56-57.

[10] International Labor Office, *Legislative Series,* 1920 (Bulgaria 1).

are explained to the recruits. Individuals who seem capable of performing specialized tasks are sent to technical and vocational schools for longer preliminary training. During the winter months, when outdoor work is impossible, the labor service provides courses for the training and development of leaders. An attempt is made to teach illiterates, of whom there are many in Bulgaria, the rudiments of reading and writing while they are in the service. Men in the regular labor service live under strict discipline, wear uniforms, and must take an oath of allegiance, but are under civilian control.

Women Included in the Service

One interesting innovation in the original labor service law was the drafting of unmarried women for service, the types of work in which women might take part being specified by administrative ruling. Such work included household duties, training in nursing and hygiene, needlework, office work, electrotechnics, gardening, preserving, raising of silkworms and bees, cattle and poultry breeding, afforestation, and vine culture. Compulsory service for women functioned during only one enrollment period. For reasons of economy, in 1923 it was suspended by an amendment to the labor service act.[11]

Administration of Labor Service

The labor service is administered by a general directorate in the Ministry of Public Works with the help of a superior council and ten district offices. The average number of workers each year is 20,000, about 50 per cent of whom work directly under the Ministry of Public Works. The men in the service are organized into eight production groups (*chetas*); each *cheta* is divided into six companies of three squads each, with three camps to a squad. This form of organization was finally established for the service in April 1923.

Work Projects

Nearly half the work done in 1930-31 was devoted to building and repairing roads and railways, the remainder being given to state prop-

[11] See below, pp. 245-46.

erties, institutions, breeding farms, workrooms for skilled workers, and forestry projects. A number of workers are also loaned to government or privately owned public utility undertakings, which then become responsible for their maintenance.

An act of June 19, 1925 provided for construction of a railway system of twenty lines and of a large number of small ports on the Danube and the Black Sea. For this construction work both regular and temporary labor service were made available. Fifteen thousand of the 25,000 men in the service in 1934 were engaged in road building, chiefly on the Bulgarian section of the London to Istanbul motor road.

Skilled workers were employed in workshops to supply and equip labor groups and to repair tools.[12] The directorate managed twelve such enterprises in 1923, six in 1924, and has carried on four since 1926. These have included a boot and shoe factory and a clothing factory at Gornia-Bania near Sofia, a forest estate (prior to 1925 there were three forest estates in operation), and brick works. The products have been used by the labor service. The directorate reported that in 1925-33 net profit from the enterprises totaled 50,123,000 leva [13] ($350,861).

Financing the Service

The capital required to operate the labor service is provided by annual credits. From June 1920 to August 1925 these amounted to 710,975,648 leva ($4,976,829) annually. From 1925 to 1933 they were 2,101,505,661 leva ($14,710,540) annually.[14] The average cost a man per day in the service was 27 leva in 1923. By 1925-26 it had risen to 49.45 leva. However, in 1933-34, it had dropped to 35.80 leva.

Compulsory Labor Week in the Schools

As preliminary training for compulsory labor service, all students in Bulgarian schools give one week of service in the spring and another week in the autumn to the school or to the municipality in which they

[12] Between 1921 and 1934, 22 per cent of the men in the labor service worked for the directorate.

[13] During this period 1 leva had an exchange value of .007 in United States money.

[14] See the *International Labor Review*, XIII, 1 (January 1926); see also *ibid.*, XXX, 3 (September 1934); and *Industrial and Labor Information*, LIII, 9 (March 4, 1935).

BULGARIAN LABOR SERVICE MEN DRILLING ROCK

LABOR SERVICE IN BULGARIA
Above and below: Labor battalions
structing railroads

live. This "compulsory labor week in the schools," as it is called, was instituted at about the same time as compulsory labor service. Regulations for student service were signed by the Minister of Public Instruction and gave detailed instructions for organizing the work.

The work to be done is determined by a committee appointed by the local school board. This committee must include an agricultural expert, an engineer, and a doctor. Preference is given to projects which can be carried on without special equipment and which are of direct value to the school itself. These projects include cleaning up the school building and grounds, leveling the grounds, planting and caring for trees and gardens, and improving the playgrounds. Older children are often assigned tasks which supplement their studies, such as mending maps, cleaning and binding library books, cleaning laboratories, and work in connection with archaeological excavations. Work done for municipalities has included making parks at Bela-Cherkova and Livnova, and planting pine trees in both these places as well as in Troyan, Kustendil, Suknidol, and Samokov.

The Minister of Education made enthusiastic comment on the results of the first compulsory labor week in the schools:

> The enthusiasm with which the young people welcomed my plan was so infectious that even the schools which did not come within the competence of the Ministry spontaneously asked to join us. Schools of other denominations (Turkish, Jewish, et cetera) did the same. The Turkish School Committee of Chumen asked me by telegram to allow the Turkish pupils and teachers to join the Bulgarians, and of course I agreed with pleasure. It was yet another proof that my plans for labor week in schools were opportune.
>
> Now we have information from almost everywhere, and I can place it at your disposal so that you may see how everything has been carried out, and what brilliant results have been obtained. The material value of what was done may be estimated at about a hundred million leva, but still more important is the pedagogic and educational value of the young people's work, of public work in common, of manual labor in the open air, and of the general eagerness of the pupils. No less valuable is the example given to the citizens of Bulgaria by these young people under the guidance of their conscientious teachers; an example which will be fully appreciated by foreigners.[15]

[15] Lazard, *op cit.*, Appendix IX, pp. 157-58.

Labor Service for the Unemployed

Labor service in Bulgaria differs from government-subsidized labor service in most of the other countries, because it was not begun in order to alleviate unemployment. It represented instead the state's need for labor which it could not otherwise obtain. It was also intended to be a national institution for training and disciplining youth.

The labor service is equipped to handle only about 20,000 men annually, although the number liable for service each year exceeds this figure by several thousand. When unemployment became prevalent in Bulgaria, it was natural to give the unemployed preference in enrollment for the labor service. In this way the compulsory labor service was able to give work to about one-fourth of all unemployed workers registered in Bulgaria in 1934.

In August 1934, however, a special labor service for the unemployed was inaugurated. This has no direct connection with the compulsory labor service, and special work projects have been assigned to it. It is financed by funds for unemployment relief, 10,000,000 leva ($70,000) having been appropriated for this purpose in 1936. Unemployed men who have families, are in good health, and are between twenty and fifty years of age may volunteer their services. About 5,000 men have done so each year since 1934. They have worked for a period of five to seven months each year under the same conditions as obtain in the compulsory labor camps. They receive about 35 leva (25 cents) a day for their work, from which ten leva are deducted for maintenance.

Conclusion

The Bulgarian labor service has been in existence since June 1920, when it was established to perform much needed public works projects and to provide a training program for Bulgarian youth. The fact that it has been continued to the present time is one indication of its success. Although it is still compulsory, there seems to be little opposition from the youth of Bulgaria or from the population as a whole.

It would seem that the Bulgarian labor service has been of considerable assistance to this small Balkan country in developing better means of communication and in providing work and training opportunities for young men who might otherwise glut the labor market. From all indications, compulsory Bulgarian labor service will continue indefinitely.

Bibliography

ALLIED and ASSOCIATED POWERS. *Treaty of Peace between the Allied and Associated Powers and Bulgaria, and Protocol.* Signed at Neuilly-sur-Seine, November 27, 1919. British Treaty Series, 1920, no. 5. London: H. M. Stationery Office, 1920. 171 pp.

RENÉ AURIC. *Étude sur le service obligatoire de travail.* Paris: Pedone, 1934, pp. 1-94.

JOHN BUCHAN (editor). *Bulgaria and Romania* (The Nations of Today). Boston: Houghton Mifflin, 1924, pp. 64-185.

"Bulgarian National Service Law," *Review of Reviews,* LXIV (July 1921), 81-83.

BOYAN CHOUKANOFF. "Bulgaria's Labor Battalions," *Current History,* XL (April 1934), 44-48.

"The Compulsory Labor Service in Bulgaria," *Industrial and Labor Information,* LIII, 9 (March 4, 1935), 260-61.

G. T. DANAILOV, *Les effets de la guerre en Bulgarie.* New Haven: Yale, 1932. 723 pp.

GEORGE DESBONS. *La Bulgarie après le traité de Neuilly.* Paris: Rivière, 1930. 462 pp.

"Deutsche Gäste bei Bulgariens Arbeitsdienst," *Der Arbeitsmann,* III, 32, 7 (August 1937), 6-7.

GUSTAV EGLI. *Der freiwillige Arbeitsdienst in der Schweiz.* Zürich: Oprecht, 1936, S. 40-41.

"Everybody Works but Father," *Saturday Evening Post,* CXCV (May 12, 1923), 30-31.

FRIEDRICH W. HEINZ. *Kameraden der Arbeit; Deutsche Arbeitslager: Stand, Aufgabe und Zukunft.* Berlin: Frundsberg Verlag, 1933, S. 73-82.

INTERNATIONAL LABOR OFFICE. *The Bulgarian Law on Compulsory Labor,* Studies and Reports, Series C, No. 3, Geneva, 1920. 13 pp.

——— *Legislative Series:* 1920 (Bulgaria 1); 1922 (Bulgaria 1); 1923 (Bulgaria 1); 1924 (Bulgaria 2); 1925 (Bulgaria 3); 1927 (Bulgaria 1).

RUDOLF KOLLER. "Arbeitsdienst und Wissenschaft," *Der Bulgarienwart,* II, 6 (1934), 5-6.

"The Labor Service in Bulgaria; Activity of Units of Unemployed, 1934-37," *Industrial and Labor Information,* LXV, 10 (March 7, 1938), 254-55.

MAX LAZARD. *Compulsory Labor Service in Bulgaria,* Studies and Reports, Series B, No. 12. Geneva: International Labor Office, 1922. 158 pp.

W. NERESOFF. "Die volkswirtschaftliche Bedeutung der Arbeitsdienstpflicht in Bulgarien," *Deutscher Arbeitsdienst,* V, 20 (19 Mai 1935), 634-37.

N. P. NICOLAEV. "Le travail obligatoire en Bulgarie," *Revue politique et parlementaire,* XXX, 338 (10 janvier 1923), 56-57.

LEO PASVOLSKY. *Bulgaria's Economic Position.* Washington: Brookings Institution, 1930. 409 pp.

HANS RAUPACH. *Arbeitsdienst in Bulgarien; Studienergebnisse der Schlesischen Jungmannschaft.* Berlin: De Gruyter, 1932. 98 S.

"Rebuilding Bulgaria," *Living Age,* No. 317 (May 19, 1923), 390-92.

"The Results of the Compulsory Labor Service in Bulgaria from 1921 to 1925," *International Labor Review,* XIII, 1 (January 1926), 83-92.

"The Results of Compulsory Labor Service in Bulgaria from 1925 to 1933," *International Labor Review,* XXX, 3 (September 1934), 365-73.

IVAN P. ROGOSAROFF. "Der Bulgarische Arbeitsdienst als Erziehungsmittel," *International Education Review,* VI, 4-5 (1937), 242-48.

"The Situation in Bulgaria; Unemployed Persons and the Compulsory Labor Service," *Industrial and Labor Information,* LI, 11 (September 10, 1934), 324.

K. D. SPISSAREVSKI. *La Bulgarie au travail; cinquante ans après.* Marseille: Société anonyme, 1929. 276 pp.

"Unemployment and Public Works in Bulgaria," *Industrial and Labor Information,* LVIII, 8 (May 25, 1936), 238.

"Working of the Compulsory Labor Service, 1933-34," *Industrial and Labor Information,* LIII, 9 (March 4, 1935), 260.

OSKAR WUDY. "Die Arbeitsdienstpflicht in Bulgarien," *Der Bulgarienwart,* I, 8 (1933), S. 11-13.

ILIA YANOULOFF. *La législation sociale en Bulgarie.* Sofia: 1926. 48 pp.

Work Camps in Switzerland

THE International Voluntary Service which came into existence in 1920 under the leadership of Pierre Ceresole, a citizen of Switzerland, and which has continued to receive considerable support from individuals in this small confederation, has been discussed in the second chapter. The camps of the International Voluntary Service, however, are not limited to Switzerland; in fact they have provided experience for only a small number of Swiss youth. If we are really to understand the labor service movement in Switzerland, we must consider the camps of the National Union of Swiss Students which came into existence in 1925, and the camps for unemployed which were organized with the assistance of the Swiss government during 1933.

In 1925 a group of fifteen students from Swiss universities decided that they would spend the summer helping to prevent the destruction of a historical castle at Mesox, Switzerland. Accordingly, they worked all summer putting in a retaining wall to prevent a stream from undermining the castle walls. They enjoyed the out-door work and the friendships which they developed, and learned much about Switzerland. They returned to their respective universities in the fall with a better understanding of Swiss people and their social and economic problems. Discussions of their experiences aroused interest, and the National Union of Swiss Students adopted the camp idea and organized the Swiss Student Voluntary Work Service.

Student Voluntary Work Service

Each summer for the past twelve years approximately 500 university students have participated in the camp programs. About 3,700 young people took part in this service during the first eleven years of its existence and worked a total of 71,000 days. About 80 per cent of the young men and women have been students at Swiss universities; the remaining 20 per cent have come from colleges and universities scattered throughout Europe and the United States. In 1935 eleven different nationalities were represented among the camp workers.

The National Union of Students and its representatives in different institutions of higher learning in Switzerland recruit young people during the spring by means of student periodicals, blackboard notices, special circulars, and moving pictures. They also send announcements about the service to colleges, universities, and various student and international organizations in other countries. Since there are far more applicants than there are places in the camps, the Union selects those who have been prominent in their respective universities and who have an interest in social, political, and economic problems. Swiss students who have traveled or studied in other countries are given preference because of their knowledge of the language and customs of foreign students who participate in the camp program. An organization known as International Student Service has been active in the development of the work camp movement, and for several years has been responsible for the exchange of student workers in camps in different countries.

Each participant is expected to spend at least three weeks in a student camp working about forty hours per week. Organization of leisure-time activities is left to the individual camps. As a rule, students have little difficulty in providing adequate amusement for themselves.

Projects for this student service must be of proved usefulness and of a character not to increase unemployment. Work projects consist largely of building roads and trails to isolated communities in the higher Alps, cleaning up after avalanches and floods, and helping to rebuild villages after fires.

The camps are financed by the federal and cantonal governments and by contributions from the universities of Switzerland or from private individuals and organizations. The federal government contributes two francs per capita for each work day, the canton contributes one franc, and the remaining one franc necessary to carry on the camps is raised by voluntary contributions. The students have attempted to collect one franc from every registered student each semester for this purpose, but this contribution does not provide more than a fraction of the quota. The commune for which the work is done is not expected to con-

SWISS LABOR CAMPS

ve:
ıstoffice and store of a camp near the Furka

t:
ımp leader, housekeeper, and an official from
ıational headquarters in a camp near Zürich

w:
ʋo French students in camp at Ausserberg

SWISS LABOR CAMPS

Above:

Even the camp pigs are housed in commodious chalets

Right:

Swiss and American students in a camp near Ausserberg

Below:

Swiss unemployed constructing road near Zürich

tribute to the project financially, though it may provide sleeping quarters and donate food.

The Ausserberg Camp

During August 1933 I visited and worked in a student camp at Ausserberg, Switzerland. I had previously spent two weeks in Germany, about seven months after Hitler had been appointed chancellor. At the International Student Service Conference at Etal, Bavaria, we had heard the late Röhm, then Chief of Staff of the Storm Troopers, try to explain the *Weltanschauung* of National Socialism. Germany was tense under the strain of dictatorship and suppressed opposition. Young Germans freely predicted a second German revolution which would rid the National Socialists of the influence of the *Junkers* and big industrialists.

It was therefore refreshing to cross the Swiss frontier and travel to Berne, the capital. From Berne I traveled to Thun; the train climbed into the Alps of Reichenbach, Frutigen, and Blausee. Hikers with their knapsacks, heavily hobnailed shoes, and pikes boarded the train for short trips, sang their songs, or waved to us as we moved through the verdant country. We paused at Kandersteg which, at an elevation of nearly 4,000 feet, is surrounded by snowcapped peaks, then plunged into the darkness of Lötschberg Tunnel. Presently we came out on the opposite side of the mountain, high up on the north side of the Rhone valley. The hillsides were dry and barren, and little vegetation managed to grow on the steep mountain slopes. Far below, the Rhone, milky-gray from the Rhone glacier, moved toward Lake Geneva. On the opposite side of the valley tiny villages clung to the mountainsides on patches of green. Several miles farther on the train stopped at Ausserberg, and a group of deeply tanned students playing *"boule"* behind the station directed me to the camp about a quarter of a mile up the mountainside. We found ourselves in a village of unpainted houses, rudely constructed from hand-hewn timbers closely fitted together and set up on posts six to ten feet high. On the ground floor were cows, pigs, or sheep, if the villager was fortunate enough to own them, and on the floor above lived the families. The flooring of none too closely fitted logs was the only partition between cattle and people.

Life here was most primitive. Perched on the side of the dry mountain, the village derived its income almost entirely from milk, butter, and cheese. Since the area received little rainfall, irrigation ditches, centuries old and dug by hand, often out of the granite mountainside, brought water from glacial streams ten or twelve miles away. Water was, therefore, the most precious resource in that vicinity, and each villager could irrigate his small patch of grass or vegetables only on certain days each week. The records of these water rights were kept in the village hall on pieces of wood about a foot long, a quarter of an inch thick, and rounded at one end. On these the family insignia or initials were carved or impressed, and along one edge cuts in the wood indicated the number of days each week that water could be diverted from the common ditch.

I was sent to the headquarters of the camp, which was located in one of the larger houses. Here I met Otto Zaugg, an engineering student from the University of Zürich and director of the student camps, who took me on a tour of the village and the work project. He explained that Ausserberg's population of about three hundred people lived for the most part in abject poverty. About seven miles above Ausserberg is Lüerig, a smaller village. During the summer most of the men in Ausserberg take the cattle to the high Alpine meadows near Lüerig, where the grass is more abundant. The problem then is to get the milk, butter, and cheese down to the lower village and the railroad. The only means of communication for centuries had been a narrow rocky path, which was very steep in places. The people of that vicinity had heard of the work of the National Union of Swiss Students and had requested that they build a path from Ausserberg to Lüerig. Their application had been favorably considered and during the summer of 1932 the work was begun.

The path was nearing completion when I visited the camp in 1933, and already the women, with great baskets on their backs, were moving up the Studentway *(Studentenweg),* as it was called, with provisions for their husbands or coming down with milk, butter, cheese, or firewood from the forests above.

There were about fifty young men and five girls in the camp. The youth slept in houses donated by the village, on straw ticks laid in rows along the floor. They ate in a room on the first floor of a large house or in the open when the weather permitted. The villagers were on friendly terms with the students, and the last night of the camp organized a celebration for them about a half mile up the *Studentenweg* from Ausserberg. A large fire was built and the villagers sang folk songs and told stories. The students put on several skits and joined in the singing. Wine of poor, bitter quality from the villagers' precious homemade stock was freely passed to the students.

Purpose of the Camps

These camps assist the villagers and give the students of Switzerland an opportunity to work with and to know the depressed groups in their own country. They permit students of different nationalities to work and live together, to discuss common problems, and thus to come to understand one another better. The student camps, like the camps of the International Voluntary Service, are ready in case of disasters to help repair the damage. However, they are not motivated by a pacifist ideology, and they restrict their work to projects within the boundaries of Switzerland.

Harvest Service

A service closely connected with the student work camps is the Harvest Service (*Service de Fanage*), which enrolled an average of 160 students each year during the period 1932-35. Requests for harvest hands come from the secretaries of agriculture in the cantons and are handled by the Student Voluntary Work Service. Students from different colleges and universities in Switzerland, who are at least seventeen years of age and in good health, volunteer during the summers to assist the poorer peasants with harvesting. The work period is from three to four weeks, and the farmer for whom work is done furnishes room and board. Other costs, such as railroad fare, insurance, and administration, are borne by the federal government, the cantons, and various agricultural organizations. The average cost per individual for a harvest season from 1933 to 1935 was 19.48 francs ($5.84). This work has continued for a period of approximately seven years now and, like the camps, gives the youth of Switzerland opportunity to study economic conditions by working and living with the depressed classes.

In recent years interest in student camps in Switzerland has lagged somewhat and there are not so many applicants as formerly. However, the student camps still provide the university youth of Switzerland with an excellent opportunity to gain practical experience and to supplement their college training.

Camps for Unemployed

The origin of the Swiss labor camps for unemployed goes back as far as 1920, about the time the labor service in Bulgaria was starting. On December 7, 1920 Waldvogel introduced a motion in the Federal Council advocating a compulsory labor service of six months for all Swiss young people. The service could be justified, Waldvogel said, on the basis of social, educational, economic, and national needs. Nevertheless, the National Council defeated the motion because, as it said, the service (1) would make an unjustifiable break in the normal progress of young people through school and into occupational activity; (2) would be opposed by the young people; (3) would interfere with military service; (4) would be too costly; and (5) would require a constitutional amendment.

In 1933, however, the unemployment problem in Switzerland became acute, especially for young men. Out of Switzerland's population of 4,000,000 there were about 15,000 unemployed young people. This number was reduced to approximately 10,000 during the summer of 1936, but rose again to about 15,000. The government of Switzerland decided to adopt the camp idea to assist in solving this problem of idle youth.

By an order of April 13, 1933 which dealt in general with relief for the unemployed, the Federal Council was empowered to make over to work camps for young unemployed, funds to the extent of, and not to exceed, two-fifths of the total outlay for maintenance, shelter, payment of pocket money, and railroad fares. Materials and tools could be included only in special cases. Cantons and communes together must

SWISS UNEMPLOYED CAMPS

Above: Mealtime. *Right:* Road construction in experimental forest. *Below:* Recreation after work

SWISS UNEMPLOYED CAMPS

Above:
Moving rock

Left:
Wash day

Below:
A pause in the afternoon's work

make a contribution at least equal in amount to that made by the federal government.

In December 1934 the Federal Council agreed to subsidize camps for older men with no fixed abode, from funds available after the needs of younger men had been met. There were fourteen of these camps in the summer of 1936.

Swiss Center for Voluntary Labor Service

Since the National Union of Swiss Students had planned and administered student camps successfully for nearly ten years, they were called upon to assist in working out plans for camps for unemployed youth. Otto Zaugg, president of student camps in 1933, was made leader of the Swiss Center for Voluntary Labor Service which administers camps for unemployed in cooperation with the Federal Office of Industry, Arts and Crafts, and Labor in Berne. The former organization is private and is composed of representatives from the federal government, the governments of cantons and communes, the National Union of Swiss Students, and private organizations of workers, factory owners, and young people.

The center provides a publicity and information service; orders camp equipment through military authorities; provides a uniform system of bookkeeping and reports; distributes funds and handles all financial negotiations; and examines projects with a view to making recommendations regarding them. If approved, a request for funds is made to the Federal Council which will not, however, grant aid unless the conditions set up by it are met as to type of project and workers employed on it.

At the head of the center is a council consisting of a president, a representative from the Federal Office of Industry, Arts and Crafts, and Labor, and one representative from each cooperating agency. This council admits new members, selects the executive committee for the year, sets up the budget, and considers reports. It convenes annually, but may meet oftener if circumstances demand or if one-third of the membership requests it. The executive committee consists of the president, at least one other member of the council, and the leader of the Swiss Center for Voluntary Labor Service.

The cooperating agencies finance their own activities and keep separate accounts. The center submits a yearly budget for common expenses, which is met by membership contributions, grants, and voluntary gifts. Although the members of the center represent varying political, religious, and economic points of view, the center itself is required to maintain complete neutrality in this respect.

There are eighteen local work service offices in various parts of the country, including seven public and four religious offices. Among the most important are the Zürich Central Office for Young Unemployed, which like the Swiss center is a coordinating agency for a number of local groups, the Evangelical Youth Conference, and Swiss Catholic Youth. The first two of these established camps in 1932, the Catholic group in 1933. These local offices present projects to the center, secure funds through it, and then assume responsibility for seeing that the project is completed.

Selection of Volunteers and Period of Enrollment

The recruiting of men is done through factories, political parties, guilds, the press, churches, and religious organizations. The local offices keep in direct touch with youth. There has been no difficulty in securing men to fill the camps, since for most of them enrollment means better living conditions, having work, and relieving an overburdened family.

Selection is left to the judgment of the local offices, but is determined largely by requirements which the government has made for the granting of financial aid. These requirements specify that the young man must be not older than twenty-four years of age, must be in good health, must have previously exhausted every possibility of finding work outside, and must remain registered with a public employment exchange during his stay in camp. The cantons try to place their own residents in local camps first, but the men often prefer to be sent out of their own communities.

The period of enrollment is limited to three consecutive months as a rule. In no case may it exceed six out of twelve months. After two consecutive months' service, a man is given a certificate which confers certain rights of priority with placement institutions.

Number and Cost of the Camps

During the summer of 1936 there were about fifty-five camps for the unemployed in Switzerland with about 2,700 men enrolled. Approximately half the camps were for young men; the others for older men. There were also several projects, or camps, which permitted men trained in the professions to utilize their abilities, thus gaining valuable experience until jobs in private industry became available.

The general expenses of the camps are paid for as follows: 40 per cent by the federal government, 40 per cent by the cantonal and communal governments, and 20 per cent by the people for whom the work is done. The cost of camps is about five Swiss francs a man a day, which includes food, clothing, insurance, room, and transportation. The camps cost the Swiss Confederation a total of 2,000,000 francs annually (about $400,000).

Administration of the Camps

The administrative staff of the camps consists of a director, an assistant director in charge of the work projects, and a housemother who is also usually responsible for the cooking. One of the greatest problems in the Swiss camps has been to obtain the services of well-trained directors. Some directors of student camps have done well as leaders of the camps for the unemployed, but a training course for other leaders has been needed. Such courses are now being provided by the central office for the Voluntary Labor Service, and are limited to fifteen or twenty men selected by the office. One requirement for admission is previous experience as a worker in a camp, although exceptions are made in favor of candidates who seem to show unusual aptitude for camp leadership. The training course includes a survey of the labor service movement in Switzerland; the organization, direction, and administration of a camp; a study of federal and local unemployment relief measures; the readjustment of the unemployed worker in the camp and his occupational reorientation; introduction to techniques required on work projects:

problems of a rural nature, silviculture, and rural settlement. Discussion and instruction are supplemented by practical demonstrations and inspection trips.[1] By the summer of 1936 all camp directors had gone through a training program.

Development of the Camp Program

At first camps for the unemployed performed only public works projects and did little to train the young men for skilled jobs. The projects consisted chiefly of building roads and trails, conserving historical landmarks, such as castles and old houses, and making historical and archaeological surveys. The second type of camp developed for unemployed in Switzerland was organized to train young men for jobs, for example, machinists, welders, clerks, masons, tailors, and barbers. An order of May 24, 1935 empowered the Federal Office of Industry, Arts and Crafts, and Labor to take necessary measures for developing public employment service and improving the state of the labor market. These measures include vocational development and rehabilitation of the young unemployed and are subsidized by the federal government, thus strengthening the policy of assisting work camps which include vocational training in their program.

The work day varies from six to eight hours, with Saturday afternoon free. The work week is forty-eight hours, but in exceptional cases may be reduced to forty hours, especially in winter. Twelve hours may be deducted for attendance at vocational classes.

In the fall of 1936, accompanied by Swiss officials, I visited camps in several parts of Switzerland. One camp, in the suburbs of Zürich, containing about sixty unemployed young men, was building a road through an area which was used as an experimental laboratory by the state forestry school. Another camp at Kemleten, near Winterthur, was building a road through a state-owned forest. Camps which perform public works projects are usually housed in barracks quite similar to those of the C C C camps in the United States. Recently the Swiss War Department has constructed special demountable barracks for the labor service, which can be assembled and disassembled very quickly.

[1] Centrale suisse, *Bulletin de renseignements,* X-XI (juillet-août 1936).

Winterthur Training Center

One of the best examples of the second type of camps, those which train men for jobs, has been conducted on the outskirts of Winterthur. It has been training young unemployed Swiss men to be machinists, electric welders, and house electricians. The camp has been housed in the oldest cotton mill on the continent of Europe. It was built in 1806, when Napoleon attempted to make the Continent independent of England, so far as manufactured goods were concerned. This training project for young unemployed Swiss began as an experiment conducted by Charles Schaer, of Winterthur, who noticed that many young men were idling about the streets of that city, and on his own initiative developed a small shop to train them to be machinists. He ran this machine shop under the direction of the city officials of Winterthur for about a year and was so successful in interesting and training young men for technical jobs that his facilities were inadequate to care for all the boys who volunteered to take his training course. He then interested the city government in the project, and with their assistance, plus additional subsidies from the federal government, acquired the old cotton mill on the outskirts of the town. The federal government paid 60 per cent of the cost of buildings and administration, the canton of Zürich 20 per cent, and the city of Winterthur 20 per cent. Most of the tools which the boys use, as well as the ten benches on which they work, have been made at camp.

The training program in the new location began in March 1935. There were two sections—one taught the young men machine welding; the other taught them how to become turners and machine-shop helpers. In September 1936 a third course was developed to train young men as electricians. There has been an average of about thirty-five men between the ages of nineteen and twenty-five enrolled in the third course and a total of sixty-five in the other two courses.

In order to enter this training center, the young men must have served as apprentices in the trade which they wish to relearn and they must be unemployed. They are selected and enrolled by the employment offices all over Switzerland.

Each training project is supervised by an advisory commission made up of representatives from the federal government, the government of the canton, and the governments of Zürich and Winterthur. The camp staff consists of a director, two women cooks, a foreman for benchmen, a foreman for turners, a foreman for mill machinery, a foreman and assistant for welding, and two electricians who direct the work of the men in the practice projects.

The director explained that while many of the young men in the training center had at one time possessed technical skills, they had been forced to work as farm hands because of lack of opportunities in their own fields, and as a result had lost their skill. Some of them had, he felt, been poorly trained as apprentices. When the men first come to camp the director starts them out measuring and gives them other practical experience in the simpler skills. They must spend one hour each week in the classroom, for the most part learning mechanical drawing. They then gradually are given opportunity to do more complicated things. Of special interest to the boys is a course in welding. This usually lasts from two to three months, depending upon the ability of the individual.

The course to train electricians had not had a chance to prove itself, but seemed to be making progress. We visited the electrical shop and saw men mounting electrical equipment on steel, tile, and wood, and learning how to install switches, plugs, and outlets.

The training center at Winterthur has been singularly successful in placing young men who have been trained in welding and machine-shop operations. After all available jobs in and around Winterthur have been filled, the men are sent to other cantons in Switzerland. The director explained that there are good job opportunities in the field of electric welding since the government is now building airplanes for national defense. He stated that more than 75 per cent of the men who had learned welding and machine operation had been placed. The school is gaining a reputation for its welders and machinists, and frequently manufacturers request the director to inform them when he has young men ready for employment.

While it is true that the training program for electricians has not been conducted for as long a period of time as that for welders and machinists, the director was concerned over his inability to place young men who became electricians. The building trades in Switzerland have been lagging, and it is very possible that jobs in this field may not be available for two or three years. In this event the young men will have to take such jobs as farmers' helpers or delivery boys, and will probably lose much of the skill they have gained.

Three farm camps in Switzerland are planned especially to train young men to become farmers' helpers. While there is a scarcity of jobs in business and industry, there seems to be ample opportunity for single men who are willing to work on farms. We visited one project near Zürich where the equipment included a farmhouse and barn which the campers have rebuilt and modernized, several cows and horses, and complete farming equipment.

General Education in the Camps

When camps for unemployed were begun, they met opposition from Socialists, Communists, and some religious groups, especially the Catholics. It was, therefore, impossible at first to attempt any comprehensive educational program. However, confidence in directors of camps has increased, and recently permission has been given to the central government to develop an "educational and cultural" program in camps. It is difficult to find leaders, however, for this phase of the camp program, because it is seldom that persons qualified for camp administration also have qualities that make good educational directors.

Technical Labor Service

The International Labor Office credits Zürich with having introduced the idea of a technical labor service in Switzerland in 1932. This is under the direction of a committee representing the Federal Office of Industry, Arts and Crafts, and Labor, the cantonal employment offices of Zürich, Aarau, and Basle, the municipal employment offices of Zürich and Winterthur, and various trade associations. An employment bureau is in charge of the technical work, and it is jointly subsidized by the Swiss Confederation, the cantons, and the city of Zürich.

The work is planned so that it will not compete with ordinary labor and will utilize and develop the particular skills available. The participants do topographical work, surveys of artistic monuments and buildings, and prepare charts and graphs. This labor service keeps in close touch with the placement service for technical workers and in this way is able to help many workers find employment in ordinary occupations.

Conclusions

The Swiss work camps for unemployed have gained great popular favor since their establishment in 1933. As indication of this, the public collection which is made annually on August 1, Switzerland's Independence Day, was donated in 1935 to the central office for Voluntary Labor Service to assist in the administration and development of the system of camps in Switzerland.

Although compulsory labor service for youth was rejected by the Federal Council in 1920, some groups in Switzerland have continued to sponsor the idea. In 1934 a conference of experts was called to consider various reports which had been made advocating introduction of the compulsory feature. By a large majority, the conference voted against the idea, at the same time urging extension of camps on the existing basis to meet the real needs of youth. The Federal Council, and the Swiss public in general, agreed with the decision of this conference.[2]

In Switzerland the tendency at present is for camps for the unemployed to continue indefinitely as a part of the program for youth. In recent years the camps organized by the National Union of Swiss Students have not been received by students either in Switzerland or abroad as enthusiastically as they were during the first eight or nine years of their existence, but they will undoubtedly be organized each summer for many years to come.

Bibliography

"Conditions in Switzerland: The Voluntary Labor Service," *Industrial and Labor Information,* LV, 11 (September 9, 1935) 303.

CONFEDERATION SUISSE. Arrêté fédéral concernant la lutte contre la crise et la création de possibilités de travail, 21 décembre 1934. 8 pp.

——— Ordonnance concernant le placement, le développement professionnel et les measures propres à faciliter la translation des chômeurs, 24 mai 1935. 7 pp.

——— Ordonnance concernant le service de travail, 24 mai 1935. 5 pp.

[2] International Labor Office, *Unemployment among Young Persons,* pp. 118-19.

GUSTAV EGLI. *Der freiwillige Arbeitsdienst in der Schweiz.* Zürich: Oprecht, 1936. 221 pp.

H. LEIBUNDGUT. "Le service de travail volontaire en Suisse," Extrait du *Journal forestier suisse,* 1936, no. 6. 7 pp.

"Measures against Unemployment in Switzerland," *Industrial and Labor Information,* LIII, 9 (March 4, 1935), 286.

"Measures against Unemployment in Switzerland; the Voluntary Labor Service," *Industrial and Labor Information,* LIV, 12 (June 17, 1935), 412-13.

CHARLES SCHAER. *Hard; das Berufslager für Metallarbeiter.* Zürich: 1936. 78 S.

SCHWEIZERISCHE ZENTRALSTELLE FÜR FREIWILLIGEN ARBEITSDIENST. *Durch freiwilligen Arbeitsdienst zurück in die Arbeit und den Beruf.* Separatabzung aus der Zeitschrift *Berufsberatung und Berufsbildung,* August 1935. Zürich. 16 S.

——— *Der freiwillige Arbeitsdienst in der Schweiz.* Zürich: Leemann, 1935. 13 S.

——— *Mitteilungsblatt,* Oktober 1935. (French and German text.)

——— *Statuten,* 1933. 4 S.

"The Situation in Switzerland: Labor Camps and Compulsory Labor Service," *Industrial and Labor Information,* L, 7 (May 14, 1934), 247-48.

Verband der Schweizerischen Studentenschaften. *Das Amt für Arbeitskolonien,* 1935. S. 18-21.

Zentralstelle für jugendliche Erwerbslose. *Hilfe für arbeitslose Jugendliche der Stadt Zürich.* Zürich, n.d. 12 S.

German Camps Before Hitler

We skidded dangerously near a water-filled ditch as our tiny car with its four bulky passengers swung out to pass a great mound of hay that had been jogging along ahead of us, nearly blocking the highway. Having cursed the peasant and his load of hay in harsh, vehement German, my Nazi driver resumed the terrific speed at which we had traveled since leaving Dresden.

This incident occurred during the summer of 1932, when we were on our way to visit German labor camps. The bent and battered fenders on our driver's car clearly showed that he was used to narrow escapes; and flying glass from a broken windshield would only have added a few scars to his already excellent collection, gained in that German university sport of "duelling." Not being accustomed to such reckless driving, I longed for the safety of the German student self-help office (*Deutsches Studentenwerk*) in Dresden, where only a few moments before I had talked with Reinhold Schairer, the director at that time, about the problem of the million and a half unemployed youth in Germany.

From conversation with Schairer and with the young men who were driving me to see the camps, I learned that during the years following the World War and after a short recovery in 1925, young Germans faced a serious unemployment problem. They wandered through their country seeking jobs in much the same way that American youth did in the United States from 1930 to 1933. Still other thousands remained at home to burden their poverty-stricken parents or the relief agencies.

The Germans who returned from the trenches and grew up after the war lived in a nation that had been poorly informed as to actual conditions behind their lines. Many of them had believed that if they threw themselves wholeheartedly into the war they were bound to be victorious, but after months, even years, in the debilitating conditions of the trenches they had to face the realities of defeat. Lack of food and clothing, especially among their civilian relatives and friends, convinced these ex-soldiers that the Central Powers had been much harder pressed than they had suspected, but they did not realize that their defeat had been overwhelming or that the whole internal organization of Germany was disintegrating. They believed that the "Fourteen Points" of Woodrow Wilson would be the basis of the peace settlement. Woodrow Wilson had talked of a "just peace," a "peace without victory," but his declarations were interpreted in one way by the Germans and in another by the Allies.

When representatives from Germany were finally called to sign the completed treaty at Versailles, the German nation was shocked by its severity. Germany was to lose her colonies, was to be divided by the Polish Corridor, was to lose her war and commercial fleets, was to be burdened by a huge indemnity, and was to take responsibility for the war. This treaty, the Germans said, was a violation of the "Fourteen Points" of President Wilson. The politically active youth of Germany rebelled against its tremendous burden. They never accepted the treaty as a just settlement. They were humiliated by the clause of the treaty that made Germany responsible for the war. Much of what is deplored in Germany today by the United States and the democratic countries of Europe is attributable in large part to the Carthaginian peace imposed on Germany at Versailles in 1919.

German youth were therefore disillusioned by the war and the peace settlement, and grew up under conditions that left many of them without food or shelter, or jobs with which these could be obtained.

During the period immediately following the World War the young Germans experienced for the first time the privileges of citizenship in a democratic state. Because of the lack of experience in self-government and the absence of democratic traditions, the serious economic conditions drove them to extreme political beliefs. Some pledged allegiance to the red flag with the sickle and hammer, while others adopted the swastika of Hitler and joined the ranks of the brown shirts. As the years passed and economic conditions became worse, one group heckled the other, and their meetings often ended in riotous fighting.

Germany's most precious resource, its young people, was being wasted. Many of the youth had been undernourished during the war and were now desperately in need of healthful labor and wholesome food to rebuild them physically. Older Germans saw the youth of the nation deteriorating and harked back to the days of compulsory military training before the World War. The youth needed to learn to live together to understand and help the German Reich regain its position of trust and respect among nations.

In 1921 Bulgaria had established a compulsory labor service, and during the early twenties some Germans had visited and worked in the Bulgarian camps. A labor service now appeared to be a desirable means of caring for some of the youth in Germany. Experimentation in this field was begun under the leadership of college and university professors, students, and various sport and Christian associations. Work service was not a strictly post-war idea in Germany, however, as we learned in the introductory chapter. In 1912 Eugen Rosenstock and some of his colleagues at Heidelberg University had proposed an "Army of Public Peace."

The idea of a system of camps in Germany, made imperative by economic conditions, gained support from the German youth movement which, even before the World War, had encouraged young people to get out into the open country and live voluntarily a life of hardships. During the war young people from fourteen to seventeen volunteered for harvest work to replace the men who were in the army. Following the war this idea of work service was discussed and even proposed by various youth organizations, among them the Artaman League (named after an Indo-Germanic deity of the soil).[1]

Origins of the Labor Service

Some German writers, especially Müller-Brandenburg, now chief of the Division of Foreign Relations and Information in the National Socialist Labor Service, would give the origin of labor service an earlier date. They insist that the colonization and development of Brandenburgia, Pomerania, Silesia, and West and East Prussia during the Middle Ages was really accomplished by what is now called labor service. Müller-Brandenburg maintains that the origins of modern German

[1] See Friedrich W. Heinz, *Kameraden der Arbeit* (Berlin: Frundsberg Verlag, 1933), S. 54; see also Otto D. Tolischus, "Young Germany Faces the Labor Draft," *New York Times Magazine*, Jan. 20, 1935, p. 5.

ꓤE-HITLER GERMAN
LABOR CAMPS

ve:

'aking lunch to the
'kers on the project

er Right:

. Nazi in voluntary
or camp

ht:

inging the bell for
ner

PRE-HITLER GER
CAMPS

Recreation in a
in northern Germ

political life are to be found in the lands won by blood and work, and that it was because of the effects of this rugged experience with nature that Prussia developed capacity for leadership and became the political center of Germany.[2]

Frederick the Great is considered by many Nazi writers on the German work service to be its greatest historical figure, and some of the projects now being carried out were planned and mapped out by him during the eighteenth century. Müller-Brandenburg names him as one of the labor service leaders, and considers that the resettlement of 70,000 people in Prussia after the Seven Years' War, and the development there of cities and industries, was the result of a type of labor service developed by Frederick the Great. The following two quotations from the Emperor's writings are frequently used by the present work service: "The poorer a land is, the more it must be cultivated," and "He who brings it about that where formerly one stalk of grain grew, henceforth two are produced, does more for his people than a general who wins a great battle."[3]

While there seems to be very little real connection between the activities of the German race during the seventeenth and eighteenth centuries and the present work service, such an alleged historical background adds to the glamour of the labor service and emphasizes its Germanic origin. This attempt to link the institutions of "New Germany" with the German "blood and soil" of the past is in accordance with accepted practice in the National Socialist state.

Voluntary Labor Service Established

Labor service in Germany really began in 1925, when the leaders of the German free corps *(Deutsche Freischar)*, a group in the youth movement, organized the first camp at Colborn, Hannover, to unite young people of their organization in "common work and common play for the mutual understanding and enrichment of their life and

---

[2] Müller-Brandenburg, *Was ist Arbeitsdienst? Was soll er?* (Leipzig: Armanen Verlag, 1934), S. 16-21.

[3] Quoted by Erich F. Berendt in *Männer und Taten* (Leipzig: Der nationale Aufbau, n.d.), I, 62.

outlook."[4] Fifty students did field and forest work on the grounds of a castle, working six hours in the morning followed by an obligatory rest period of two hours. The remainder of the day was devoted to lectures, singing, and discussions. The outdoor labor and wholesome food made these students physically strong; an educational and recreational program built up their morale. The informal interchange of ideas and the practical experience of working with their hands had distinct educational implications for students whose lives had been spent in the realm of the theoretical.

After the first camp of 1925 no camps were organized for three years. It was not until 1928 that another camp was developed, at Löwenberg, Silesia. This camp brought together students, young workers, and peasants[5] for three weeks during the summer. In the spring of the next year a similar camp was organized under the auspices of the *Deutsche Freischar,* a group which continued to organize camps in 1929 and 1930. By 1931 some thirty work camps had been organized, which brought together the unemployed from industries, farms, and universities.

Working side by side in camp tended to make the young people realize that political and class distinctions were artificial and that they had enough in common to cooperate as citizens of Republican Germany. The young intellectual found that physical labor removed many of his impractical tendencies. The youth of Germany from the different classes were brought under a common roof and taught to work together.

In the meantime the depression had spread over the nation, paralyzing industry and trade. The already serious conditions in Germany grew worse. The number of unemployed increased, and private groups, such as Christian, sports, and student organizations, were unable with their own means to expand the system of camps to meet the increasing need for help. Finally, to help solve the unemployment problem, the government decided to subsidize the camps.

---

[4] There is a difference of opinion among German writers as to which camp was really the first to demonstrate the value and desirability of labor service. On the basis of the information available to us we believe that the camp at Colborn is the forerunner of the system of camps in Germany.

[5] Osgood Nichols and Comstock Glaser, *Work Camps for America* (New York: Day, 1933), p. 9.

An emergency order issued June 5, 1931 concerning unemployment insurance and relief made the Federal Institution for Employment Exchanges and Unemployment Insurance "responsible for the promotion of voluntary labor service" for those in receipt of unemployment benefit, especially those persons under twenty-five years of age.[6]

On July 16, 1932 another emergency decree[7] was made public which increased the government backing of the voluntary labor service (*Freiwilliger Arbeitsdienst*) and appropriated about 60,000,000 reichsmarks ($14,000,000) for this work. The federal government immediately began to subsidize private camps of all kinds, provided they could meet certain conditions, in order to provide the unemployed with work, room, board, and work clothes.

Visit to a Camp

It was one of these camps, just beginning to receive the support of the government, that we were on our way to see that morning when a load of hay nearly landed our small Opel in the ditch. About an hour after leaving Dresden, we turned off onto a narrow road through the woods, and a short descent into a valley brought us to the foot of a newly constructed dam. To the left on a small rise stood the barracks where the contingent of youth was housed. Along the small stream of water that came from the base of the dam some fifty bronzed young Germans were busily engaged in constructing a stone spillway. Stripped to the waist and deeply tanned, they seemed healthy and in high spirits. A small car on steel rails brought the stone from the stream bed a hundred yards below. Four husky fellows pushed the car up the slight grade to a point near the workers, dumped the load of rock, and then rode back down the hill talking and joking. A burst of laughter greeted a splash, when one young worker lost his footing and slipped into the water.

These young men seemed normal and happy. They did not have the hopeless look of the unemployed I had seen in Münich, Breslau, Dresden, Hamburg, and Berlin. Here there were no party emblems, no bitter disputes ending in fist fights. My guide informed me that it

[6] International Labor Office, *Legislative Series*, 1931 (Germany 5).

[7] *Ibid.*, 1932.

was only after several weeks in camp under excellent leadership that these young men returned to normal condition and attitude.

We talked to some of the boys as they worked. Erich, broad-shouldered, blue-eyed, and blond, had never had a steady job. His father had been killed during the World War and his family pauperized. After he finished school, he worked at odd jobs on the neighboring farms. Then the lights of the capital attracted him. He left Saxony and made his way to Berlin, then to Hamburg, but was unsuccessful in finding work. Finally, he returned to the vicinity of Dresden and heard of the voluntary labor service camps, immediately applied, and for the first time found something satisfying and worthwhile to do. He said he enjoyed working in the camp and hoped to remain the maximum period permitted—forty weeks.

The camp quarters were not luxurious, but the barracks of rough lumber were clean and well built. Army cots with blankets were arranged in orderly rows, and underneath each cot were the personal belongings of the occupant. The meals were prepared by the youth under the direction of an unemployed army cook. Food was plain but wholesome, and no restriction was placed on the amount each individual could have at a meal. A large wood-burning stove in each of the rooms provided heat.

Organization and Administration of Camps

Three types of German camps existed at that time—open, half-open, and closed—if we translate the German into English. In the open type of camp the youth merely worked on projects with other men, while living and eating at home. These camps were not considered satisfactory, as it was very difficult to develop any *esprit de corps* in them. In the half-open camps the youth lived at home, but took their meals at camp. The closed camps were resident camps in which the young men both lived and ate. These were generally thought to be the most desirable, and there was a steady and successful movement to make all camps of this type. The youth remained in the service night and day and thus developed more of an understanding of the problems of their fellow workers and felt that they were part of an organization run by and for youth. In April 1933 nonresident camps were abolished.

'RE-HITLER GERMANY

ver right:

Campers staging amateur
amatics in a church

ht:

Mending clothes in the sun

ow:

Girls collecting brush to
e ditches

wer right:

Breakfast

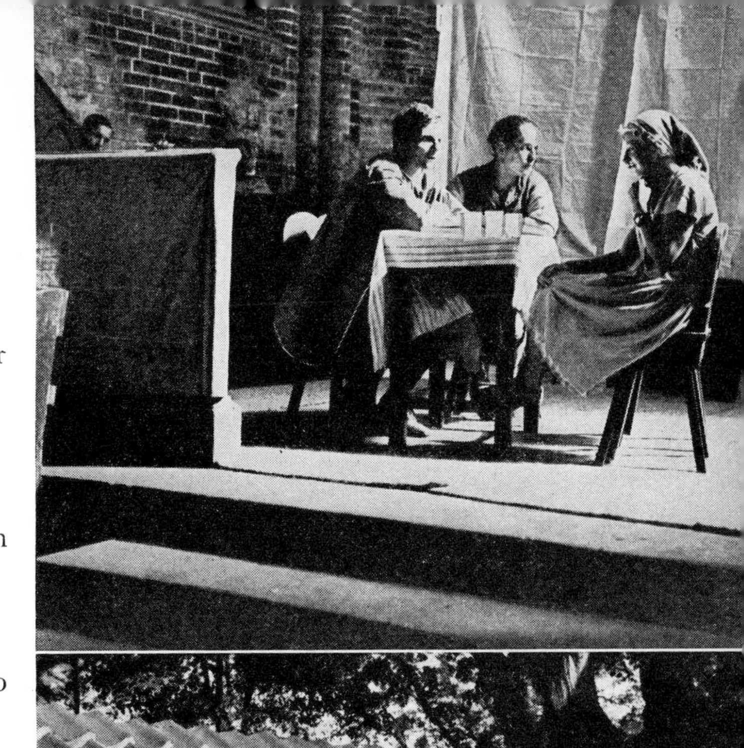

PRE-HITLER GERMA
LABOR CAMPS

Above:

Adult education in
camp, a discussion

Left:

Boys and girls working
gether

Lower left:

Departure from the ca

The law setting up the camps provided that all Germans under twenty-five years of age could volunteer for such work, but that for every twenty-five persons in a camp, one above that age could enroll. This provision was planned to admit unemployed intellectuals into the camps to assist in planning and executing the educational program.

An emergency decree stated that if a youth left a camp before he had worked out his contract, he forfeited his right to unemployment insurance, but from my observations, this penalty was hardly necessary. Experts in the *Studentenwerk* estimated that half a million young Germans would have entered the camps in 1932 had they been given the opportunity.

By November 1932 the camps contained about 285,000 young Germans between the ages of eighteen and twenty-five who received for their services about 25 pfennigs (6 cents) a day, besides room, board, and work clothes. The small sum of money was not considered a salary or compensation for the work done, but merely pocket money to purchase candy, tobacco, or other incidentals. For some of the German youth, work in the voluntary labor service *(Freiwilliger Arbeitsdienst)* was simply a relief job, but the majority of those who volunteered for this service were motivated by a spirit of devotion to duty and a desire to perform constructive work for their country. The cost of the camps was about 2.14[8] reichsmarks (51 cents) a man per day, including the 25 pfennigs (6 cents) per day given to the workers as pocket money.

The voluntary labor service was administered by a government commissioner in the Ministry of Labor. Friedrich Syrup was the first man to occupy this position. His subordinates in the thirteen state offices and the 363 local bureaus cooperated by supervising the local camps. The actual selection of the work projects, the recruiting of the workers, and the selection of the leaders were left in the majority of instances to the local bureaus.

Organization of the labor service was entrusted to two types of administrators: a work sponsor (*Träger der Arbeit*), responsible to the Reich who provided tools, machinery, and financial assistance; and a service sponsor *(Träger des Dienstes),* responsible for recruiting the workers, equipping the camp, and organizing its life. The *Träger der*

[8] At this time the reichsmark was worth about 23 cents.

Arbeit was never an individual citizen, but usually a local government authority, a farmer's cooperative, or a federal department. The *Träger des Dienstes* was usually a religious or charitable group, athletic or sport club, youth or employees' organization.

The camp leader, chosen by the *Träger des Dienstes,* was responsible for camp discipline and administration and the carrying out of the project. With the help of the students he organized a program for the constructive use of the campers' leisure time. Leaders were often selected from the ranks of the unemployed, but since rare personal qualities were needed, it was sometimes necessary to find them among the employed and to give them a salary of from twelve to fifteen dollars per month besides room and board. The most popular leaders, however, were those who, like the youth, had volunteered to enter the service. At first it was possible to choose these leaders carefully, but soon the quick growth of the movement made it difficult to select and train them properly.

Prior to the introduction of training for camp leadership by the state, the leaders were chosen from among camp participants, and anyone showing special ability for camp management and organization was a potential candidate for a leader's position. Gradually, however, the organizations in charge of the voluntary labor service transformed the most suitably located camps into training centers for leaders.

Training of Leaders

By a decree of September 5, 1932 [9] the state opened schools for camp leaders in the various districts. Requirements for admission were that candidates must have taken active part in the voluntary labor service and have shown special ability for the work. Selection of the men to be trained was in the hands of the district school commissioners. The candidates, who came from many different organizations and varied in age from twenty to fifty years, had to apply by handwritten letter through the Employment Exchange, giving their life history and references from the *Träger des Dienstes.*

The courses for leaders which lasted from four to six weeks included

[9] Reichsanstalt für Arbeitsvermittlung und Arbeitslosenversicherung. *Reichsarbeitsmarktanzeiger,* 1932 Nr. 17, 7. September, Dienstliche Mitteilungen Nr. 77.

demonstrations by experts, interchange of experiences, with general discussions on camp management, camp hygiene, technical problems, sports, and leisure-time activities. The schedule was similar to that of a regular camp, but practical work was shortened and theoretical studies were extended. Short courses, varying from ten days to two weeks, were given for leaders already in charge of camps.

Women Volunteers

When these camps were first established in Germany, young women were permitted to volunteer for the *Freiwilliger Arbeitsdienst.* Frequently there were fifteen or twenty young women in each camp of a hundred men, doing the cooking, sewing, and other work around the camp. Some camps were set up for women alone, and in these the volunteers raised vegetables for other camps or for the poor, repaired the clothes of the workers, took care of children, and did the housework in poor people's homes and general social service work in the slum areas of cities. From my own observation it seemed that the camps composed of both men and women had a better morale than had those composed entirely of either sex. In a camp at Cismar, Germany, a little village near the old Hanseatic city of Lübeck, where I worked during the summer of 1932 there were about twenty young women and eighty men. We were housed in an old Cistercian abbey, which had been converted into a summer camp by a Christian association. The behavior of the men and the general morale of the camp were much better than in the camps composed of men only, which I had visited earlier in the summer.

When the girls first came to Cismar they were assigned to the kitchen and to work around the camp. After a few weeks they rebelled against such work (this was before the *"Kinder, Kirche, Küche"* program of Hitler), stating that they wanted to go out into the woods and do the same type of work the men were doing. The men agreed to this and took their turn in the kitchen. The women were thus able to emancipate themselves from the humdrum of camp housekeeping.

These young women who demanded the right to do the same work as the men soon found that with rights come duties. The project in the camp at Cismar involved the draining of a forest, and the work consisted largely of clearing brush and digging ditches. This required wading in mud, decayed leaves, and brackish water up to our knees. The girls found that wielding an ax or a pick and shovel under these conditions was not so enjoyable as they had expected. Some of them frankly admitted that they could not do the work; others stuck to the job in spite of painful blisters and backaches. The men finally convinced them that it was not necessary for them to use picks, axes, and shovels. Since the project required the clearing of brush and small trees before the ditches were dug there was quite a bit of material to be burned, and the young women realized their desire for hard labor in the open air by turning to this work.

Life in the Camps

The youth in the camps devoted their mornings to public works projects. They built roads, drained land on a small scale, regulated lesser streams, prepared land for agricultural settlement, did forestry work, and built gardens for the poor. The type of work done was restricted by law to projects which promoted the general welfare, could not be done by regular laborers, and did not compete with or take work from employed workers.[10]

Our afternoons and evenings were devoted to educational recreational programs adapted to the different types of workers. An attempt was made, however, to impress all workers with their duties and responsibilities to the social order and to help them to understand their place in the life of the community. The methods by which this program was carried out varied in the different camps from the formal lectures of *"Herr Doktor"* to informal discussions in which the authority met his listeners on an even plane. As would be expected, the informal discussions proved to be the most usual and effective type of instruction. The speaker or leader of the discussion group was urged to spend at least a day in the camp where he was to speak, in order to familiarize himself with the condition and attitudes of the youth and the types of men and women who were in that particular *Arbeitslager*.

When the discussion groups were first attempted, it was essential to start with the most elementary subjects. If the camp was composed mainly of students, it was not hard to organize discussion groups; if,

[10] International Labor Office, *op. cit.*

IN A PRE-HITLER CAMP IN NORTHERN GERMANY

bove:

Enjoying the sun and food during a rest eriod

ight:

An effigy of the author made by his room-
ıates

elow:

Marching home from work in a forest

PRE-HITLER GERMAN
CAMPS

Above:
Ready to work in camp
Heiligenhafen

Left:
Drainage work being
by campers near Dresden

Below:
The members of a s
camp near Lübeck

however, the camp was composed of unemployed workers and peasants with only a few students, discussion was far from easy. To arouse the interest of the workers and the peasants it was necessary to select subjects which came within their immediate experience, and this was sometimes difficult.

The first few discussions were devoted to explanations of the foundations of the state and society; then problems of the locality were considered; then more complicated matters beyond the immediate experience of some members of the group were taken up. Care was taken not to proceed too rapidly, if a large number of students whose knowledge was naturally greater than that of the others were included. The unique feature of the discussions was that members of different classes of society expressed their opinions on subjects of common interest.

The first camp in Silesia owed its existence to the distressing conditions of the Waldenburg district. The first subject for discussion, therefore, was "social conditions in an industrial community." Another camp in the same area discussed "the trend of population towards the cities." A third camp talked of "the breakdown of the agricultural community." The first camp in northern Germany considered "men and work in our times." Subsequent camps dealt with the relationship of city and country.

In every group problems which touched the lives of the volunteers were considered. For example, in Upper Silesia a camp composed of workers, peasants, and students was established, and a discussion program for the afternoons was outlined. The volunteers, having been recruited from that immediate area, could be most readily interested in matters that came vividly into their experience. What were the questions which met this requirement? First, there were the problems of industry and unemployment as they affected the area from which the recruits were drawn. The great majority of the volunteers had experienced unemployment and were familiar with the industries of that area. A study of their personal unemployment problem led to a consideration of the unemployment problem in the whole of Germany. Then the question naturally followed, "Why this unemployment?" Someone immediately suggested the Treaty of Versailles. It was vigorously maintained that the Treaty of Versailles unjustly destroyed the economic unity of Upper Silesia and ruined industry. Passionate discussions followed. Then a consideration of the Treaty of Versailles was necessary. Who drafted it? What does it contain? How does it affect Germany and the world? The members of the group were inevitably brought to a consideration of the World War and the question of war guilt. Thus peasants and unemployed workers of limited experience were led by successive steps from a consideration of their immediate problems to those of national and international importance.

A sincere attempt was made at this time to permit all sides of a question to be presented for discussion. The leaders of the camps were usually young members of the Social Democratic Party who had taken responsibility for a camp because they hoped the German youth who were already being swayed by the blasts of party propaganda from the Communists and National Socialists might be guided along a liberal democratic course to a cooperative solution of Germany's problems.

While working in the camp at Cismar I became acquainted with a Communist who came to the camp believing passionately in the "class struggle." After six weeks of living in a camp with her political opponents she frankly admitted that she had modified her ideas and believed that it was possible to cooperate with other classes in rebuilding the German Reich. These were the days prior to the National Socialist victory, and the daily press almost invariably described clashes between storm troopers and "Reds." Yet in this camp I was sharing the same room with two Communists and two National Socialists. The adherents of each party criticized the political ideas of the other, but did not resort to violence. Peasants and workers were taught to understand their position with relation to society, while students gained respect for the discipline of physical labor, and through contact with the soil lost many of the qualities which Hitler has justly ridiculed as "sterile intellectualism." By cooperating with the people in the surrounding communities and inviting them to participate in discussions, dramatic productions, choruses, and other activities, the camps were developing into what might be called folk schools.

Evenings in the camps were devoted to such activities as storytelling, description of travels, plays, and music. Even the uneducated man from the factory or farm was sometimes found to be a master of storytelling. In every camp the fine old German songs were sung spontaneously during meals, going to work, on the work projects, and returning to camp. There was also group singing under the direction of leaders. Wherever we went we marched; whenever we marched we sang.

The work of the youth in dramatics was especially fine. The leaders of the camps encouraged the free play of imagination and spontaneous expression. Because of the variety of assistance needed to produce a play, this type of artistic effort was singularly successful in bringing out the talent of the youth. It made for creative unity, removed the inhibitions of the lower classes, and opened the way to frankness and a closer comradeship. At first it was difficult to interest the workers and peasants in artistic expression, because it had played no part in their daily lives. Some of them considered it a waste of time. After participating in a few small productions, however, they entered into the activities with vigor and enthusiasm, and very often a play with instrumental music and singing was produced the last night of the camp season. Frequently the people living in the surrounding community were invited to the production, and in this way the camps fostered some of the arts.

Conclusion

The system of labor camps existing in Germany before Hitler came to power was developed because of the conviction of liberals, workers, and educators that the conditions among youth had to be improved if Republican Germany was to survive. The original camps were established at great personal sacrifice by individuals in these groups, who believed that by bringing together the various classes of youth and providing them with work, food, and clothing, as well as the opportunity to exchange ideas and discuss social and economic problems, youth would learn to cooperate in rebuilding Germany.

The backers who gave their time and money so unselfishly to these projects were correct in the belief that the labor camps would assist greatly in breaking down the class hatreds and the political rivalries that existed among German youth. If the camps had been developed on a large scale by the government at a much earlier date undoubtedly they would have prevented a great many youth from becoming enthusiastic Nazis.

The better labor camps developed by Republican Germany had not only completed work projects of great value by 1932 but had become an important part of the educational system. They were so successful and popular that during the last few months of 1932 plans were developed to encourage all students who contemplated higher education to spend an orientation period of several months in them. While these youth were in contact with the rugged forces of nature, they were to be provided with a counseling service. It was hoped that the camp program would direct some of the youth to occupations that did not require them to attend the already overcrowded universities.

At this stage in their development the camps were not without their critics. The Communists fought against the *Freiwilliger Arbeitsdienst* because they feared that it would wipe out class distinctions and permit general class understanding; therefore their representatives in the *Reichstag* opposed subsidies to the *Arbeitsdienst.* National Socialists, on the other hand, were not friendly toward the voluntary camps under private or government auspices because sometimes loyal and devoted Nazis going into the camps lost their fervor for the party. However, Hitler and his followers favored a compulsory labor service, because they saw the possibilities of these camps as propaganda centers, and talked of developing them under their own auspices.

Labor camps were only one project among others which were developed to assist the youth of Germany. But these efforts, intended to help the youth to live normal lives, reached only a part of them and did not compensate for the economic conditions that followed Germany's defeat in the World War. In their want and bewilderment the youth sought a definite program of action that promised results. Both the Communists and National Socialists made fantastic promises, while the more moderate parties controlling Republican Germany temporized, debated, split into numerous factions, and finally failed to carry through a program of action that produced tangible results. That the democratic nations did not give post-war Germany an opportunity to develop and enjoy a reasonable degree of prosperity so that her youth could have lived normal lives was a world tragedy.

Bibliography

C. W. Gray. "Voluntary Labor Service in Germany," *Monthly Labor Review,* XXXV, 4 (October 1932), 802-6.

Friedrich Wilhelm Heinz. *Kameraden der Arbeit; Deutsche Arbeitslager: Stand, Aufgabe und Zukunft.* Berlin: Frundsberg Verlag, 1933. 157 S.

Kenneth Holland. "German Work Camps," *School and Society,* XXXVIII (July 8, 1933), 55-58.

Georg Keil. *Vormarsch der Arbeitslagerbewegung.* Herausgegeben vom Deutschen Studentenwerk. Berlin: De Gruyter, 1932. 133 S.

Hertha Kraus. *Work Relief in Germany.* New York: Russell Sage Foundation, 1934. 93 pp.

Osgood Nichols and Comstock Glaser. *Work Camps for America; the German Experience and the American Opportunity.* New York: Day, 1933. 31 pp.

G. Priesemann. "Das Arbeitslager, ein Weg zur Volksbildung." *Deutsche Rundschau,* 231 (Mai 1932), S. 112-16.

"Voluntary Labor Service in Germany," *Industrial and Labor Information* XLIII, 3 (July 18, 1932), 101-3.

Ernst Wendler. "Das freiwillige Volksdienstjahr; Auftakt und Symbol der deutschen Erhebung," *Deutsche Rundschau,* 288. (Juli 1931), S. 62-67.

The National Socialist Labor Service

ON THE second day of the National Socialist Party Congress at Nuremberg in 1937 nearly 50,000 bronzed young Germans between the ages of eighteen and twenty-one marched past the reviewing stand, with the carriage and precision of an army. Instead of guns they carried brightly polished shovels. This particular Congress was dedicated to "Work," and the compulsory German labor service, in which more than 300,000 young Germans were enrolled, provided a living symbol of this slogan.

Of the numerous spectacles provided by the congress, this marching of the labor service was characterized by many observers as the most thrilling and inspiring. One observer described it as "a demonstration of the dignity of labor, the joy of work in unison, the glory of making the Fatherland a better place in which to live." He stated further, "onlookers, native and foreign, responded wholeheartedly to its appeal." [1]

While the labor service was given an especially prominent place in the 1937 party congress because of the emphasis on work, the uniformed labor battalions of young men and women were also very much in evidence at the 1938 Nuremberg Congress and marched past Hitler and the applauding multitudes along with the other representatives of the so-called "New Germany."

The close connection between the labor service and the National Socialist state is indicated by the oath which every young person takes on entering the labor service:

> I swear that I will dedicate myself in unbreakable allegiance to the Leader of the German Reich and the German people, that I will unconditionally obey him and all the leaders designated by him, that I will resolutely fulfill all my duties of service and that I will be a good comrade to all members of the National Labor Service.[2]

[1] Frederick T. Birchall in the *New York Times,* September 9, 1937.

[2] "Zweite Verordnung zur Durchführung und Ergänzung des Reichsarbeitsdienstgesetzes," (1. Oktober 1935), Artikel 13, *Reichsgesetzblatt,* I, S. 1215.

The National Socialist party considers the labor service one of its most important achievements. This attitude was expressed by Hitler himself when he addressed the labor service at the 1937 Nuremberg congress:

> The greatest thing accomplished by National Socialism in reaching the community goal has been the foundation of the labor service. We can never again visualize Germany without the *Arbeitsdienst*. Nor shall it ever disappear; and the knowledge that through all eternity you and the comrades succeeding you will shoulder a spade, that weapon of peace, is to us a guarantee of the security of our country and of our nation.[3]

The labor service has been described as "one of the three great pillars of the National Socialist educational and fighting body" which "stands between the Hitler Youth and the Storm Troops." It has also been said that, "What the Hitler Youth does for German youth, the labor service shall carry further and perfect, and after six or twelve months send worthy fighters into the Storm Troops. This task the labor service can and must perform."[4]

In the following quotation Müller-Brandenburg explains the relationship among the three divisions of the party organization:

> The road which the labor service travels is practical work on German soil for folk and state, and education of German youth in its ranks to be conscious bearers of the National Socialist idea. The labor service will be the door from the Hitler Youth to the Storm Troops; it will be the door through which each young German will step into complete participation in the life of the people. In practice the labor service is, in the best sense of the word, National Socialism of deeds, an honor service which each young German must have for practical experience.[5]

Movement Toward Compulsory Service

As stated in the preceding chapter, when the German universities, and private organizations, and later the Republican government, were developing work camps in an attempt to care for youth and to bring different classes of young people together in cooperative endeavor, some of the Nationalist Socialists were not favorably inclined toward

[3] Birchall, *op. cit.*

[4] Müller-Brandenburg, *Soldaten der Arbeit* (Leipzig: Seeman, 1934), S. 42.

[5] *Ibid.*, S. 7.

this effort. Hitler and his followers, however, realized the possibilities of the camps for training and developing ardent National Socialists, and a system of Nazi camps was proposed. At the same time, plans were laid to expand this system to include all young men when the National Socialist party should take over the government.

A movement to make the labor service compulsory, however, had been under way for several years before the National Socialists came into power. As early as 1924 Arthur Mahraun, head of the Young German Order, published a brochure, "Concerning the Introduction of a Universal Equal Labor Service Obligation." [6]

In 1928 the Nazis introduced a bill in the Reichstag to establish a compulsory labor service but it was defeated by the Social Democrats, who feared competition with free labor. Another attempt to make the camps compulsory through legislation was instituted in 1930 by the Economic party, which submitted to the Reichstag a bill that had been drafted after study of the Bulgarian labor service law. The proposed bill did not permit commutation of service and required that the unemployed be called up first.[7] The bill also provided a three-month prison sentence for anyone refusing to serve, and recommended that military sports and patriotic instruction be provided in camps. Like the earlier proposal of the National Socialists, however, this bill did not become a law.

In January 1933 President Hindenburg made Hitler chancellor, and shortly thereafter Konstantin Hierl became leader of the labor service. Hierl had been laying groundwork by planning a labor service and his first step as leader was to coordinate all existing camps under Nazi control. Then on January 7, 1934 the camps were transferred from the Ministry of Labor to the Ministry of the Interior. When this was done the movement toward making the service compulsory began to make real progress. Professional organizations started to make admission for membership dependent upon the possession of a labor pass, showing that the candidate had spent a required number of weeks in the labor service. In the spring of 1934 the Na-

---

[6] Friederich W. Heinz, *op. cit.*, S. 53; see also Otto D. Tolischus, "Young Germany Faces the Labor Draft," *New York Times Magazine*, January 20, 1935, pp. 5, 19.

[7] René Auric, *Etude sur le service obligatoire de travail* (Paris: Pedone, 1934), p. 141.

tional Union of German Students *(Deutsche Studentenschaft)* decided that labor service should be required of every student before he could matriculate at a university. In Würtemburg a compulsory term of labor service was introduced for anyone who proposed to become a university teacher, while Saxony was the first state to insist that its entire public service personnel should have experience in the work camps. Employers were "urged," which in many cases meant "ordered," by the National Socialists, to give employment preference to holders of labor passes.

According to Theodor Wilhelm and Gerhard Graefe, this tendency to favor manual labor for students, teachers, and other professional classes grew out of a desire of the German people to "return to the laws of life." [8] These two writers maintain that an "overemphasis of the intellect," a tendency "to identify life with knowledge," to believe "that education could be restricted to the development of the intellect, and . . . could only be effected through the medium of instruction," excluding feelings, will, soul, and emotions, caused German youth to revolt against "this theory of teaching and the kind of school which resulted." The young longed for "finite values." They did not want "merely to be instructed"; they wanted "to be led." [9] Wilhelm and Graefe maintain that young Germans accepted the dictum of Hitler that "the German youth of the future must be slim and strong, as fast as a greyhound, as tough as leather, and as hard as Krupp steel." [10]

It is probable that the majority of the youth did not rationalize their feelings and desires to the extent these writers claim. Rather they were unemployed, dissatisfied, and frequently lacked the basic necessities of life. Faced by these difficulties they were critical and established institutions and grasped at any plan or program that promised better conditions.

Labor Service Becomes Compulsory

On July 1, 1935 a law was passed making the labor service compulsory for all young Germans of both sexes for a six-month period, as

[8] Theodor Wilhelm and Gerhard Graefe, *German Education Today* (Berlin: Terramare, 1936), pp. 3-5.

[9] *Ibid.*, pp. 6-7.

[10] *Ibid.*

"an honor service for the German people." Failure to perform this service means loss of citizenship. According to the law, the aims of the service are: "to educate German youth in the spirit of National Socialism and . . . to awaken in them a feeling of national unity and a true conception of labor, above all a proper esteem for manual labor."[11]

Thus, according to the law of 1935, all young Germans of both sexes are obliged to enter the service.[12] As a rule they are called to camp during the summer they complete their nineteenth year, but provision is made for voluntary enrollment at the age of eighteen, making it possible for students who contemplate university courses to enter the labor service when they complete their preparatory school work.

The five groups of persons excluded from the labor service by law are: (1) those who have been sentenced to a penitentiary or to hard labor; (2) those who have lost their civic rights; (3) those subjected to the regulations of public safety and personal improvement according to Article 42A of the penal code;[13] (4) those excluded from the National Socialist party because of dishonorable conduct; and (5) those punished in court because of activities detrimental to the state. Exceptions to the regulations for the third and fifth groups may be allowed by the Minister of the Interior. Individuals who have lost the right to hold public offices can be called to the labor service only after the lapse of the term of their exclusion. Persons who are not able-bodied are excluded from the service. Non-Aryans or persons married to non-Aryans are also excluded from the work camps, although non-Aryans declared worthy of serving in the army may be admitted into

[11] Reichsarbeitsdienstgesetz vom 26. Juni 1935, *Reichsgesetzblatt,* I (27. Juni, 1935), S. 769.

[12] The labor service is not yet sufficiently expanded to include all girls. It is now compulsory only for those girls who intend to go to colleges and universities, though in the *New York Times* of January 3, 1939, it was reported that the number of young women was to be increased to 400,000. It is doubtful, however, if any such number will be actually enrolled.

[13] *Strafgesetzbuch* für das Deutsche Reich in der Fassung der Strafgesetznovellen vom 26. Mai und 24. November 1933 und mit den für die Praxis wichtigsten strafrechtlichen Nebengesetzen; *Textausgabe* mit Verweisungen und Sachregister; Fünfte Auflage (Mannheim: Deutsches Druck- und Verlagshaus, 1934), S. 14.

the labor service. The latter cannot, however, hold any positions of leadership.[14]

Numbers in the Camps

During the chancellorship of Heinrich Brüning (1931-33), when work in the camps was voluntary, the number of young people in them reached as high a figure as 285,000.[15] When they were taken over by the National Socialist regime, the number increased as the compulsory feature was extended. At present the average strength is about 300,000 youth. This number was authorized[16] by a decree of September 26, 1936, but that many youth were not to have been enrolled until the beginning of October 1939.

Aims of the Labor Service

What is the National Socialist government trying to accomplish with this labor service which it considers so important? To aid in obtaining an official answer to this question an interview was arranged for me with a high official of the German labor service.

As I drove to the new headquarters of the labor service on Schinkelstrasse, Berlin was bedecked with thousands of red, white, and black swastika flags and banners in celebration of the Olympic Games. At the entrance to the building stood a young work camp member in full khaki uniform, with cap, black knee boots, and the swastika and work service armband. As I crossed the threshold he clicked his heels, gave the Nazi salute, and shouted, "Heil Hitler!" In the anteroom I noticed three more young members of the labor service in full uniform and a fourth wearing an officer's cap, who seemed to be in charge. I made it known whom I wished to see and after considerable telephoning by the labor service men, I was escorted to the second floor. After reporting to several other men, we finally arrived in the official's office, where I was asked to sit down.

---

[14] Reichsarbeitsdienstgesetz vom 26. Juni 1935, *Reichsgesetzblatt,* I, Abschnitt II, S. 5-7.

[15] The monthly average for 1932 was 122,041 persons. See *Statistisches Jahrbuch für das Deutsche Reich,* 1932.

[16] *Jahrbuch des Reichsarbeitsdienstes,* 1937-38 (Berlin: Volk und Reich Verlag, 1937), S. 34.

I saw before me a short, heavy-set, middle-aged man with blue eyes and sandy blonde hair. He wore the labor service uniform with the insignia of an upper labor leader *(Oberarbeitsführer)*. While my guide explained my interest in labor camps, especially their educational aspects, I had an opportunity to glance around the office. On the wall hung pictures of Hitler and Hierl, a large photograph of orderly rows of men with shovels silhouetted against the sky, and a large map of Germany showing the locations of the camps.

This official spokesman for the labor service began his explanation of the educational aspects of the work camps by stating the case of the leaders of the Third Reich against the terms "student" and "education" as he said they had been used by Republican Germany. "We do not teach the men in the work camps theory; we teach them how to live, how to live in the camp and when they return to their homes."

I asked, "What can be said to be the general aims of the program in the camps?"

He replied that the aim is to train young men for the "New German State," the "Germany of Adolf Hitler." The first emphasis, he explained, is on physical development.

The speed and enthusiasm with which he spoke had gradually increased, and at this point he rose from his desk to demonstrate how the young men were taught to use their shovels and picks, so that they would achieve balance and symmetrically developed bodies.

The secondary emphasis, he said, is on bringing together the youth of Germany, regardless of their social, political, or economic standing, to live and work together and thus to break down class feeling. The law states that by the time they are nineteen years old all youth must have spent six months in a labor camp. A restricted budget and difficulty in finding work projects and leaders prevented the labor service from including young women in any large numbers.

The third aim of the camps, my informant explained, is to develop respect for manual labor. The motto of the labor service is *"Arbeit adelt"* which translated means "work ennobles." It is felt by the leaders of the National Socialist party that during the 1920's, because of unemployment, a generation of Germans grew to manhood without learning the value of a day's work. Others, especially

NAZI GERMANY

ve:
azi labor battalion returning
uarters

t:
uilding an outdoor theatre
ve the Rhine valley

w:
abor service men marching to
r work project

NAZI GERMANY

Left: Nazi labor service m ceiving physical training. A Guard at attention, entranc labor service camp. *Below:* service men weaving on which they have built

those from aristocratic families, because of their wealth and position, had never done any work and consequently looked down upon men who had. Then there were the students and intellectuals. Hitler has heaped ridicule upon the so-called "sterile intellectualism" of Germany before 1933, and it is hoped that the labor service, by requiring the attendance of all young men and women who plan to go to a college or university, will remove the impractical tendencies of these young people, giving them a better understanding and appreciation of manual labor.

The fourth aim of the labor service, he went on, is to give the youth an understanding of German culture. Every camp is named for some prominent German. There is Camp Moltke, Camp Schiller, Camp Goethe, Camp Hindenburg, and so on. Frequently camps are named after men who lived in the vicinity of the camp, and in these instances it is possible for young workers to visit the birthplace of the camp patron or buildings or places where he lived, worked, or fought. Special instruction is given concerning the contribution of the camp patron to German culture. A considerable amount of material is sent out from Berlin, and this is read in the camps by the leaders at times when the work camp members are assembled.

The official went on to say that the final aim of the labor service is to weld German youth into a body of young people imbued with a love for their country and willingness to sacrifice everything for Germany. Repeating what the National Socialists have said innumerable times in their propaganda, he continued by saying that during the years following the war the German youth were divided in their allegiances. Some were Communists, some Social Democrats, others members of the Center party, and still others members of parties on the extreme right. They could not agree on a program, and meanwhile Germany deteriorated. Then came Hitler with his definite aims and promises. Having captured the imagination and enthusiasm of many of the youth, Hitler, this Nazi asserted, is now uniting them in devotion to the Fatherland.

I made the remark that the Civilian Conservation Corps in the United States did not have similar aims; that there was less regimentation in the American camps than in the German work camps; and that no attempt was made to mold young Americans into a body of youth giving absolute devotion to the state. I said that, as a matter of fact, there was no definite nationalistic philosophy back of the American camps, and that each corps area, even each CCC district and individual camp, developed its own program and was permitted a considerable amount of freedom of choice. The labor service official replied:

> It is unwise to think that any system of camps, or plan for one, can, or should, be copied in another country. Each nation should develop its own system independently. It is interesting to know about labor service developments in other countries, but it is not wise to try to adopt *in toto* the plan of any other country. I do feel, however, that in the work camps it is possible to develop a new generation of youth with definite cultural ideas. This is possible in the United States just as it is in Germany. The CCC camps might be a means of bringing together all of the divergent groups of youth in the United States and making them one.

Work Camps Visited

Arrangements were then made to take me out to see some work camps in the vicinity of Berlin. Two days later, at 9:45 in the morning, I was at the *Arbeitsdienst* office, and shortly thereafter in an official beswastikaed car we were en route to visit some of the camps. Unfortunately it began to rain shortly after we started our trip, but this did not impede us.

About eighty kilometers from Berlin our driver, who was in the full uniform of a worker, turned off the paved road onto one that had been transformed into a sea of mud by the heavy rain. After driving through this for about a quarter of a mile we reached the entrance to the camp. The gates were thrown open, and we drove into a camp quadrangle where a leader commanded three workers in full uniform who were standing in line at the gate, to shoulder arms, their shovels in this instance, and salute. On our left the leader of the camp stood at attention with arm extended in Nazi salute.

When the labor service official from Berlin alighted from the car, the leader again saluted and reported. Both then clicked their heels, gave the Nazi salute, cried, "Heil Hitler," stepped forward, clicked their heels, shook hands, stepped back, clicked their heels, again gave the salute, and again cried, "Heil Hitler." When the leader of that district *(Gau)* arrived in a second car, the same procedure was repeated by the guards at the gate and by the camp leader.

After being provided with raincoats, we were shown the camp. The buildings were set in a quadrangle. On our right as we entered was the combination dining room, or mess hall, and recreation room with the kitchen attached. The recreation room was attractively decorated with greenery and flowers. At one end hung a four-foot picture of Hitler, and just in front of it stood a high altarlike table. When we entered the room for the first time there were only flowers on the table, but when we returned from our inspection there was a guest book which we were asked to sign. At the other end of the room hung a picture of Hierl, and along either side of the room were pictures of other leaders of the National Socialists. As we entered the kitchen, the men working there came to attention and gave the Nazi salute, at the same time crying, "Heil Hitler!" The men in the camps always stood at attention during our inspection unless given permission to stand at ease.

On the south side of the quadrangle a second building was given over to the officers and a small hospital. The officers' quarters were decorated in good taste and compared favorably with the average officers' quarters of the CCC camps in the United States. The notable difference, however, was that the rooms of the officers in the German camps contained many pictures of German political leaders.

After visiting the hospital, we walked over to a long barrack on the west side of the quadrangle. This was divided into three sections, each containing beds for sixteen men, a troup (*trupp*) and its leader. Every bunk in the camp was neatly made and covered with blue and white calico. Closer inspection disclosed that the bunks were wooden boxes about seven feet long, two feet wide, and six inches deep, in which were placed straw ticks.

As I was specially interested in the educational program, we were next taken to the library. In the bookcases which the young men themselves had made we found some 400 books. There were many on biography, and also a goodly supply on the "New Germany." This room, like almost all the others, contained pictures of Hitler and various lesser lights in Nationalist Socialist Germany. The educational program is conducted in the combination recreation-dining room, in the library, or in any other rooms that are available.

While we were at the camp we were given a list of the topics considered during that week. On Monday a troop leader read a statement on *"Das Diktat von Versailles"* (the Dictate of Versailles). On Tuesday another statement was read by a different leader on *"Hitler auf der Wacht"* (Hitler on Guard); on Wednesday, "Gregor Mendel" was the topic; on Thursday, the *"Kanonenboot 'Iltis'"* (Gunboat "Iltis"); on Friday, *"Friedrich von Logau"* (a German poet of the seventeenth century famous for his maxims); and on Saturday, a statement on Austria.

After inspecting the camp we started toward the work project, which was situated about a half mile away. A large ditch was being dug to straighten the meandering course of a stream and to drain the adjacent land to make it suitable for cultivation. On our way to the project we met the members of the camp returning from their work, marching in military formation, carrying their shovels erect as though they were guns. The district leader cried, "Halt," as the campers approached, and after the usual saluting and reporting on the part of the group, he cried, "Heil Hitler!" which the young men repeated with sufficient strength to be heard for a good half mile.

It was then suggested that I ask them questions. In order not to embarrass them by asking penetrating questions I suggested that a tall, blonde young student tell me about the work project, and he explained about the drainage ditch which the group was digging. I asked about the food, which he said was fine. The *Gau* leader, who had been standing at my elbow all this time, then broke in asking the boy to tell me about the comradeship in the camp. The lad hesitated and then replied that they made many friends and that a fine comradeship existed. The *Gau* leader then said, "Oh, that is fine, that is very fine!"

Then the leader gave the order, "Forward march!" and these young soldiers of the soil marched off in the rain singing as only Germans can sing. The leader followed their every movement with great pride and said with fervor, "There goes the New Germany. There goes the Germany that the *Führer* has developed."

I remarked that the marching workers looked to me very much like a military formation. I mentioned that I had watched the men drilling on a Sunday morning near Lübeck and at Altstadt, both in northern Germany, suggesting that six months' compulsory labor service prepared the men for the two years of military service that follows immediately thereafter. The leader denied that the camp training was military. There are no arms in the camps, he said. The marching simply prepares the men for service in the "New Germany" and is "soldierly" not military.

On the way to the headquarters for that particular district we discussed the labor service as a permanent part of German life. The leader said that the service would never be abandoned. "We who have organized and developed it have put too much of our idealism into it ever to let it die. It is also very popular with the German people, and they will not let it come to an end." He then spoke of what he termed the "chaotic" state of the system before Hitler came into power and all the camps were coordinated and reorganized by Hierl.

This district leader had traveled rather extensively. He had visited the CCC camps, and said he had noticed when he was in the United States that American young people did not know whether to go to the left or to the right politically. They, too, he said, needed a great leader.

After visiting the district headquarters and two other camps, I again entered the car with the Berlin official As we drove back to Berlin I said that there was much talk in the United States of war in Europe, and that many people thought Germany to be the greatest menace to peace. The six months of compulsory labor service and two years of military training were thought to be preparing youth psychologically and physically for war. He was emphatic in denying that the camps were militaristic. "The camps are work camps," he said, and he drew from its sheath his twelve-inch dagger (standard equipment for all leaders of the labor service) to show me the motto, *"Arbeit adelt"* (work ennobles) engraved on the steel blade. "Germany does not want war," he continued. "We who are in charge of the camps know what war is and do not want to send our young men into the trenches. The *real* people (*das Volk*) in all the European countries do not want war. They want only to live and to cultivate their little pieces of land."

He repeated what he had said in the office two days previously concerning the purposes of the camps, but emphasized especially that the camps were organized to fight communism and bolshevism. In typical Nazi fashion he stated that: "The true people do not want war," he said, "only the Bolshevists and Communists." He dwelt upon the alleged threat of communism in Germany from 1919 to 1933, asserting that it was still a danger, although on being questioned he admitted that it had been largely stamped out. The danger of communism in other near-by states, however, was very great, he said, especially in Czechoslovakia and France. "It is against communism and bolshevism that the camps are organized." In correspondence since that time he has emphasized that General Franco in Spain has been fighting against communism just as Hitler and Mussolini have in Germany and in Italy.

Organization and Financing of Camps

Each of the camps visited with the Berlin official was made up of about 160 men. This is the usual size. The camp leaders are called upper fieldmasters (*Oberfeldmeister*). The men in a camp are subdivided into three platoons, each of which is led by an under fieldmaster or a fieldmaster.[17] The platoon (*Zug*) is further subdivided into three troops (*Trupps*), of fifteen men each, officered by a leader or upper troop leader (*Obertruppführer*). Of the one hundred and sixty or more men, eighteen are leaders, all of whom have gone through a period of training in government schools before assuming responsibility in the camps.

Five to ten camps form a *Gruppe* and one camp in each *Gruppe* is the so-called key camp (*Stammlager*), which is larger than the others. The key camp contains 220 recruits who are chosen from the most loyal members of the Hitler Youth. Its function is that of the skeleton corps of a regiment in an army. The groups in each province are organized into work districts (*Arbeitsgau*), the leaders of which take orders directly from Hierl.

A decree published on April 13, 1938, provided for the extension of the work service to Austria, by dividing the new era into three regions

[17] The rank of fieldmaster corresponds to our sergeant.

or districts containing a total of 150 camps. This expansion of the service brought the total number of districts to thirty-five, each of which is composed of from four to eight groups.

The workers in the camps under the Republican government were housed for the most part in old factories, schools, army barracks, and other public buildings. Under the National Socialist regime about half of the 1,200 camps are in specially constructed barracks quite similar to those used for the CCC camps in the United States. Most of the specially constructed buildings are portable and are built of lumber from state forests.

The camps are usually located within four or five miles of the work project. No trucks are available for transportation, so that the time required for marching or bicycling to work is deducted from the seven-hour work day. If the distance is greater than can be covered in an hour's marching, the work sponsor must provide transportation.

The schedule in a German camp is generally as follows:[18]

6:00 A.M.	Reveille
6:05– 6:15	Physical exercises
6:20– 7:15	Washing, bedmaking, early breakfast
7:20	Flag parade
7:30	March to work
7:45–10:00	Work
10:00–10:30	Breakfast
10:30– 2:00 P.M.	Work
2:00– 2:15	March back to camp
2:30– 3:20	Dinner, free time
3:30– 5:00	Games
5:10– 6:00	Instruction in civic duties
7:00	Orders issued for the next day
7:15– 7:45	Supper
7:45– 8:15	Cleaning of clothes, equipment, etc.
8:15– 9:45	Various forms of entertainment
10:00	Taps

The camps are financed by the Reich government. It is estimated that the total cost of maintaining 300,000 men in the camps and pro-

[18] Fritz Edel, *German Labor Service* (Berlin: Terramare, 1937), p. 12.

viding them with work materials is between 360,000,000 and 390,000,000 reichsmarks ($144,000,000 to $156,000,000) a year.[19] In 1933 the voluntary labor service had between 180,000,000 and 190,000,000 reichsmarks ($54,900,000 to $66,500,000) from the government. The appropriation for 1936-37 was 250,000,000 reichsmarks ($100,000,000),[20] and was carried as a separate item in the national budget. This sum does not include the contributions to the program made by the work sponsor. To justify the cost of labor service it is argued that the expense is no greater than relief or unemployment benefit would be, and that the work has economic value.

The cost a man per day according to German official sources was estimated in 1933 to be 2.14 reichsmarks (65 cents). Of this amount 82 pfennigs (25 cents) went to subsistence and 25 pfennigs (8 cents) to pocket money. The average cost a man per day at present is about 2 reichsmarks (80 cents). About 85 pfennigs (34 cents) a man per day is now being spent for food. No wages are paid to the labor service youth for the work he performs. Each worker continues to receive 25 pfennigs a day. With this he buys boot polish and soap as well as tobacco, candy, and other extras.

Leadership in the Camps

In developing the camp system the National Socialist government has paid special attention to the selection and the training of leaders and has developed a well-organized routine through which candidates for leadership must pass. According to Hierl,

> The labor service leaders must know how to obtain unquestioning obedience from their subordinates and to maintain the strictest discipline and order. But they must combine this quality with a fine sense of justice and a fatherly concern for the welfare of their men, and, in character, they must be, not instructors, but true educators.[21]

---

[19] Otto D. Tolischus, "Young Germany Faces the Labor Draft," *New York Times Magazine,* January 20, 1935.

[20] Information received from Müller-Brandenburg. The average exchange value of the mark was 24 cents in 1932, 31 cents in 1933, 39 cents in 1934, and 40 cents in 1935. Its present par value is 40 cents.

[21] Wilhelm and Graefe, *op. cit.,* p. 23.

NAZI GERMAN LABOR SERVICE

bove:

Washing up after work

ight:

Group of Nazi labor service men

elow:

Nazi laborers marching to their roject in marshland

NAZI GERMAN LABOR SERVICE

Above:

Gardening near a camp

Left:

A road-marker for a camp (the scription reads: "With tired bones, buddies go home, leave us alone")

Below:

Cleaning the quarters on Saturd

All candidates for the lower group of leaders must have successfully completed a two-year probationary period in the labor service. If accepted they must sign up for a ten-year period.

A special system of schools has been organized for leaders beginning with the troop leader school (*Truppführerschule*), of which there are sixteen, where the lower and middle groups of leaders are trained. The course lasts three months and is planned for two groups of men—those who have performed military service and those who have not. The second system of schools, of which there are five, are the fieldmaster schools (*Feldmeisterschulen*). These are open to men who have attended the troop leader school, have completed their military service, and have demonstrated their ability as leaders through practical work in the camps. This second course lasts for eight months. From the standpoint of the future of the leaders this second system of schools is the most important, since it is during this period that it is decided whether or not a man has the ability to hold higher positions in the labor service.

The third system of schools is known as the district schools (*Bezirkschulen*). Of these there are five. After practical experience as a platoon leader (*Zugführer*), the graduate of a fieldmaster school may attend a three-month course at a district school to be trained for leadership of a camp (*Abteilung*). Here again the process is highly selective, and only those men showing special ability are permitted to graduate. Finally, there is the national school (*Reichsschule*) at Potsdam, near Berlin, where the best members of the personnel, after having successfully completed terms of practical experience in camps or in other positions of responsibility, are trained to become the administrators and planners of the whole German labor service.[22]

Müller-Brandenburg, in his book, *Soldaten der Arbeit,*[23] devotes several pages to a description of the ideal leader in the labor service. He must have a fervant faith in National Socialism, a spirit of devotion and self-sacrifice, and an understanding of young people. Without these no one is qualified for the work or will be retained in it. Leader-

[22] *Jahrbuch des Reichsarbeitsdienstes,* S. 78, 79.

[23] S. 36-42; see also *Arbeitsdienst in 13 Staaten* (Zürich-Leipzig: Orell Füssli Verlag, 1938), S. 24-25.

ship demands constant devotion to duty and willingness to do without comforts. An official in a labor camp must be leader, comrade, teacher, and helper to his men.

Hierl, in addressing the *Reichschule* on May 13, 1933, stated:

> A labor service leader particularly must be a real fanatic in fulfilling his duty . . . but the true leader is above all he who has power, not only over the wills, but also over the hearts of his followers. The leader in the labor service especially needs this power over hearts, for he is to be a folk teacher, a teacher of German Socialism, that is of real German folk community.[24]

Although the camps are organized along military lines and give a semblance of military organization, in 1934, according to German reports, 46.4 per cent of the leaders were nonmilitary men. Only 7.7 per cent of the leaders were army officers, and only 23.7 per cent of them had been in the armed forces during the World War.[25]

With this elaborate training program Germany has taken steps to insure a highly trained personnel who look to the camps as a career. This is in contrast with the situation in the United States where, because CCC camps have not been made a permanent part of American life, the personnel often consider the work in the camps a stopgap until more permanent positions become available in public or private organizations.

Work Projects

The work projects now being carried on by the labor service are for the most part long-term programs of public works. Hermann Tholens, Chief of the Planning Office, is at present the administrator. The avowed aim of this aspect of the program is to win "bread freedom" for Germany.[26] Germany lost 13 per cent of her land by the Treaty of Versailles, together with 9.5 per cent of her population. In addition, the famine that came toward the end of the war indelibly impressed upon the Germans the danger and hardships resulting from a lack of

[24] Müller-Brandenburg, *Was ist Arbeitsdienst? Was soll er?* (Leipzig: Armanen Verlag, 1934), S. 11.

[25] Beintker, *Der deutsche Arbeitsdienst in Frage und Antwort* (Leipzig: Armanen Verlag, 1934), S. 48.

[26] *Ibid.*, p. 2; see also Tholens, "Der Reichsarbeitsdienst im Kampf um die Brotfreiheit," *Jahrbuch des Reichsarbeitsdienstes* (Berlin: Volk und Reich, 1936), S. 37-40.

foodstuffs. To produce an adequate food supply on a reduced acreage requires both reclamation of waste land and improvement of existing productive land. It is estimated that by these means the agricultural product of the nation can be increased one-sixth.[27] But in spite of Germany's need for land and her desire for "bread freedom," the economic aims of the camps are secondary to the aim of training the youth for the "New Germany."

Between 1933 and 1936, 70 per cent of the members of the labor service were engaged in reclaiming land and carrying on soil improvements, 15 per cent were at work on forestry projects, and another 15 per cent on land settlements and assistance at the scenes of catastrophes.[28] A statistical summary of the work accomplished in 1933-36 shows that about 300,000 acres of land were secured against floods, 60,000 acres were made arable, 750,000 acres were drained, and 400,000 acres of land already under cultivation were made more accessible by the construction of roads. Along the North Sea coast the government has a ten-year program intended to wrest thousands of acres from the tidal marshes. Outstanding drainage projects are located at Emsland on the Ems River, at Sprottebruch in Lower Silesia, and at Havel-Rhinluch, about thirty miles northwest of Berlin. Once the lands have been reclaimed, the labor service assists in settling agricultural families there.

Labor Service Relationship to the Party

On September 10, 1936, Hierl was appointed *Reichsleiter,* that being one of the highest political positions in the National Socialist party under the *Führer.* This appointment indicates the close relationship existing between the labor service and the National Socialist party.[29]

In spite of a close relationship, members of the labor service allegedly are not permitted to engage in party activity, although they may become party members. They may accept purely honorary offices in the party, but they must ask permission to do so. This permission, however, is not ordinarily refused.[30] The men in the labor service also take an

[27] Edel, *op. cit.,* pp. 18-19.

[28] *Ibid.,* pp. 21-22.

[29] *Der Arbeitsmann* (2. Januar 1937), II, 1, S. 7.

[30] *Der Reichsarbeitsdienst, Verlag für Recht und Verwaltung,* Sections 17 and 20, Berlin, 1937.

active part in demonstrations and assemblies of the National Socialist party. As has been stated previously, they are especially in evidence at the annual party rally in Nüremburg, where, dressed in full uniform and armed with highly polished shovels, they march with the same precision and bearing as the German army (*Deutsche Armee*). In 1934, 52,000 members of the labor service passed in their first review before Hitler at the National Socialist Party congress. Since 1934 they have paraded annually with the other party units.

Educational Program of German Labor Service

As the Berlin official said in the interview previously described, the primary aim of the labor service in Germany is to train the young men for the Nazi state. The National Socialist government regards the labor service as a folk school for the nation, and considers the training aspects of the service of greatest importance. In 1934 Hierl told the German Student Union:

> Should one take away the educational idea of the labor service, or push it into the background, he would rob the labor service of its soul. . . . In the entire scheme of the education of our people to a National Socialist outlook on life (*Weltanschauung*), a very special educational task falls to the labor service.[31]

The aim of this educational program is to train the young men and women "for the national community" and to give them a "true conception of work. He who leaves the labor service after a half year must know that he has a duty to his people and country, and that work is noble."[32]

In some ways the labor service is taking the place of older educational institutions in Germany.

> The school must realize that even though its methods of teaching were fundamentally altered, as a place of instruction it can make only a small contribution to education as a whole. Labor service, for instance, will perhaps for many years play a far more decisive part than the school in the training of the youth of this country.[33]

[31] *Soldaten der Arbeit,* S. 11.

[32] *Jahrbuch des Reichsarbeitsdienstes,* 1936, S. 35.

[33] Wilhelm and Graefe, *op. cit.,* p. 7.

The elements of the program which contribute to these educational aims are: (1) the practical work program; (2) the teaching of German history from the Nazi point of view and of National Socialist political theories; (3) the leisure activities built around the promotion of a German culture, for example, folk dancing, folk and camp songs, games, and theatrical performances (four evenings each week are devoted to this sort of activity); and (4) the physical training program.

Political and Cultural Instruction

While the whole camp life is considered educational, about one hour per day is given over to instruction in National Socialism and its policies, including readings from Hitler's *Mein Kampf* and other Nazi books. Articles from the *Völkischer Beobachter* are also read and interpreted. The lectures usually have such topics as "Germany and Austria," "Italy and Her Mission in Abyssinia," "Spain's Liberation from Bolshevist Liberalism." Short statements on the lives of the different men who, in the opinion of the National Socialists, have made great contributions to Germany are read to the men when they are in retreat formation. Naturally the words of Hitler, Goering, Goebbels, and other dignitaries in the National Socialist state are most frequently quoted.

The labor camp leaders claim that the emphasis is not placed on what the National Socialists call "theoretical subjects," but rather deals with German history, art, and culture, as they are related to the developments of the last few years in Germany. Since 60 per cent of those enrolled in all camps are peasants, workers, or artisans (regulations permit that no more than 40 per cent of the men assigned to any one camp be students), the educational program is conducted on a rather elementary level. Like the rest of the labor service, the educational program is coordinated and directed from Berlin.

Libraries

The official budget provides a fixed amount for the purchase of books for labor service camps. The Ministry of Education has been issuing a series of lists of suggested titles for purchase, by camps and schools, through the columns of the *Amtsblatt des Reichs und Preussischen Ministeriums für Wissenschaft, Kunst and Volksbildung* since early in 1934.[34] A selection of every seventh title from a sample list follows: *Almanac of the National Socialist Revolution,* edited by Wilhelm Kube; *Germanic Culture,* by Gustav Menz; *The National Socialist Revolution, 1914-1933,* edited by Walther Gehl; *Theories of Human Heredity,* by von Verschuer; *Fiery Ring around Germany, Youth Edition,* by Werner Beumelburg; *Brief History of National Socialism,* by Johann von Leers; *The National Socialist Youth Movement,* by George Usadel; *Surveying and the Estimation of Distance,* by Andreas Staub; *Judaism and Leadership, The National Socialist Mission,* by Wilhelm Müller-Walbaum; *Military Education in the New Spirit,* by Hans Willi Ziegler; *The New Germany in Verse,* by Hans Gille.[35] These and the remaining titles on this list may be classified roughly as follows:

History		16
Pre-war	6	
Post-war	10	
Military science		14
National Socialist theory and practice		11
Race hygiene		11
Biography		9
Hitler	7	
Other	2	
Literature and culture		8
Youth		5
Agriculture		1
Total		75

In looking over the libraries I noted that a large number of books had been donated by persons residing near the camps. These consisted

[34] John W. Taylor, *Youth Welfare in Germany* (Nashville: *Baird-Ward,* 1936), pp. 109-12.

[35] The German titles are: *Almanach der nationalsozialistischen Revolution; Germanische Kultur; Die nationalsozialistische Revolution, 1. August 1914 bis 1. Mai 1933; Erblehre des Menschen; Sperrfeuer um Deutschland, Jugendausgabe; Kurzgefasste Geschichte des Nationalsozialismus; Die nationalsozialistische Jugendbewegung; Messdienst und Entfernungsschätzen; Judentum und Führertum—Von der Sendung des Nationalsozialismus; Wehrerziehung im neuen Geiste; Das neue Deutschland im Gedicht.*

chiefly of biographies of men prominent in German history. One is impressed with the large number of books by the leading figures in the National Socialist hierarchy. A copy of Hitler's *Mein Kampf* is to be found in every camp. Books and pamphlets by Streicher, Rosenberg, Goebbels, and other National Socialist leaders are also very much in evidence. However, in going through books and library cards in the camps visited, I was impressed with the fact that very few of them had been read. Even *Mein Kampf* had not been signed out by many of the workers. This situation is in contrast with the interest in reading among the workers when the camps were administered by the Republican government. This apparent lack of interest on the part of the camp workers in the writings of National Socialist propagandists may mean that not all German youth are avid readers of a monotonous diet composed of Nazi theories concerning inferior races, Nordic supremacy, unscrupulous enemies, and the menace of communism.

Instructors

The instructors for the educational program are drawn almost entirely from the personnel in the camp. Sometimes well qualified campers themselves lead discussion groups, but only if they are loyal National Socialists and are accepted as capable leaders by the German authorities.

In the days of the voluntary camps individuals from the surrounding communities frequently led or joined in the discussions and activities of the campers. Now, however, except for local party officials, few outsiders participate in the camp program. The educational program is almost entirely planned from Berlin. As would be expected, little opportunity is given for local initiative or imagination on the part of the instructors. They are required to follow directions or orders in conducting the programs, and in many cases simply carry out the instructions sent from Berlin.

Physical Development

Special attention throughout the whole labor service is paid to physical development of individuals. On this aspect of the camp program greater emphasis is placed in Germany than in any other country, with the possible exception of Bulgaria. Emphasis on the physical in contrast to the intellectual is typical of the greater part of Germany today. To quote Hitler:

> The educational work of the National Socialist state must consist in the first place in the training of healthy bodies and not in the mere teaching of knowledge. Mental training is a matter of secondary importance. . . . A people of scientists, psychologically degenerated, weak-willed and cowardly pacifists will not be in a position to insure its existence on this earth.[36]

The program for training healthy bodies consists of four steps. First, each boy entering the service is given a physical examination. Whatever treatment is shown to be needed is then given under the supervision of the camp physician in so far as is possible. Physical exercises are next required, including gymnastics with and without apparatus, light athletics, and games. The purpose of these exercises is not to provide sports for enjoyment, but to develop bodily strength and to inculcate respect for discipline. Finally, the youth are required to have military drill with maneuvers (*Geländesport*), thus getting practical experience in the use of terrain during military movements.[37]

Health

The aim of the health program in the labor service camps is to teach the men how to develop their bodies and how to keep well. It also includes instruction in racial purity, the effects of narcotics and intoxicants, the prevention of accidents, and first aid.

Each member of the labor service up to and including the chief labor leader (*Oberstarbeitsführer*) is entitled to free medical care, to dental care in acute cases, and to free hospitalization and treatment. The other members of the labor service are entitled to free medical, dental, and hospital care only when it is established that treatment is necessary because of injuries received while on duty. Treatment is ordinarily given in the room of the camp physician, who is available at all times. Serious cases are committed to the hospital.[38]

---

[36] Adolf Hitler, *Mein Kampf*, 261-262. Auflage (München: Zentralverlag der NSDAP, 1937), S. 452.

[37] Beelitz, "*Körperliche Ertüchtigung*," *Der Arbeitsdienst ein Bildberichtbuch* (Berlin: Freiheitsverlag, 1935), S. 21-23.

[38] *Jahrbuch des Reichsarbeitsdienstes*, 1936, S. 42 ff.

Lack of Vocational Education

While it is the purpose of the camps to train the young men for the "'New Germany," no attempt seems to be made to train them for any special type of occupation. It is true that some of them learn the rudiments of a limited number of jobs while they are on the work projects, or conducting camp activities, but only incidentally.

A partial explanation of this is the fact that outside of the labor service there exists a well organized program of vocational education and rehabilitation for youth up to the age of eighteen years who are not in school. For unemployed youth up to the age of twenty-five years and sometimes older, voluntary vocational courses are provided. However, the labor service does emphasize the importance of manual labor and tries to interest those who had intended to take professional training in finding a vocational interest elsewhere. This, of course, is a result of overcrowding in the professions in Germany, and follows the plan of the camps under Republican Germany.[39]

When young Germans complete their labor service, together with the two years of compulsory military training, they must rely largely on their own resources to find a place in society, even though the holder of a labor service certificate is given preference for a position over other applicants without this credential. In addition, special inducements to settle on the lands newly reclaimed by the service are given to young men with labor service experience.[40]

Military Training

The military training varies with the different structures of the camps. According to reports of refugees from Germany,[41] the key camps, composed entirely of Hitler Youth, have more intensive military

[39] Walter M. Kotschnig, *Unemployment in the Learned Professions* (London: Oxford Press, 1937), pp. 203-5.

[40] Die Deutsche Studentenschaft, *Der Arbeitsdienst in der Welt* (Hamburg: Hanseatische Verlagsanstalt, 1935), S. 65-66.

[41] It seems fair to use here material on the German camps from some of the German refugees. While they may be biased against the National Socialist regime, the reports from the German government and statements from labor service officials are for the most part obviously "official," uncritical, and specially prepared for public consumption.

training than the others. Marching, cross-country maneuvers, technique of attack, tank defense, and hand-grenade throwing, they also say, are practiced in all the camps.

The camps in Germany are administered by the Department of the Interior rather than by the Department of War, but their military character is indicated by the following facts: (1) they are conducted along rigid disciplinary lines, with individuals subordinated to camp officers; (2) military punishments for offenses are used; (3) the physical training program is designed to build these men up physically and is based on the type of military exercises that makes a good soldier; and (4) the *Arbeitsmann* is taught to march and handle his shovel in the same fashion as a gun. It is also significant that the six months of compulsory labor service are followed immediately by two years of compulsory military training. In driving and walking through Germany one frequently sees the members of the labor service engaged in military drill. In spite of official denials, this is military training, if only of a preliminary or preparatory type. The labor service has properly been termed "the army's prep school."[42]

Discipline

The punishments in the camps for oversight or disobedience are military in nature. The most severe penalties are imposed for intentional disobedience.

> The culprit is locked in a dark room without furniture for three or four days, and wakened every hour. Then his labor service uniform is ripped from his back in the presence of his comrades. The flag of the camp is lowered. The whole body of . . . men is disgraced and all privileges removed. The disobedient one is taken away by guards to another camp.[43]

Punishments for less serious offenses consist of standing guard rigidly with shouldered spade for two or three hours, loss of free time, or an extra hour of drill.

---

[42] Fritz M. Marx, *Government in the Third Reich* (New York: McGraw-Hill, 1936), p. 106; see also Brady, *The Spirit and Structure of German Fascism* (New York: Viking, 1937), p. 180.

[43] Albion Ross in the *New York Times,* March 7, 1937.

Attitudes Toward Labor Service

It is difficult to determine the attitude of the young Germans toward compulsory labor service. The press is under such rigid censorship and expressing an opinion contrary to the "official viewpoint" is so dangerous that it is almost impossible to get a frank statement from anyone within the borders of Germany. In a conversation between the writer and a member of the labor service in Germany the latter said, "You see that motto there under the labor service insignia *Arbeit adelt?* Well, there are a lot of us that would rather remain just good common men." Refugees from Germany allege that the compulsory nature of the camps and the regimentation have made the labor service unpopular with as high as 60 per cent of the German youth. Undoubtedly many of them react against the eternal saluting, clicking of heels, "Heil Hitler"-ing, marching, and propagandizing that goes on in the camps.

To anyone visiting the camps it is obvious that not all the boys are satisfied with life there. One is especially impressed with the tenseness reflected on the faces of the young men. The laughing and joking and the lightheartedness that characterize the camps in other countries, or those in Germany before Hitler came into power, does not exist. The men sing in the Nazi camps, but not in the spontaneous manner of the youth in the labor service during 1931 and 1932.

It can also be said that students who plan to go to the universities often resent the fact that they must spend a half year in a compulsory labor camp and then two years in military service before they can begin their studies. This means that the young men who plan to work for advanced degrees must postpone attending universities until they are twenty or twenty-one years of age, so that a student taking a four-year course will not graduate until he is twenty-four or twenty-five years old. Then, too, while the youth are spending the two and a half years in labor or military service, they are given little opportunity to think for themselves, or to do any studying. They become accustomed to the regimentation and to the emphasis on physical development, and lose any habits of study and critical analysis they may have had. As a result, when they matriculate at the universities, dulled and uncritical as their minds have become under the training of National Socialism, they have difficulty in adjusting themselves to the life of a student and lower even the National Socialist standards for German universities.

It is difficult to obtain accurate information on conditions in the labor camps in Germany. Usually one must choose between material that is obviously government propaganda and statements of refugees or other individuals definitely opposed to the regime. A leader of the labor camp movement prior to Hitler who is trustworthy and seems to be objective in his analysis of conditions gave me his impression about the Nazi camps as follows:

> In the case of the labor camps as with other phases of the National Socialist program the Nazis have taken over an idea from the days of the Republican government and made it their own. Before the Nazis seized the power in Germany they talked a great deal but did very little about the development of labor camps. When they finally came into power, they took over the labor service that had been created prior to their time. The institution continues at the present time, but the liberal spirit under which the camps were developed in Republican Germany is gone.

He went on to say that he had received reports from young men who had attended camps in many different parts of Germany.

> The outstanding impression they gave me of the camps is one of almost unbearable boredom. There is no educational program. The camps have only the uninteresting diet ground out by the Nazi propaganda machine. By forcing all youth into the camps and giving the young men an overdose of propaganda, the Nazis are not succeeding in making good National Socialist followers out of their *Arbeitsmänner*. Instead the German youth who have been in the camps feel that they have undergone a kind of slavery.
>
> In the voluntary labor camps before Hitler the youth did not mind working without pay. There was a community spirit in the camps, the opportunity to learn and to take part in the self-government program developed in the camps. Now all this has been changed. The quality of leaders for the National Socialist camps has declined pitifully. Most of them are petty semimilitaristic officials, interested more in their pay, careers, and family life than in the boys and the camps. Most of them are incapable of carrying on any kind of an educational or recreational program and even admit that they prefer to give the men military exercises (*Wehrsport*), which will make them very tired and willing to go to bed early in the evenings and so not embarrass the officers by asking for anything educational.

NAZI GERMANY

e:

laying games dur-
leisure

t:

rainage work in
shland area

w:

azi labor service

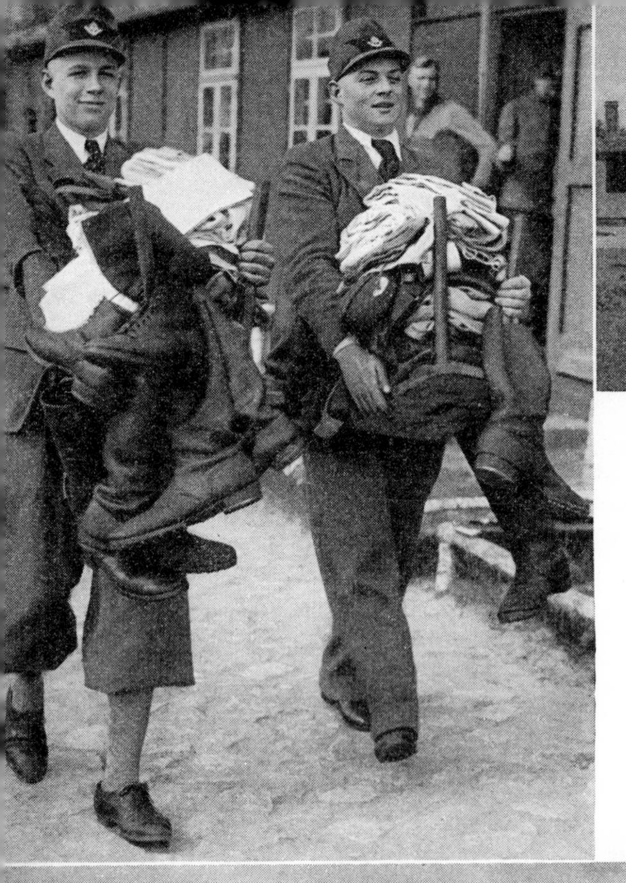

NAZI GERMAN LABOR SERVI

Left:
New enrollees with their outfi

Above:
A camp with the slogan of the labor service *"Arbeit adelt"* (wo nobles)

Below:
Land reclaiming on the Nort coast

According to this former German leader of the labor service,

> If it is the spirit that really makes a movement, then it is not possible to say that a labor camp movement exists in Germany at the present time since the camps have become merely a preparatory school for army life, an institution to teach German youth to drill, to accept unthinkingly the propaganda of Herr Goebbels, and not a folk school for the education of young people.

Conclusions

Officials in Germany state emphatically that the work service is a great success, and that it will continue so long as National Socialism does. Undoubtedly there are some constructive results of the camp program which should be considered if just appraisal is to be made of the German compulsory labor service.

First of all, the labor service brings together, as did the earlier camps of Republican Germany, but on a larger scale, representatives of the different classes of youth. Consequently they force all young men, and some young women, to live and work together for a period of six months.

The camps undoubtedly benefit the young men physically. While the food is plain, and to an American not very appetizing, it is wholesome. It is unofficially reported that the young Germans bring food back with them from home to supplement the meals in camp, and that high school and college students depend to a considerable extent on this supplementary diet. The work out of doors, the regular hours of camp life, and the sports and recreational activities, however, all contribute to the development of a stronger and more vigorous German nation.[44]

From an authoritarian point of view the camps seem for the most part to be carefully organized and efficiently run. According to the best figures available this is done with an expenditure for food, shelter, and medical care slightly less than the cost per man in the CCC camps. In considering the total cost of the camps in the United States, it should

[44] According to Goetze of the Reich labor service staff, 83.4 per cent of the labor service enrollees gain weight during their period of service, 6.8 per cent maintain the same weight, and the remaining 9.8 per cent lose weight. *Der Arbeitsmann* (3. Juli 1937), S. 5.

be remembered that the enrollees receive about twice as much as the German youth for spending money each month, and that about $300 a year goes to the family of the CCC enrollee, whereas no such amount goes to the family of a boy in a German camp. The amount of work performed by the men in the CCC is greater than that performed by the German youth. In part, this is due to the use of machinery in the CCC.

Some young Germans undoubtedly enjoy the satisfaction derived from hard work and gain a healthy respect for manual labor. Since the upper classes in Germany have generally looked down on the ordinary worker, this result is important.

The Germans learn neatness, promptness, and the desirability of keeping regular hours. These virtues should be the results of any well-organized camp program, but they deserve mentioning.

The camps provide satisfying work for many youth who would otherwise be unemployed. Upon attaining power Hitler was pressed to solve the unemployment problem, which he had promised to eradicate. As one way of providing the youth with something to do he continued and expanded slightly the labor service already developed by the Republican government.

Finally, the land reclamation and road-building programs are of real value to Germany. The use of this land will assist Germany in producing more foodstuffs within her frontiers. A great deal of the work, nevertheless, is chiefly of military value.

On the other hand, the dangers and destructive results of the camps far outweigh their constructive achievements. The programs undoubtedly train the men both psychologically and physically for war. The atmosphere of the camps is military, and frequently hostile. German youth are taken during their impressionable years to be taught that unthinking obedience to Hitler and willingness to lay down their lives for the "New Germany" are the highest ideals.

The minds of the youth are poisoned by the campaign carried on in the camps against non-Aryans, and especially against the so-called "Jewish communism," a term often indiscriminately applied to all opposition, both within and without Germany. The young men in the camps are taught that as "true Germans," in contrast with "Communists, Jews, internationalists, liberals, and pacifists," they belong to a superior race and are decreed by a Nordic destiny to lead Europe, if not the world.

The youth are taught the glorification of the physical as against the intellectual. They are taught to look with disdain upon the use of peaceful methods for the settlement of disputes, as well as the institutions that have been developed to achieve these ideals. Germany, they are taught, must be strong, and her youth are the main girders of that strength. This leads the youth to a feeling of false confidence in the purely physical that would then seem to demand a trial of strength, when men and steel could be pitted against the forces of other nations.

The camps are compulsory; they subject the individuals who participate in them to a regimentation which subordinates them to the collective will. Little opportunity is given the youth to develop as individuals, or to use their imagination or initiative except along prescribed National Socialist lines. When the youth finally complete their labor and military service, and no longer have every hour of the day organized for them, refugees allege they frequently have difficulty in regaining that initiative.

The camps provide no religious training and are essentially anti-Christian. They prevent or interfere with church attendance by arranging drilling, hikes, and other organized activities for Sunday.

In general, it seems that the labor service, together with the other German organizations, is conditioning youth for what is believed to be an inevitable conflict with any nation or force that seems to stand athwart the grandiose destiny of Germany.

Bibliography

BEINTKER. *Der Deutsche Arbeitsdienst in Frage und Antwort.* Leipzig: Armanen Verlag, 1934. 64 S.

ERICH F. BERENDT. *Männer und Taten; das Losungsbuch des Reichsarbeitsdienstes,* Zwei Bände. Leipzig: Der nationale Aufbau, n.d., S. 424, 452.

ROBERT A. BRADY. *The Spirit and Structure of German Fascism.* New York: Viking, 1937. Chap. V, "Training the Youth to Become Soldiers of Labor."

G. S. COX. "In a Nazi Labor Camp: A Spartan Routine," *New York Times Magazine,* October 28, 1934, pp. 7, 18.

AUGUST DAHM. *Arbeitsdienstrecht; Reichsarbeitsdienstgesetz nebst einschlägigen Gesetzen und Verordnungen.* Berlin: Stilke, 1936. 123 S.

WILL DECKER. "Methoden der Erziehung im Reichsarbeitsdienst," *International Education Review,* VI, 4-5 (1937), 280-81.

Deutscher Arbeitsdienst für Volk und Heimat; Die Führerzeitung des Deutschen Arbeitsdienstes, V, 15-26 (14. April-30. Juni 1935).

FRITZ EDEL. *German Labor Service.* Berlin: Terramare, 1937. 32 pp.

HERBERT ERB. *Der Arbeitsdienst, ein Bildberichtbuch.* Berlin: Freiheitsverlag, 1935. 120 S.

German Youth in a Changing World, 4th edition. Berlin: Terramare, 1936. 47 pp.

C. W. GRAY. "Compulsory Labor Service in Germany." *Monthly Labor Review,* XXXVII, 2 (August 1933) 286-87.

STEFAN HEYM. "Youth in Hitler's Reich," *Nation,* CXLII (June 27, 1936), 836-40.

KONSTANTIN HIERL. *Grundsätzliches zur Arbeitsdienstpflicht;* Vortrag gehalten am 20. Januar 1934 vor der Deutschen Studentenschaft, Berlin. München: Zentralverlag der NSDAP, 1934. 15 S.

W. HISCHE. *Deutscher Arbeitsdienst als Erziehungsgemeinschaft.* Zweite Auflage. Leipzig: Teubner, 1935. 49 S.

WALTER HOHMANN. *Geländesport und Schule.* Leipzig: Armanen Verlag, 1933. 20 S.

KENNETH HOLLAND. "Work Camps for the Youth of Germany." *School and Society,* XXXIX (February 17, 1934), 213-15.

"Institution of Compulsory Labor Service," *Industrial and Labor Information,* LV (July 15, 1935), 100-101.

ISAAC L. KANDEL. *The Making of Nazis.* New York: Teachers College, Columbia University, 1935. 143 pp.

KARL KAUFMAN. *Praktische Winke für den Zeugmeister und den Quartiermeister im Reichsarbeitsdienst. . . .* Leipzig, 1936. 125 S.

HERMANN KRETZSCHMANN. *Bausteine zum Dritten Reich; Lehr-und Lesebuch des Reichsarbeitsdienstes.* 3. Auflage. Leipzig: Der nationale Aufbau, n.d. 635 S.

HERMANN KRETZSCHMANN und FRITZ EDEL. *Der Reichsarbeitsdienst in Wort und Bild.* Berlin: Deutscher Verlag für Politik und Wirtschaft, 1936. 83 S.

FRITZ M. MARX. *Government in the Third Reich.* New York: McGraw-Hill, 1936, pp. 106-8.

MÜLLER-BRANDENBURG. *Soldaten der Arbeit.* Leipzig: Seeman, 1934. 56 S.

————. *Was ist Arbeitsdienst? Was soll er?* 2. Auflage. Leipzig: Armanen Verlag, 1934. 51 S.

————. *Jahrbuch des Reichsarbeitsdienstes,* 1936, 1937, 1938. Berlin: Volk und Reich Verlag.

MÜLLER-BRANDENBURG und T. SCHEFFER. *Heimat und Arbeit; Monatshefte für pädagogische Politik.* Berlin: Beltz, 1928.

————. *Passing through Germany.* 10th edition. Berlin: Terramare, 1936.

KARL RAU. *Jugend im Dienst, Briefe und Berichte deutscher Arbeitsdienststudenten.* Berlin: Stalling, n.d. 92 S.

BRUNO RAUECKER. *Social Policy in the New Germany.* Leipzig, n.d. 39 pp.

REICHSARBEITSDIENST. *Der Arbeitsmann;* Zeitung des Reichsarbeitsdienstes für Führer und Gefolgschaft. Berlin, 1935.

————. *Dienststrafordnung, Durchführungsbestimmungen, Beschwerdeordnung.* Berlin, 1936. 48 S.

REICHSARBEITSDIENST. *Unser Lager als Heim; Bilder aus den Abteilungen der Rhöngruppe 224 des Reichsarbeitsdienstes.* Gersfeld-Rhön, n.d. 31 S.

A. C. RINGLAND. "The CCC in Germany," *Journal of Forestry,* XXXIV (June 1936), 554-61.

Rund um den Spaten. Leipzig: Der nationale Aufbau, 1935. 55 S.

GERHARD SACK. *Die Entwicklung des freiwilligen Arbeitsdienstes in der nationalen Revolution.* 54 S.

WILHELM SCHLAGHECKE. *Das Heim im Reichsarbeitsdienst.* Frankfurt: Bechhold, 1936. 78 S.

HERBERT SCHMEIDLER. *Verwaltung und Wirtschaftsführung im Reichsarbeitsdienst.* Leipzig: Der nationale Aufbau, 1936. 80 S.

KURT STAMM. *Der Reichsarbeitsdienst; Reichsarbeitsdienstgesetz mit ergänzenden Bestimmungen und Erläuterungen.* 2. Auflage. Berlin: Verlag für Recht und Verwaltung, 1937. 400 S.

STATISTISCHES REICHSAMT. *Statistisches Jahrbuch für das Deutsche Reich,* 1933-36.

HELMUT STELLRECHT. *Soldatentum und Jugendertüchtigung.* Berlin: Junker und Dünnhaupt, 1935. 23 S.

JOHN W. TAYLOR. *Youth Welfare in Germany.* Nashville: Baird-Ward, 1936. 259 pp.

OTTO D. TOLISCHUS. "Young Germany Faces the Labor Draft," *New York Times Magazine,* January 20, 1935.

————. "Universal Compulsory State Labor Service in Germany," *Monthly Labor Review,* XLI (November 1935), 1218-20.

RODERICH VON BISTRAM. "Der deutsche Arbeitsdienst," *Europäische Revue,* X, 9 (September 1934), S. 583-89.

AXEL VON GRAEFE. *Shoulder Spades! A Tale of the German Labor Service.* Leipzig: Bibliographisches Institut, 1936. 87 pp.

ARTHUR VON MACHUI. "Wirtschaftliche Bilanz des deutschen Arbeitsdienstes," *International Education Review,* VI, 4-5 (1937), S. 288-91.

HANS-JOACHIM VON SCHUMANN. *Die nationalsozialistische Erziehung im Rahmen amtlicher Bestimmungen.* Berlin: Beltz, n.d. 46 S.

MILDRED S. WERTHEIMER. *Germany under Hitler.* World Affairs Pamphlet No. 8. New York: Foreign Policy Association and World Peace Foundation, 1935. 48 pp.

C. J. WHITE. "Extension of Compulsory Labor Service in Germany," *Monthly Labor Review,* XL, 4 (April 1935), 883.

THEODOR WILHELM and GERHARD GRAEFE. *German Education Today.* Berlin: Terramare, n.d. 33 pp.

The Austrian Labor Service

FOLLOWING the Armistice, Austria, along with the other Central Powers, was in a chaotic condition economically and politically. Like Germany, Austria was left depleted by the World War and the peace terms of the Allies, saddled with an indemnity, and reduced to impotence. With her economic system so hopelessly crippled and with tariff walls in the Succession States preventing her from exporting enough goods to pay for imports of food, coal, and other necessities, it is not surprising that Austria's economic life became gradually paralyzed after 1928. No nation of Europe suffered more severely from the effects of the world crisis which began in 1929.[1]

Austria had planned to introduce compulsory labor service in 1918 to carry on the economic life of the country. After the war the idea of labor service continued to exist, especially among student and youth organizations and a small group of men and women who belonged to the Union for Compulsory Labor Service (*Bund für Arbeitsdienstpflicht*). As early as 1926 Odo Neustädter-Stürmer urged the adoption in Austria of a system similar to the Bulgarian Labor Service. At first little interest was evidenced in these suggestions, but continuing and widespread unemployment eventually forced Austria to adopt such projects.[2]

In 1932 a few unemployed young people under the leadership of J. Diakow, an ex-lieutenant colonel of the staff, founded the first Austrian labor camp in the neighborhood of Vienna, demonstrating their conviction that it was an honor to work voluntarily in the service of one's country and far preferable to the demoralizing effects of inactivity. The idea then began to meet with general approval, and soon afterward a special section of the Ministry of Social Administration was established to direct the camps for young people.[3]

---

[1] Vera M. Dean, "Austria: the Paralysis of a Nation," *Foreign Policy Reports*, VIII, 22 (January 4, 1933), 256-58.

[2] *Der Oesterreichische Arbeitsdienst*, I, 5 (Oktober-November, 1935), S. 1-2; Second International Work Camp Conference, "Labor Service in Austria," p. 2.

[3] League of Nations, Assembly, 16th Ordinary Session, *Fifth Committee*, p. 24.

Voluntary camps were legally established by the government on August 18, 1932, a year after Germany had begun to subsidize camps. The law was subsequently modified by orders of April 10 and December 23, 1933. By an act of October 19, 1934 the labor service was reorganized and all private organizations which had been responsible for work camps were combined in a state organization, known as the Austrian Labor Service (*Oesterreichische Arbeitsdienst*).[4] The two general aims of the camps were to provide constructive activity for unemployed young people and to train the youth for existing jobs.[5]

In 1934 the following types of camps were in operation:[6]

Type of Camp	*Per Cent*
State camps	28
Other public institutions	45
Land settlement associations	4
Youth organizations	2
Others	21

On January 31, 1936 organizations which were sponsoring the labor service camps included: Union of Working Youth (*Verein Jugend in Arbeit*), Union of Child Care Centers (*Verein Kinderpflegeheim*), Catholic Aid Society (*Caritas Socialis*), Federal Union of Catholic Girls (*Reichsverband der Katholischen Mädchenvereine*), and Catholic Women's Organization (*Katholische Frauenorganisation*).[7]

Administration and Financing of the Camps

After January 1, 1935 the camps were coordinated under the Austrian labor service and the country was divided into nine administrative districts. Franz Keller was appointed director of the service by the Federal Minister of Social Administration, and in 1937 Hans Rott was named state secretary for the labor service. The Austrian labor service performed the duties previously carried out by the labor service organizations (*Träger des Dienstes*), except in special instances

[4] International Labor Office, *Legislative Series*: 1932 (Austria 4); 1933 (Austria 3); and 1934 (Austria 8).

[5] Franz Keller, *Der Oesterreichische Arbeitsdienst,* II, 1 (Januar 1936), 3.

[6] International Labor Office, *Unemployment among Young Persons*. p. 98.

[7] Akademischer Arbeitsdienst der Hochschülerschaft Oesterreichs, *Geschlossene Lager des Freiwilligen Arbeitsdienstes per 31. Jänner 1936.* Mimeographed.

when the work was done in private camps. The Federal Minister of Social Administration was required by law to make final decisions on a number of important matters regarding the labor service. He also issued standing orders for its management, was responsible for its supervision, and issued general rules regarding the amounts of grants to be made to labor service organizations.

While in principle the camps were voluntary, the law provided:

> An unmarried unemployed person under the age of twenty-five years who without good reason fails to avail himself of the opportunity to engage in voluntary labor service may be refused emergency benefit or deprived of it in conformity with rules to be issued by the Federal Minister of Social Administration.[8]

The camps were financed from relief or benefit funds or by grants from the federal treasury. The payment of unemployment benefits was discontinued during the period of the enrollee's stay in camp, when a block grant was made.[9]

Government expenditure for the labor service from 1933 to 1936 was as follows:

1933	6,000,000 schillings[10]	($925,200)
1934	12,000,000 schillings	($2,254,000)
1935	10,000,000 schillings	($1,883,000)
1936	4,000,000 schillings	($754,000)

In the 1939 Austrian budget 6,000,000 schillings were earmarked for the labor service.

The Austrian camps cost about 3.40 schillings (64 cents) a man per day, of which the government paid between one and two schillings (19 to 38 cents). The work sponsor (*Träger der Arbeit*) provided the balance. The 3.40 schillings were distributed among various items of expense as follows:[11]

---

[8] Order of the Federal Government to Amend the Act Respecting Voluntary Labor Service, December 23, 1933. International Labor Office, *Legislative Series,* 1933 (Austria 3), p. 3.

[9] International Labor Office, *Legislative Series,* 1933. (Austria 3), p. 2.

[10] *Der Oesterreichische Arbeitsdienst,* II, 2 (Februar 1936), 6-7. The average exchange value of the schilling was 15.4 cents in 1933, 18.7 cents in 1934, 18.8 cents in 1935 and 1936. On July 30, 1937 its exchange value was 18.7 cents.

[11] Diakow, *Der Arbeitsdienst Oesterreichs* (Vienna 1934), S. 9.

RE-HITLER AUSTRIA

mbers of labor camp re-
ng from church service

use being constructed by
participants

cer team of a labor camp

PRE-HITLER AUSTR

Above:

Camp workers of a mine

Left:

House constructed w the help of campers

Below:

Building low-cost ho near Vienna

Item	*Per Cent*
Camp construction Camp furnishing Transportation costs	8.8
Food	43.0
Clothing	17.5
Sickness and accident insurance	8.5
Small articles of equipment	5.0
Pocket money	14.6
Smoking articles	2.6
Total	100.0

Selection and Enrollment of Youth

Those eligible for admission to camps were classified as follows: (1) labor service volunteers who received unemployment insurance; (2) those who no longer received unemployment insurance payments or emergency relief and who were needy; (3) other indigents under the age of twenty-five years who had a preferential rating at their unemployment office; (4) unemployed professional forest workers who satisfied the relief requirements; and (5) professional agricultural and forest workers who were particularly needy, provided that they were employed in work which was promoting agriculture.[12] The majority of the youth in the camps were under twenty-six years of age, but men over twenty-six years were admitted if they could be employed as leaders or assistant leaders.

The young people went into the camps for a period of forty weeks. When they left camp at the conclusion of this period, they were required to wait two years before they could enroll for another forty-week period. The following groups were exempt from these enrollment requirements: (1) volunteers who could be employed as camp leaders or assistant leaders; (2) settlers who were erecting buildings for a community if they would gain their livelihood largely from the development; and (3) volunteers above twenty-five years of age, but under twenty-eight years, who belonged to a private camp, or to the same age group in other camps, provided they had completed a course at a higher educational institution.[13]

---

[12] International Labor Office, *Legislative Series,* 1933 (Austria 3), Sec. 3, p. 1.
[13] *Ibid.,* pp. 2-3.

In 1934 approximately 13,000 men were enrolled in the work camps each month. In 1935 the average number of persons occupied in the labor service was 12,900. On January 1, 1936, 3,940 men were registered in 101 government and 43 private camps. This decrease in number was the result of a sharply reduced appropriation for camp expenses, brought about by the transfer of funds used by voluntary work camps to those which provided military training. On October 10, 1937, only 2,874 men, including the leaders, were enrolled in 87 camps.

Training of Leaders

Camp leaders were selected and trained in accordance with special instructions published by the Ministry of Social Administration and the Ministry of Education, which stated that to be accepted the men had to "be healthy, intelligent, of good moral character and possess a certain gift of leadership." They were also required to have spent at least twelve weeks as voluntary workers in a labor camp or have acquired the necessary experience for such work in other ways. The applicants for positions as leaders also had to agree to remain at the call of the labor service for not less than one year.[14]

The training of leaders was divided into several stages. Those men who seemed likely candidates for leadership were first sent to a training camp of the lowest rank. When they had passed the required examinations, they were employed as subleaders in a work camp. If after this experience they seemed fitted for further training, they were sent to a training camp for intermediate service, and if successful there and in the practical experience which followed in camps, they were later sent to the higher service camp. At least one year's experience in the Austrian Labor Service was required before a man could become a camp leader.

Persons selected under the conditions described above received training as leaders for eight weeks or more in resident labor camps. The course included practical as well as theoretical training. The law required that there must be 120 hours of the latter. In order to

[14] International Labor Office, *Unemployment among Young Persons*, pp. 124-25.

test the physical endurance of the candidates, nine hours of practical manual work was required daily of the men. The theoretical training of leaders included: (1) preparation for the duties of leadership (a consideration of the aims and ideals of the voluntary labor service, administrative and technical problems, and equipment and management of a labor camp); (2) a general course in physical culture and instruction in certain sports; (3) problems of management which included treatment of young persons, importance of good living conditions, food, etc.; (4) development of *esprit de corps;* (5) character training of young workers; (6) general education; (7) special problems of present-day Austria which included a consideration of the Austrian Corporative State — its Christian, German, and social aspects, as well as its fundamental principles; (8) the training of youth in the spirit of the corporative state; and (9) community life in camps.[15] Examinations were held at the end of the course for prospective leaders.[16] Once appointed, the camp leaders could serve for an unlimited period of time.

A Camp for Leaders

When in Vienna I visited a camp for directors on the outskirts of the city, which had enrolled about fifty young men who were preparing for service in the work camps in Austria, despite the fact that already there were more trained leaders than there were available jobs. The camp was apparently well staffed, but the location was unattractive and the buildings were of only mediocre quality. In September 1936 the camp was moved into an old Viennese palace where facilities were much better.

The work supervised by these directors consisted mainly of helping

[15] The educational offerings in a camp that I visited were as follows: (1) a technical course taught by engineers from the central office in connection with the work projects, fourteen hours a week; (2) financial administration, four hours a week; (3) character education (*Lebenskunde*), three hours a week; (4) commercial law, two hours a week; (5) civics, three hours a week; (6) use of leisure time, four hours a week; (7) sanitation, four hours a week; (8) sports, four hours a week; and (9) military education without arms, four hours a week, making a weekly total of forty-two hours. All who conducted these courses, except the sanitation officer, came from the central office in Vienna.

[16] International Labor Office, *op. cit.*

the people of limited income in Vienna to build their houses. In co-operation with other workers about fifty houses had been built. Since the camp officials felt that it was desirable for the prospective leaders to have work experience, some type of work project was carried out in the schools for leaders. The work performed by the candidates not only proved valuable experience for them, but made it possible for the state to give the courses free of charge and to pay the men from one to two schillings (20 to 40 cents) a day.

A schedule used in a leaders' training camp, where theoretical courses were emphasized, was:

5:55 A.M.	Reveille
6:00– 6:30	Setting-up exercises
6:30– 7:00	Making beds and cleaning rooms
7:00	Breakfast
7:25	Flag salute
7:30– 9:30	Lecture or discussions
9:30	Second breakfast
10:00–12:00 M.	Training courses
12:00– 2:50 P.M.	Lunch and rest
2:50	Orders for the next day
3:00– 5:00	Lecture courses
5:00– 5:30	Rest
5:30– 7:30	Courses
7:45	Supper and rest
8:00– 9:00	Free
9:00	Silence in sleeping rooms
10:00	Lights out [17]

Organization of Camps

The Austrian camps, while generally thought of as valuable from a disciplinary standpoint, were not part of the military training program. However, the Federal Compulsory Service Law *(Bundesdienstpflichtgesetz)* of April 1, 1936 provided that all male citizens between eighteen and forty-two years of age must serve the state in either military or labor service. And in 1937 the money appropriated by the

[17] In camps where practical work was performed, the periods from seven-thirty in the morning until noon and from three until five o'clock in the afternoon were spent on the work project.

federal government for the labor service was, in the original estimates, allocated for use in nonmilitary organizations *(Bundesdienstpflicht ohne Waffe)*.[18]

Each camp was under a sponsor who had two assistants—one in charge of the food and finance, and another in charge of the work program, or the technical phases of the camp. In appearance many of the Austrian camps resembled the WPA projects and the federal transient camps operated from 1933 to 1935 in this country. All men accepted in the camp had to be registered in the employment centers before entering the work service.

The camps visited varied in size. The one near Vienna (constructing low-cost houses) enrolled nearly 500 men, while the one near Alt-Aussee (operating a government-owned salt mine) had only ten enrollees. The men were housed in various types of barracks and in abandoned or rented public and private buildings. From 1934 to 1937 the Austrian camps averaged about thirty enrollees each.

Both "open" (nonresidential) and "closed" (residential) camps were in operation in Austria, but after January 1937 government funds were available only for closed camps. The men were given 50 groschen (9 cents) and five cigarettes a day, and were provided with two uniforms and two pairs of shoes.

All volunteers were required to undergo a medical examination before admission to a camp. While in the camp they received free health service and were covered by sickness and accident insurance. In addition they were protected by labor legislation applicable to all workers in Austria, which regulated hours of work and protection of life, health, and safety of employees.

Work Projects

The work of the men in the camps consisted of such projects as street and road building, forestry, stream regulation, soil improvement, suburban and rural settlement, recreational improvements, operation

[18] *Lehrlings-, Jugend- und Berufsfürsorge,* XIV, 2-3 (Februar-März 1937), 24.

of government-owned salt mines, and relief work. The men worked eight hours a day.

According to the regulations governing the work service, all projects had to be approved by competent local authorities[19] and had to have public utility value and to be supplementary, that is, of a type that would not have been performed without labor service. The decision of the local authorities was subject to review by the Federal Minister of Social Administration.

One camp visited near Vienna enrolled 470 men, none of whom slept in the camp. They did eat at the camp, however. Their work consisted of building houses for people of low income, and helping the families who were to live in them with the landscaping and planting of gardens. By the fall of 1936 the camp had completed, or partly completed, 360 houses, most of them two-family dwellings.

WORK PERFORMED BY THE AUSTRIAN LABOR SERVICE, 1935–37 [a]

Work Project	Number of Camps			
	1935	1936	1937	Total
Highway building	48	21	23	92
Service road building	45	36	28	109
Hydraulic construction	67	39	23	129
Melioration projects	28	13	7	48
Settlement construction	5	7	5	17
Various restoration projects	27	17	27	71
Total	220	133	113	466

[a] "Drei Jahre Oesterreichischer Arbeitsdienst," *Der Oesterreichische Arbeitsdienst,* IV, 2 (Februar 1938), 3.

[19] From my observations in Austria it seemed that after the suppression of the Social Democrats in February 1934 less care was taken to select projects for the camps that did not compete with private employment. By using the workers on low-cost housing projects and the operation of salt mines (salt is a government monopoly), competition with ordinary labor certainly occurred. See *Foreign Policy Reports,* XI, 15 (September 25, 1935).

PRE-HITLER AUSTRIA

e:

istrian camp members re-
ng to quarters

:

oad construction

v:

ospective leaders of Aus-
camps

PRE-HITLER AUSTRIA

Above:

Group of campers who operat
government-owned salt mine

Left:

Campers' living quarters of the
mine project

Below:

From left to right, student le
of labor camps, director of educa
for all Austrian camps, directo
leader training center near Vie

Time Spent on Work Projects by the Austrian Labor Service, 1935–37[a]

Work Project	Number of Work Days			
	1935	1936	1937	Total
Highway building	339,028	217,473	197,541	754,042
Service road building	241,343	230,130	235,816	707,289
Hydraulic construction	598,411	247,941	125,022	971,374
Melioration projects	144,123	82,217	61,217	290,557
Settlement construction	43,853	144,919	44,961	233,733
Various restoration projects	131,284	175,889	153,872	461,045
Maintenance	82,577	94,628	49,674	226,879
Total	1,580,619	1,196,197	868,103	3,644,919

[a] "Drei Jahre Oesterreichischer Arbeitsdienst," *Der Oesterreichische Arbeitsdienst*, IV, 2 (Februar 1938), 3.

Secondary Work Performed by the Austrian Labor Service, 1935–37 [a]

Type of Work	Number of Hours Spent on Work
Surveying and mapping	109,700
Leveling	147,300
Intellectual workers service	44,500
Instruction	88,064
Distress work	114,900
Maintenance of tools	270,122
Guard duty	100,800
Building management	519,300
Building inspection	840,900
Additional work	978,000
Total	3,213,586

[a] "Drei Jahre Oesterreichischer Arbeitsdienst," *Der Oesterreichische Arbeitsdienst*, IV, 2 (Februar 1938), 4.

Educational Program

The work itself was regarded as a valuable means of training the youth to become useful members of society; therefore this aspect of the camp program was emphasized most. Special attention was also given to physical exercise and physical education.

The physical exercise program consisted of setting-up exercises in the morning, and games and sports in the afternoon. Premilitary training was also a part of the camp program. In the evenings, courses on elementary subjects, shorthand, letterwriting, and so forth, were available, as well as lectures and discussions. Camp members were provided with reading material by the central library maintained by the national organization. Conducted tours and excursions and the observance of festivals served to vary the camp routine.

Employment Service

Youth who were able to obtain employment were permitted to leave the camps at any time. All records of the men were filed in the administrative offices and classified according to their work experience. This plan facilitated locating the men with special training when jobs were available. When a man left camp, he was given a certificate of service, somewhat like that given an enrollee when he leaves a CCC camp. This evidence of camp experience was usually of assistance to the young men in obtaining jobs.

Student Work Camps

As in other European countries, students from colleges and universities in Austria were active in the labor service movement. The first Austrian work camps were student camps, and were begun as early as 1925. Then during the summer of 1932 the Austrian Student Labor Service *(Studentische Arbeitsdienst Oesterreichs)* was founded and financed by subsidies from the colleges and universities *(Hochschulen)* and by contributions from the participants. This organization maintained camps in the country to help the farmers build their roads.[20]

The Austrian National Union of University Students was able to

[20] *Der Arbeitsdienst in der Welt,* S. 91-92.

place students in camps and also in libraries, laboratories, and scientific institutions as apprentices. Students from foreign universities were also accepted by the labor service camps during the summer months.

Present Trends in the Labor Service

In the legislative debates on the 1939 federal budget for Austria, labor service duty *(Arbeitsdienstpflicht)* was considered for the first time. State Secretary Rott expressed the opinion that the problem of labor service for youth would be the next one for the Austrian labor service officials to attack.[21] The official labor service publication, *Der Oesterreichische Arbeitsdienst,* insinuated that it might not be long before labor service in Austria, as in Germany, would become compulsory and that it would perform a similar function of training young men in "soldierly" habits, preparatory to the period of compulsory military training which they owed to the state.

Now that Germany has taken over Austria and incorporated it into the German Reich, a labor service similar to that in Germany is being developed there. *Der Arbeitsmann*[22] of April 9, 1938 describes a trip of *Reichsarbeitsführer* Konstantin Hierl to Austria to select sites for six camps and to plan for the development of the National Socialist labor service. In the April 30, 1938 issue of the same paper[23] an article describes the ceremony which took place commemorating the founding of the first National Socialist camp in Austria, on April 20, 1938, Hitler's birthday, and was attended by representatives of the various National Socialist organizations, the local work service officials, and several hundred peasants and townspeople. The camp was named the Adolf Hitler Camp.

Conclusion

Before Austria became a part of Germany, the labor service was designed primarily to assist the Austrian youth who were in a serious economic state. At first the camps were voluntary and in many ways similar to the labor services in democratic countries. As pressure from

[21] *Der Oesterreichische Arbeitsdienst,* III, 12 (Dezember 1937), 4-5.
[22] *Ibid.,* IV, 15, S. 7.
[23] *Ibid.,* IV, 18, S. 11.

Fascist Italy on the south and Nazi Germany on the north became stronger, the tendency was to move in the direction of an authoritarian state, and this was reflected in the Austrian labor service program.

When the Social Democrats were a strong force in Austria, the labor service had been careful not to compete with ordinary labor, but after the ousting of the Socialists and the establishment of the Dollfuss and Schuschnigg regimes less attention was paid to the rights of labor. As a result, it seems that the service was used more and more to build low-cost houses, construct roads, and operate government-owned salt mines, thus competing with ordinary laborers and tending to lower the wage scale in Austria. Now that the country is a part of Germany, the labor service of Austria has been incorporated in the National Socialist labor service and has lost its identity in the sea of red, white, and black swastika flags.

Bibliography

VERA M. DEAN. "Austria: the Paralysis of a Nation," *Foreign Policy Reports,* VIII, 22 (January 4, 1933), 256-66.

A. D. DIAKOW. *Der Arbeitsdienst Oesterreichs.* Vienna: Waldheim-Eberle A. G., 1934. 11 S.

INTERNATIONAL LABOR OFFICE. *Legislative Series,* 1932 (Austria 4); 1933 (Austria 3); 1934 (Austria 8).

Lehrlings-, Jugend- und Berufsfürsorge; Organ der Lehrlingsberatungsstellen der Oesterreichischen Arbeiterkammern und des Amtes für Berufsberatung und Lehrstellenvermittlung des Landesarbeitsamtes in Wien. Vienna: Gewerkschaftsbund der Oesterreichischen Arbeiter und Angestellten, XIV, 1937.

"New Law Regulating the Organization and Training of Austrian Youth," *School and Society,* XLIV (December 5, 1936), 733.

Der Oesterreichische Arbeitsdienst, III, 7 (Juli 1937). Vienna.

"Reform of the Austrian Labor Service," *Industrial and Labor Information,* LIII, 4 (January 28, 1935), 123.

FRITZ RAGER, "The Settlement of the Unemployed on the Land in Austria," *International Labor Review,* XXIX, 3 (March 1934), 384-97.

OTTO SIEGEL. "Die organisatorischen Grundlagen des österreichischen Arbeitsdienstes," *Deutscher Arbeitsdienst,* V, 20 (19. Mai 1935), 637-38.

"The Voluntary Labor Service in Austria," *Industrial and Labor Information,* LIV, 3 (April 15, 1935), 117.

MILDRED S. WERTHEIMER. "Austria Establishes a Fascist State," *Foreign Policy Reports,* XI, 15 (September 25, 1935), 181-88.

Projects for the Unemployed in Great Britain

My home is in Liverpool. I was born and brought up there. I have been living a terrible life these last few years, without regular work. My mother, she's slaved all her life, and now that I'm a grown man I can do absolutely nothing for her. I receive only five shilling transitional benefit, and I hand that over. My brother, he's a man too, and he's doing nothing; and then there's my two sisters doing nothing, and my father, a ship's painter, glad to take half a day's work. . . .

At home, now, we live in terrible low conditions. We have three rooms, and the mother and two girls sleep in one, and the brother and father and I sleep in the other. We have no bedclothes. What I put over me in winter is a Territorial Army greatcoat, and I throw my clothes on the bed to keep me warm.

. . . There seemed to be no future or anything. I wanted to get married, but what was the good without a job? So that's all finished. I became moody and fed up, and wandered around the streets. Many times I thought of suicide. There was just no chance to get a start.[1]

England, like the other countries of Europe during the post-war years, had a large number of unemployed, many of whom could tell stories of their experiences similar to the one quoted above. The crisis of 1929 and the depression years that followed increased the numbers of the unemployed and permitted a generation to pass through adolescence and come to their majority without work experience and frequently without adequate vocational training. There were also large numbers of older men who, because of extended periods of unemployment, lost their skills, and even lost the desire and ability to work.

British concern with the problem has been increased by the fact that unemployment has become an apparently permanent factor in certain sections of the country, especially in the southwest of Scotland, on the northeast and northwest coasts of England, and in south Wales. These

[1] Anthony Divers, "Time to Spare," from *Time to Spare; What Unemployment Means, by Eleven Unemployed,* edited by Felix Greene (London: Allen & Unwin, 1935), pp. 47-48.

"depressed areas" were once flourishing manufacturing and mining centers in which lived a large proportion of highly specialized workers. But most of the mines can no longer be worked with profit to their owners, and after the war the demand for the products of the heavy industries, in which a large share of the capital of these districts was invested, steadily decreased both at home and in the foreign markets. Even in the good years of 1924 and 1929 there were 500,000 unemployed in the depressed areas.

In 1937 a revival in the heavy industries, the government rearmament program, and an increase in foreign trade combined to give the "special areas" the best year they had known since the beginning of the depression, and the number on their unemployment rolls decreased twice as rapidly as in the whole of England and Wales. Yet in March 1937, 62 per cent of the total number of unemployed men between the ages of eighteen and sixty-four in the United Kingdom were in the depressed areas. Coal mining, which is of particular importance to these areas, accounted for 35 per cent of the total unemployment.[2] Although the immediate prospects for the depressed areas seemed quite hopeful, *The Economist* pointed out at the beginning of 1938 that their 1937 pace of recovery would probably not be maintained and that the case for special measures to alleviate their difficulties was as strong as ever.[3]

During the first few months of 1939 the total number of unemployed in Great Britain exceeded 2,000,000 in spite of the tremendous rearmament program, and the number in the depressed areas was disproportionately high.[4]

The revival of industry in the depressed areas has provided employment for some of the young men who until recently presented, in the words of the Commissioner for the Special Areas in England and Wales, "the most tragic aspect of the problem of the special areas and one fraught with great danger to the state." In his second report[5] the Commissioner stated that in the areas there were about 11,000 men between

[2] *Ministry of Labor Gazette,* "Unemployment in the Special Areas," XLV, 7 (July 1937), 254.

[3] *The Economist,* CXXX, 4924 (January 8, 1938), 53-54.

[4] *New York Times,* February 16, 1939.

[5] Commissioner for the Special Areas, *Second Report,* (February 6, 1936), Cmd. 5090, pp. 68-71.

the ages of eighteen and twenty-one. Of these about 7,000 had been unemployed more than three months. Many of them had practically never worked, their fathers had not worked for years, and they had come to accept state support as normal.

To alleviate and ameliorate this unemployment problem in the depressed areas and elsewhere in England, a variety of projects or "schemes" was developed, chief among them being: (1) the government training centers, begun in 1925; (2) the instructional centers, established in 1929; (3) the junior instruction centers, started in 1918; (4) the juvenile transfer scheme, and (5) various private projects for students, intellectuals, and the unemployed. While not all these projects are camps in the strict sense of the word, they are sufficiently like camps to be considered briefly here.

Government Training Centers

One of the first plans that suggested itself as a remedy for the circumstances described above was a program of vocational training. It was thought that this would help to meet the needs of the large number of men who, because of war and economic depression, had never learned a trade or had lost their proficiency at the one they had followed before their work was interrupted. The first government training centers offering vocational training to the unemployed were opened by the Ministry of Labor in October 1925.

The organization of the government training centers gained some impetus from the industrial training scheme which was put into operation immediately after the war, primarily for disabled ex-service men prevented by their disabilities from resuming their former occupations. Under this scheme, between August 1919 and December 1934, 88,000 men were trained to earn their livings. This number included 6,000 young men who were physically fit but who had been prevented from learning a trade because of their war service. The government training centers now provide means by which young men can be taken from the depressed areas where they have no prospect of employment and trained for skilled jobs in other parts of the country where they may be able to earn their living.

Eligibility and Selection of Enrollees

The men hear of the centers through the employment exchanges and through printed bulletins issued by the Ministry of Labor. Candidates for admission to the centers must be without prospect of regular employment in their own trades and willing to accept an offer of suitable employment in any part of the country. Preference is given to men between the ages of eighteen and thirty-five who live in the "scheduled" depressed areas or certain other districts of extensive unemployment. Normally, only single men are accepted, but married men, men with dependents, or any men between thirty-five and forty-five years of age may be considered if they are especially fitted for training. It is considered desirable to admit to the training centers only those men who seem likely to profit from the training offered. Men who were trained some years ago, and men who have served an apprenticeship in a trade taught at a center, may be admitted under certain conditions for short review courses if they have been unable to get a start in industry.

The trainees are chosen from the candidates by a committee on selection in accordance with the standards required for each course. This panel usually includes an assistant manager from one of the centers. The men remain in the centers for approximately six months. There are no set periods for recruiting new trainees, and every week new men enter the centers and others complete their training.

The training center program was sharply reduced between 1931 and 1933 because there were so few jobs available during those depression years. It has been a consistent policy of the centers to admit only as many men as can reasonably be expected to be placed in positions. Since 1934, however, the program has been making steady progress. In 1935, 7,205 men completed training at the nine centers then in operation; an additional 3,955 were in training at the end of the year. During 1936, 14,250 men were admitted to training and 10,693 completed the course. During 1937, 16,092 men were admitted to training; in December 1937, 5,821 were enrolled in the centers. Late in 1937 arrangements were made to train soldiers for jobs in industry during the last six months of their color service. To provide for these men, the Ministry of Labor increased its training places to more than 7,500. The number in attendance at each center has ranged from 210 to 830, depending on the available work space.

Care of the Men

For the most part the government training centers are nonresidential —that is, the men do not live in them. Since most of the men have left their own homes to take the course, they must live in lodgings near the center. Care is taken by the management of the center to see that these are located in a suitable neighborhood.

No special care for the health of the trainees is provided, but the men work under healthy conditions, and are given a substantial midday meal free of cost by the center.

Cost of Training and Payments

During training the men continue to receive the unemployment benefit to which they are entitled, or such allowances as may be granted by the Unemployment Assistance Board. The Ministry of Labor recently stated[6] that the cost of the training is 31 shillings ($7.75) a man per week, which includes a midday meal at the center, an allowance of 5 shillings ($1.25) a week for personal expenses, and the cost of instruction, materials, et cetera.

The centers are under the direction of managers and assistant managers appointed by the Ministry of Labor. These men receive no special training for their work, but all of them have had industrial experience. They receive a salary of 600 to 800 pounds ($3,000 to $4,000) a year.

Courses at the Centers

In the early experimental centers started in 1925 and 1926 the training given was intended to develop "handymen" rather than skilled workmen. However, by 1928 the work was related to industrial demands, and this relationship has been maintained, the goal being always to have an actual job for each trainee. Consequently, the courses given

[6] In reply to our questionnaire.

at the centers have varied from time to time, as the available job opportunities have changed with shifting industrial conditions.

The training consists of an intensive course of practical and theoretical instruction given by skilled craftsmen. Among the trades which have been taught at the centers are: bricklaying, plastering, tile fixing, carpentry, painting, gas and hot-water fitting, wood-machining, cabinet-making, upholstery and French polishing, coach bodybuilding, coach trimming, coach painting, machine operating, fitting and turning, instrument making, electric welding, oxyacetylene welding, panel beating, sheet-metal working, metal spinning, metal polishing, motor mechanics, hairdressing, hotel waiting, terrazzo working, glass-tube welding and blowing, and cooking. The men keep regular factory hours and put in a forty-four-hour week, but very little of the work done in the centers is productive in a monetary sense.

At certain centers new classes have been opened to train those men from the instructional centers who are likely to become successful builders' laborers and factory laborers. Efforts have also been made to encourage unemployed skilled engineers to take review courses.

The educational program in the centers is directly related to the main object of vocational training, and aims to increase the trainee's capacity to profit from his training. Some centers have an educational officer, but this is not generally the case. The time given to vocational or related training varies from one to two hours a day, and all the men attend the classes, especially in the early stages of their training. Regularity and promptness in attendance at the centers are made compulsory in order to give the men a feeling of actual job conditions.

In addition to work in mathematics, which is given special emphasis, lectures on theoretical aspects of various trades are also given by the instructors. While the centers do not expect to turn out skilled craftsmen, definite standards of trade proficiency are set up and periodic tests are given. If a man cannot meet the standards he is transferred to another trade or to an instructional center.

Results of the Program

The government training centers have achieved outstanding success in placing their men in regular employment. Except for the years from

1931 to 1933, when jobs were abnormally scarce because of the economic depression, more than 90 per cent of the men completing the courses have either been placed in jobs by the centers or have found work for themselves. In 1936 more than 97 per cent entered industrial employment as what the Ministry of Labor terms "improvers," with every prospect of being able to establish themselves and to become fully skilled workmen. This success is of course largely due to the fact that the number of men admitted to these centers, as well as the type of courses selected, have been correlated with the number and types of job opportunities in industry.

It is the opinion of the Ministry of Labor that the men usually welcome the opportunity afforded by the training program. However, in 1936 the Commissioner for the Special Areas in England and Wales reported that large numbers of men in the special areas refused to apply for admission to these centers, a situation which he did not explain, but which he termed deplorable.[7] The 1936 report of the Ministry of Labor contains the admission that it is difficult to find suitable men for "refresher" courses (short retraining courses) in engineering, who are willing to accept employment away from home.

The Ministry of Labor has made no special effort to educate public attitude regarding this training program, but believes that on the whole opinions are favorable. A certain amount of criticism has been made in the House of Commons by the members of the opposition. There is also some opposition to the centers from trade unions who claim that the centers turn out half-trained men who go into factories at full rates of pay, thus tending to break down the arrangements for apprentices.

In general the Ministry of Labor considers that the training centers have served very well the purpose for which they were set up, and that the results of the program have been satisfactory from the standpoint of the improved physique and morale of the men and of their increased ability to secure and keep employment.

---

[7] *Third Report* (October 27, 1936), Cmd. 5303, pp. 127-28. See also *New York Times*, February 23, 1939.

Instructional Centers

The instructional centers, which were inaugurated in 1929, have passed through several stages of development. At first the Ministry of Labor proposed to train men from the depressed areas for manual labor and then to transfer them to other parts of the country where jobs were available. For this reason, these centers were at first called "transfer instructional centers." As in the case of the training centers, a definite attempt was made to place the men in actual jobs, and as a result the number admitted to the instructional centers was limited, and the candidates selected were restricted to those capable of hard work. Placement became more and more difficult, however, partly because of the dearth of jobs, but also because of the hostility of both employers and other laborers to men from the centers. The result was a gradual closing down of these projects during 1931 and 1932.

In June 1932 it was decided to abolish any element of compulsory attendance in connection with the centers and to throw them open to any unemployed who wished to be reconditioned physically, regardless of the prospects for future employment. This led to an extension of the program, and in 1933 summer camps were introduced.

This policy has received many criticisms from those who feel that there is little to be gained by getting men in good physical condition and giving them some work experience when they must return to the same depressing environment from which they came. One of these critics has been the Commissioner for the Special Areas in England and Wales. In his second report, made in February 1936, the Commissioner stated that he believed the centers to be right in principle, but inadequate in results. He urgently recommended that unemployed men between eighteen and twenty-one years of age who had satisfactorily completed a course should be given some assurance of employment, at least for a year. This could be done, he believed, by a program of public works.[8] In October of the same year the Commissioner reported that nearly 40 per cent of those attending centers from the special areas were being placed in jobs.[9]

[8] *Second Report* (February 6, 1936), Cmd. 5090, pp. 69-70.
[9] *Third Report* (October 27, 1936), Cmd. 5303, p. 125.

Publicizing the Centers

In order to attract men to the centers it is necessary to publicize them in areas of unemployment where there may be eligible men. Films are shown, announcements are made over the radio, individuals are invited to visit the centers to become acquainted with the work, and leaflets and posters about the centers are issued by the Ministry of Labor. Men are also urged by officials of unemployment exchanges to take part in the instructional centers. Between August and December 1935 approximately 64,000 men on the unemployment register in the special areas of England and Wales were urged to enter the instructional centers, and 70.7 per cent of those under twenty-one years of age, and 67 per cent of those between twenty-one and twenty-five years of age, either refused or did not attend after having accepted the offer.[10] On February 22, 1939, Prime Minister Chamberlain stated:

> I am disturbed by what I hear of young men who won't attend instructional centers when they are given the opportunity of doing so and are thus defeating the efforts of those who are trying to help them.[11]

Eligibility and Selection of Enrollees

At first men were recruited only in the depressed areas, but as facilities have expanded, unemployed persons in other areas have been invited to attend the instructional centers. Officers of both the Ministry of Labor and the Unemployment Assistance Board participate in the selection of candidates. An attempt is made to select only those men who seem likely to profit from the training program. During the first three years of their existence the primary aim of the centers was to train men for jobs, and care was taken to select only those sufficiently strong to stand the hard labor involved. However, in 1932 when the aim of the centers was changed, it became possible to recruit other unemployed who, by a program of lighter work, were built up physically so that they could stand up under the exacting demands of jobs in private industry.

To be eligible for an instructional center a man must have been un-

[10] *Ibid.*, pp. 127-28.

[11] *New York Times*, February 23, 1939.

employed at least three months and have been receiving unemployment insurance or an assistance allowance. The men remain in the camps from eight to twelve weeks, and the practice is usually to have ten-week courses in the summer camps and twelve-week courses in the year-round centers.

When the instructional centers were first established, the enrollees were limited to those between nineteen and thirty-five years of age. Later, however, the upper limit was removed. At present the majority of the men are between the ages of eighteen and thirty-five, but a few are accepted up to the age of forty-five.

Successful candidates for places at the instructional centers are required to undergo a free medical examination by officers of the Ministry of Health. As a result of efforts of the Commissioner for the Special Areas in England and Wales, a certain number of men from those areas who need medical treatment are being admitted to the centers.[12] Between September 1935 and January 1936, 624 applicants from the Special Areas were refused admission to instructional centers on medical grounds.[13] This is approximately 13 per cent of the total number admitted to the centers during those months (no figure is available for the number of applications for admission). On March 26, 1936 the Minister stated that between December 1935 and the end of February 1936, 17 per cent of the applicants had been rejected for medical reasons.[14] A medical orderly resides in each center and local physicians attend the camps as required. An infirmary with beds for about six men is attached to each center.

The number of unemployed who enroll in the instructional centers is still small. From 1929 to 1936 only about 76,000 men enrolled in the projects. The number has increased, however, from year to year and during 1937 approximately 21,000 men received instructional center experience in some twenty-nine instructional centers. The centers and

[12] *Ibid.*, pp. 120-30.

[13] Minister of Labor in the House of Commons, February 20, 1936; see also Commons 308:2006.

[14] Commons 310:3183-85.

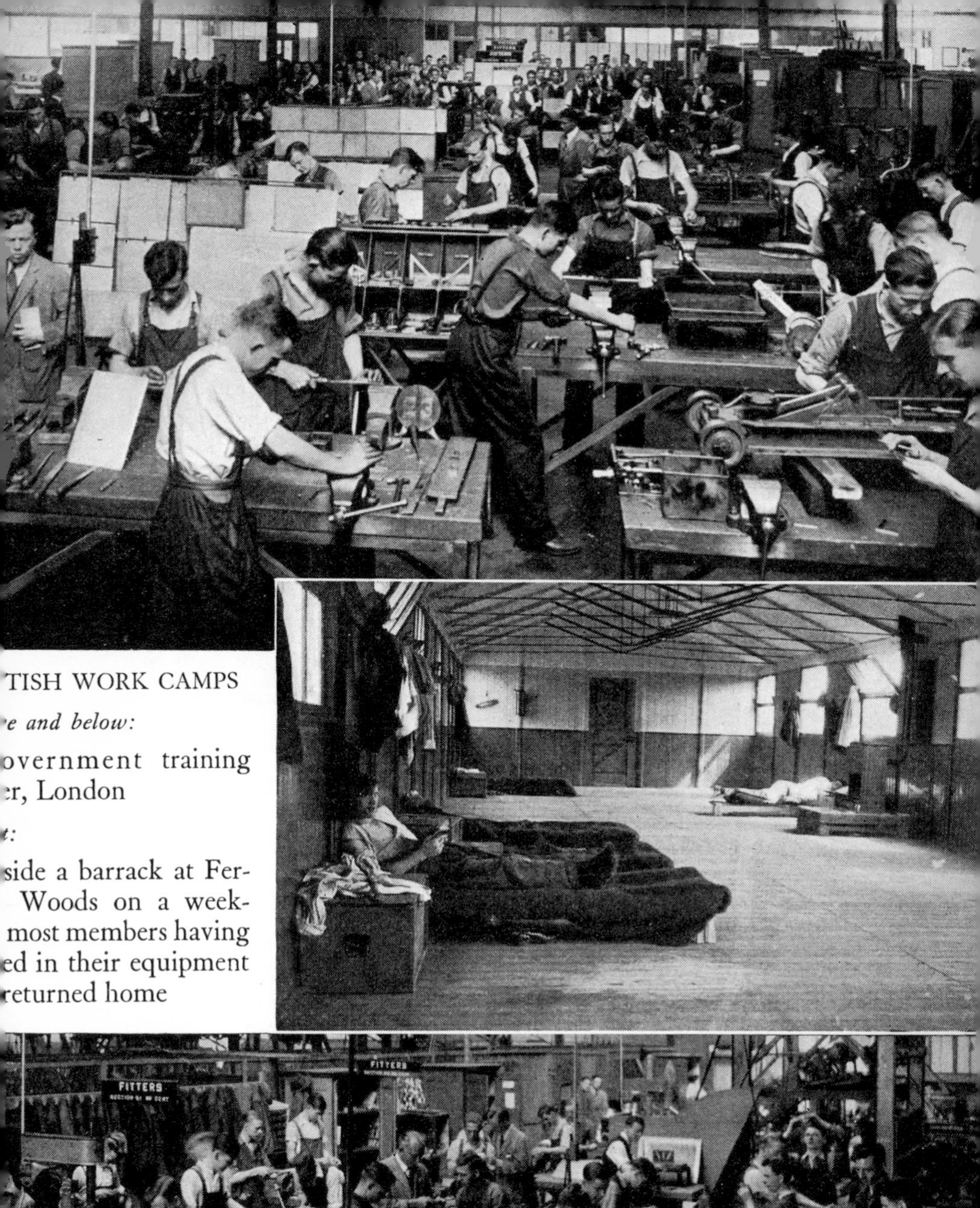

TISH WORK CAMPS

e and below:

overnment training
er, London

t:

side a barrack at Fer-
Woods on a week-
most members having
ed in their equipment
returned home

BRITISH WORK CAMPS

Above:

Training center for unemployec London

Left:

Barracks and flower garden in Ca Fermyn Woods

Below:

Training auto mechanics at Wad

the summer camps had a total enrollment of between 3,000 and 4,000 men. The unemployed do not enter the instructional centers at any particular time, but come and go from week to week.

Administration and Organization of Centers

The centers are administered by the Ministry of Labor. The Unemployment Assistance Board and the Ministry work together in deciding general questions of training policy, and officers of the Board participate in recruiting and selecting men for the instructional centers.[15]

The cost of the centers is approximately 14 shillings, 4 pence ($3.56) a man per week, not including unemployment benefit. The total cost is about 23 shillings ($5.75) a week.

The directors of the centers are officials of the Ministry of Labor and are selected from the staff of the Ministry. If they have not already had experience in the centers when appointed, they take a course of about a month's duration. They receive a salary of from 400 to 600 pounds ($2,000 to $3,000) a year. Since the centers are under the Ministry of Labor, they are entirely nonmilitary in character.

While the men are in the centers they continue to receive whatever unemployment benefit they are entitled to, as well as an allowance for their dependents. Out of this sum they pay for their board and lodging, leaving them about 4 shillings ($1.00) a week if they are living at the center or 5 shillings ($1.25) a week if they are living in a private residence near by. The men also receive traveling expenses and their work clothes.

Each center contains from 150 to 200 men, the tendency being toward the larger number. In order to harden them the men in the centers are usually housed in "hutments" during the first week or two. During the summer some of them live in tents, but in the nonresidential centers they live at home or in lodgings near the center. Both residential and nonresidential camps are used. Since the first instructional center was established, more than two thirds have been residential.

[15] Ministry of Labor, *Report for 1935*, p. 31.

Work Projects

The work projects of the centers consist of clearing forests, making roads, establishing drainage systems, timbering, excavating, building bridges, and leveling. The work is of a nature to add to the resources of the nation, but of a type which could not have been done without state funds. The men work forty-four hours per week.

Educational Program

Education is given a definite place in the instructional centers, since they are designed to build up men mentally and physically and to overcome the effects of long periods of unemployment. Sometimes the program is directed toward training the men for actual jobs, but in general no attempt is made to give vocational training for special types of work. Ordinarily during the first week at a center the men are given schoolroom instruction, consisting chiefly of a review of elementary school subjects. During stormy weather, when outdoor work is impossible, they are taught rough carpentry, simple metalwork, and boot and shoe repairing. This training is not for the purpose of producing skilled craftsmen, but to give the men a "feeling for tools."

The instructors for these courses are the educational and welfare officers of the Ministry of Labor. All the men entering the instructional centers must participate in the educational program.

The program in the instructional centers builds up the men physically and raises their morale, thus making it possible for them again to obtain employment. They are not placed in jobs directly from the camps, however, but must return home and seek work through the labor exchanges. All men entering the instructional centers are registered in the employment exchanges, since all of them are receiving unemployment benefit or relief, and to receive either they must be capable of and available for work.

Employment after Leaving the Centers

Various measures have been taken to assist the men to obtain employment after leaving the centers. It was found that employers were prejudiced against men from the centers because they felt that they were inferior workmen. Consequently, in 1930, to avoid dismissal of men from jobs without good cause, the Ministry of Labor arranged with three private organizations to employ men from the instructional centers, under the supervision of the Ministry of Labor officials. In return for this concession, a certain proportion of wages paid was returned to the employers by the Ministry. This plan was reported to work very well and was continued.[16]

In his third report (October 1936) the Commissioner for the Special Areas in England and Wales stated that employment preference was being given to men from the areas who had attended the instructional centers, those under twenty-five years of age being given first choice. Some of the men who have received the general training of the instructional centers are urged to go to a government training center to improve their skills and, as a result, their prospects of employment.

The Minister of Labor told the House of Commons on February 20, 1936 that from July 1 to December 31, 1935 approximately 18 per cent of the men from the special areas who had attended instructional centers were placed in employment after leaving the centers.[17] Another statement made to the Commons July 30, 1936 indicated that during the first six months of that year 30 per cent of all those leaving the centers had found employment, and in the month of June the rate was about 44 per cent. The Minister attributed this in large part to the trade recovery.[18] However, during 1936 work was found for an average of only 25 per cent of those attending the centers. Those who return to their homes and do not find jobs may enroll in a center again after nine months have elapsed.

Attitude of Men toward Centers

The Ministry of Labor states that while there is still "a certain amount of skepticism and apathy . . . in general the men are satisfied with the conditions of life in the centers."[19] Many erroneous ideas about the centers circulate among the unemployed, especially the idea that they

---

[16] See reports of the Ministry of Labor for these years.

[17] Commons 309:620.

[18] *Ibid.*, 315:1750.

[19] Ministry of Labor in reply to our questionnaire.

are army recruiting centers and are preparing men for participation in the next war.

A radio speech made by a man from Liverpool probably expresses the attitude of most men who have attended the centers:

> . . . When I first heard of these instructional centers I was suspicious of them—nearly all of us unemployed men were. We swore we wouldn't go to such places. I'd heard the general opinion of them at that time—that it was an army recruiting scheme, and that it was preparing for the next war—that they sent young fellows to get them fit for war. So I didn't do anything about it, and went on looking for a job in Liverpool, but with less and less hope. . . .
>
> But anyway I applied to the manager of the Exchange. He refused me the first time because I'd been ill, but I applied again. This time I was successful, and ten days later I was sent off to Fermyn Woods.
>
> The work's not really hard though we're expected to do our share. I expected strict army discipline, but there's none of that. We go out in the morning about eight o'clock, and work until four thirty, with a break for lunch at midday. The kind of work varies a good deal, but mostly it's on reafforestation, that is, clearing ground and planting saplings. But there's carpentry as well, and metal work, and keeping the lawns decent. Often there's a bit of painting to be done.
>
> Our big meal is in the evening after work. The grub is fine, and plenty of it. . . . I only got a hot meal once a week at home; I get one every day here. I hate to think of going back. . . .
>
> I hadn't any decent clothes when I came here. My boots were falling apart, and the only coat I had was torn and in a very bad condition. They fix us up with corduroy trousers, and a pair of boots. . . .
>
> . . . The staff was really kind and helpful. They go to endless trouble on our behalf. And they ask nothing in return other than we play the game with them. I am very glad of this opportunity of being able to pay a public tribute to them. There's no punishment, but a fellow can be sent home. That's the worst thing that can happen to him.
>
> . . . It's a curse on this country that so many should go hungry. When I think of the thousands of young chaps like myself waiting to be given a chance it seems a disgrace. A center like this restores some faith in human kindness. We don't feel set apart no longer.[20]

Junior Instruction Centers

According to the 1932 report of the Royal Commission on Unemployment Insurance, approximately 700,000 juveniles (boys and girls four-

[20] *Time to Spare,* pp. 48-57.

teen to eighteen years of age) leave school in Great Britain during a normal year. For a number of years these young people provided a source of cheap labor because they were not participants in unemployment insurance, and therefore employers did not have to contribute to the insurance scheme for them.

Two recent legislative changes have helped to alter this situation. First, the Unemployment Insurance Act of 1934 provided that the minimum age for participation in insurance should be the school-leaving age (not less than fourteen years). Second, the school-leaving age, except in certain specified cases, will be raised to fifteen years on September 1, 1939. As a result, the juvenile workers no longer constitute the cheap labor that they once did, and their numbers will eventually be reduced by keeping them out of the labor market for an additional year.

Since the passage of the Unemployment Insurance Act of 1934, the maintenance of junior instructional centers has been compulsory in areas where juvenile unemployment affects a sufficiently large number of young people to justify taking the action. In other places the unemployed are accommodated, as far as possible, in existing educational institutions.

These junior instruction centers were originally organized by local education authorities with the aid of funds made available from the Exchequer through the Board of Education and the Scotch Education Department. From 1918 to 1930 they were on a temporary basis, but in 1930 they were made permanent. The Minister of Labor is responsible to Parliament for the efficiency of the centers, but he is required to work "in close cooperation with the Board of Education," and the board's inspectors are "responsible for inspection on the educational side of the scheme."[21]

Aim of the Centers

The aim of these centers is "to prevent the demoralization which so soon threatens boys and girls when they are unemployed and have nothing to occupy their hands or their minds." The National Advisory

[21] Ministry of Labor, *Memorandum on the Establishment and Conduct of Courses of Instruction for Unemployed Boys and Girls, England and Wales* (ACM. 1), 1934, p. 5.

Council for Juvenile Employment has pointed out, however, that "the object is not merely to keep the boys and girls off the streets and give them something to do." The more definitely constructive purposes of the centers are:

> . . . (1) to give the boys and girls a real interest in life, (2) to keep their minds and figures active and alert, and their bodies fit, (3) to teach them something which will be of real use to them whether at home or at work, (4) without trying to train them for specific occupations, to give them the type of mental and manual instruction which will help them to become absorbed or reabsorbed into employment as soon as an opportunity may occur.[22]

It is to be noted that no specific vocational training is given in the junior instruction centers. Some English educators, however, advocate vocational training in the centers. Referring to the refusal of many unemployed young men in the special areas to apply for admission to government training centers, the *Times Educational Supplement* has said:

> This seems to point to the need of earlier vocational training—training which might well be given in the junior instruction centers when boys and girls are more receptive and more responsive to discipline after leaving school. The junior instruction centers should form preparatory courses for senior work.[23]

Enrollment in Camps

The trend in England is toward including more and more of the juvenile unemployed in the centers as facilities become improved and sufficiently expanded to take care of them. In many areas there is not sufficient unemployment to justify the establishment of centers, but in these places the education authorities are urged to make other arrangements whereby the young unemployed may receive instruction.

According to the law, attendance at an instruction center is required of any boy or girl fourteen to eighteen years of age who is capable of and available for work. Failure to attend, or misbehavior which results in dismissal from the center, may be followed by disallowance of un-

[22] Ministry of Labor, *op. cit.*, p. 4.

[23] *The Times* [London] *Educational Supplement,* November 26, 1934, p. 421.

employment benefit. According to the Education Act, fines and imprisonment may even be the result. In actual practice, however, the centers are not universally compulsory, and attendance is required only where such action is reasonable. The boys and girls attending the centers are not limited to any definite period of enrollment and may remain in the center until they find work. The number of enrollees participating in the program of a given center depends upon the fluctuations of employment opportunities.

Housing of Centers

These juvenile instruction centers are nonresidential, the boys and girls continuing to live at home. The housing of the centers varies according to the resources of different communities. The buildings used include well-equipped technical institutes and day continuation schools, unused elementary schools, church halls, rooms in cooperative stores, a vacated railway station, private houses, boys' clubs, miners' institutes, Y.M.C.A. premises, empty factories and warehouses, converted stables, and a part of a workhouse built in 1838. In several places temporary barracks have been erected.

Problem of Health

In the 1934 memorandum on the establishment and conduct of courses of instruction, the Ministry of Labor stated that it was not possible to arrange for routine medical inspection of boys and girls attending courses, but that it was hoped the education authorities would arrange to have one of their school medical officers examine and treat boys and girls attending courses and recommended for medical advice by the superintendents.

In his report of March 1936 the Commissioner for the Special Areas in England and Wales expressed his concern at the high percentage of rejection on medical grounds for juvenile transfer centers and instructional centers, and recommended that medical inspection and treatment be made available for all boys and young men attending all forms of centers. In his next report, October 1936, the Commissioner noted that the Ministry had developed the medical service recommended in his previous report by making it possible for the local education authorities to expand their facilities to those attending junior instruction centers.

On February 27, 1936 the Minister of Labor admitted in the House of Commons that 57 per cent of the trainees at four instruction centers in the County of Glamorgan had been found to be suffering from malnutrition. The local education authorities, he said, had no power to provide free meals, but in this case free milk was being distributed.

Financing of Centers

At the present time 75 per cent of the funds for approved expenditures for junior instruction centers are paid by the British government. If the instructors are certificated teachers, the standard rates of pay are applicable, although the rates for other leaders vary widely. The salaries of superintendents are also unstandardized and generally below those paid in other branches of educational service. As a result, the present grants for these centers are not sufficiently large to permit the payment of salaries which will attract teachers of first-rate ability.[24]

Those young people attending the centers who have reached the age of sixteen, or who have continued in school for one year after the legal withdrawing age, receive unemployment benefit. For younger children, dependents' benefit is paid to their parents or guardians. In instances where such expenditure is justified, the children's carfares to and from the centers are paid.

Personnel for Centers

Each center is directed by a superintendent appointed by the local education authority.[25] The majority of the superintendents are trained teachers, and in 1934 all of those in Wales and in London were from this group. In the North, many were craftsmen or technical workers, while others had been instructors in evening schools.

---

[24] Valentine A. Bell, *Junior Instruction Centers and Their Future; A Report to the Carnegie United Kingdom Trust,* p. 33.

[25] The local education authority in Great Britain discharges functions similar to those of local boards of education in the United States.

Since the success of the individual centers depends largely on the type of leadership obtained, considerable thought has been given to the qualifications of the superintendents. It would seem that the principal requirements for the position are "organizing ability, power of leadership, tact, and a thorough understanding of local industrial conditions and juvenile employees."[26]

The Ministry of Labor concurs in the opinion of the National Advisory Council for Juvenile Employment "that the greatest care should be taken by education authorities in the selection of the staff, and that the teachers should be appointed, not so much on their academic qualifications, as on their ability to handle boys and girls above the age of fourteen and to develop a sense of *esprit de corps* among those attending the courses."[27]

Because of the fluctuating conditions and temporary character of the centers, and the size of the grants to carry on the work, it has been difficult to attract trained men teachers already employed. As a result, the majority of the instructors in the boys' centers are either skilled craftsmen or unemployed teachers, most of them middle-aged.[28] It has not been difficult to obtain instructors for the girls' centers, as there has been a sufficient supply of married women teachers available for these positions.[29]

However, the Ministry has suggested that in courses where attendance is for more than fifteen hours a week, if possible there should be one teacher to each twenty-five pupils. If, however, one-third of the instruction is in practical work, the Minister of Labor will authorize the employment of one teacher to each twenty pupils. Where attendance is for only fifteen hours a week, and different sets of pupils attend in the morning and the afternoon, one teacher is usually employed for twice as many pupils. If the number of boys and girls in attendance drops below the specified figures, the authority is required to reduce its staff accordingly.

---

[26] Bell, *op. cit.*, pp. 30-31.

[27] Ministry of Labor, *Memorandum*, *op. cit.*, p. 15.

[28] Bell, *op. cit.*, pp. 34-35.

[29] *Ibid.*, p. 36.

Curricula of Centers

The Ministry of Labor has approved the suggestions of the National Advisory Council for Juvenile Employment regarding suitable curricula for centers. These recommendations cover a practical curriculum for boys' centers, a practical curriculum for girls' centers, and a general curriculum for all centers, in addition to recreational activities.

The National Advisory Council suggests that the practical subjects selected for instruction in boys' centers should have some connection with the trades and industries of the area. This "local bias" is advocated not for the sake of giving trade training, but as a means of arousing interest in trade operations with which the boys already are familiar. In addition, the council recommends that handicrafts such as woodworking, metalworking, and weaving should be taught. In girls' centers it is recommended that the training be related to homemaking, and practical cooking and sewing are advocated. Hygiene is considered a basic subject.

The general curriculum, according to the council, should normally include English, workshop arithmetic (for boys), history and civics, drawing and painting, and household arithmetic. Methods used should not be limited to verbal instruction. Books should be made available and reading guidance given. In general, while giving consideration to a balance between practical and ordinary school subjects, the greatest elasticity is recommended, so that the program may be adapted to the needs and interests of the group attending any special center. Some school studies are recommended for the fourteen- to sixteen-year-old group, while for the older boys and girls greater emphasis is placed on practical subjects. All teaching should be informal.

The amount of time devoted to the educational program was limited to not less than three nor more than six hours. The officials in charge of the centers prefer that the courses be given during the daytime, but where this is not possible, evening courses are acceptable.

Physical training, organized games, and recreation are considered important adjuncts of the center, but should not encroach upon the time given to other things. If possible, games should be played outside of hours, and every effort made to develop "team spirit."[30] As early as

[30] Ministry of Labor, *Memorandum, op. cit.*, pp. 33-34.

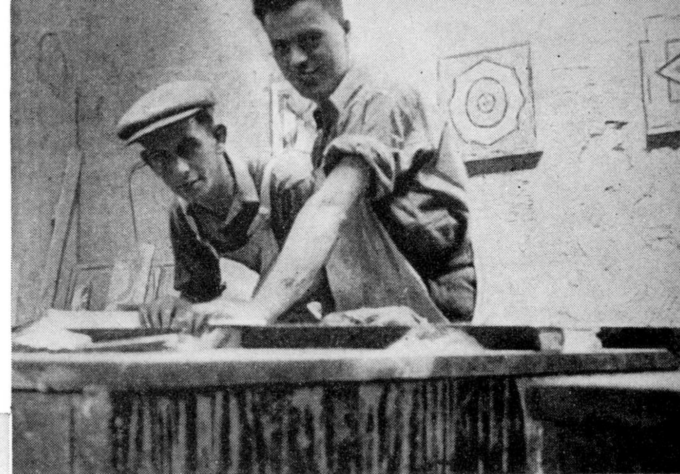

BRITISH WORK CAMPS

ve:

itch construction by British pers

t:

ile-laying as vocational train- at Waddon

w:

amp Fermyn Woods

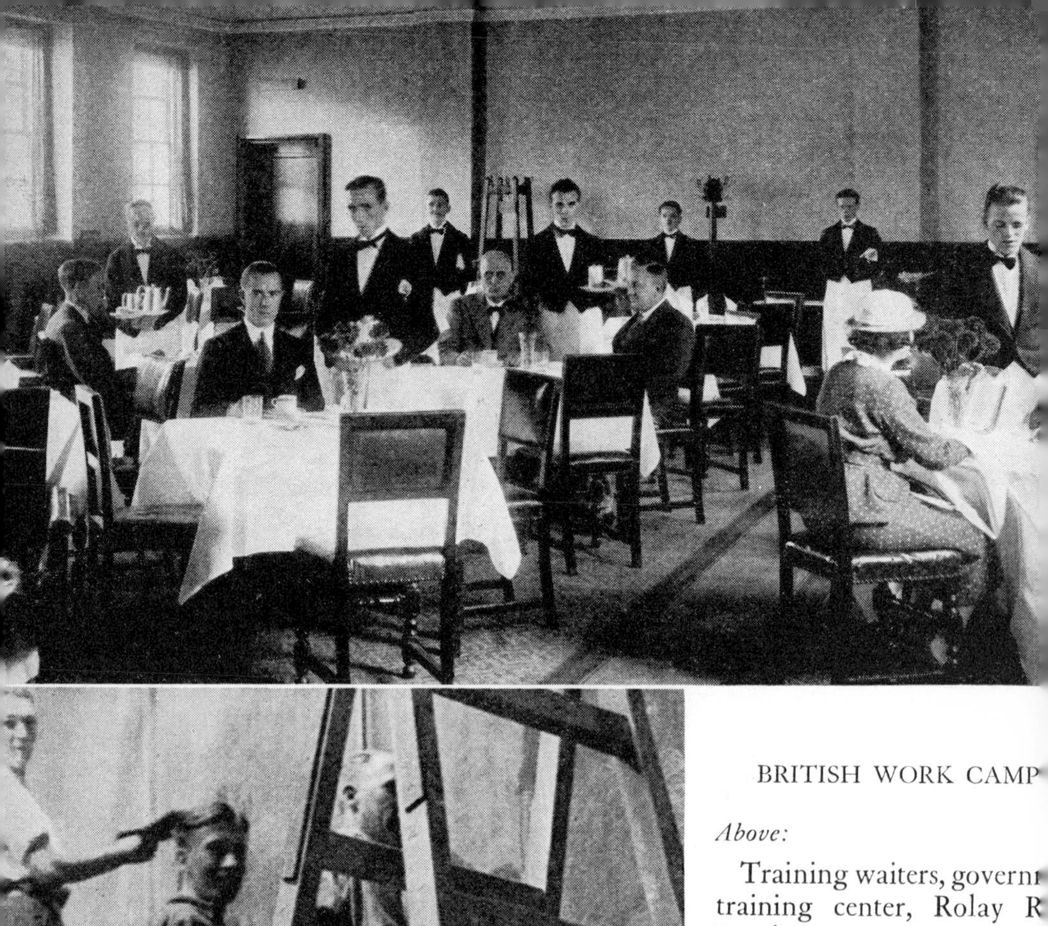

BRITISH WORK CAMP

Above:

Training waiters, governı training center, Rolay R London

Left:

Learning house painting training center, Waddon

Below:

Officer's quarters at c Fermyn Woods

1934 these recommendations of the National Advisory Council were to a large extent already effective.

Attitude of Public

In a discussion of young people in the depressed areas, the *Times Educational Supplement* of November 17, 1934, pointed out that one of the most difficult problems in the program for assisting young people to secure work was to gain the confidence of their parents. Another difficulty is that parents are often unwilling to have the older boys and girls transferred to other areas, because their unemployment pay then will not be available to increase the family budget.

This parental indifference, fear, or hostility has been overcome in several districts by officials connected with the centers, who have made efforts to gain the support and interest of employers, parents, and the general public. Exhibitions of work done in the centers have proved helpful.[31]

In 1936 one superintendent, whose experience was probably typical, reported that the attitude of the boys and girls toward the program during the first few weeks of 1923 was one of "sullen antagonism." Gradually, however, the youth have come to regard the centers as suitable places to go when they are unemployed. An atmosphere like that of a club has been created, and "the center has become a 'friendly' place, more desirable than the street corner."[32]

Results of the Program

Among the superintendents there is an opinion that the existence of the centers definitely has reduced the number of juvenile offenses against the law because attendance at the centers helps to keep children out of trouble.

While the children eligible for the centers are still in school, data concerning them is collected on a "school-leaving card." These students are supplied with information about job opportunities, and before leaving school are interviewed by an employment committee. All these

[31] Bell, *op. cit.*, pp. 60-62.

[32] Ministry of Labor, *Report for 1926*, p. 76.

resultant data are available to the officials in the junior instruction centers for use in planning programs for the participants.

Boys from depressed areas who enter the centers immediately after leaving elementary school and remain in them for a considerable length of time show marked development. However, in areas where there is a demand for juvenile labor and the fluctuation in numbers at the centers is considerable, the results are not so evident. Many of the centers in these areas do not even run courses of instruction, the superintendents being merely able to keep the boys occupied and working for the short time they attend.[33]

The juvenile workers remain in the centers until they have found a job, or one has been found for them, or until they reach the age of eighteen, 40 per cent of them being placed through the employment exchanges. Every effort is made to steer them away from blind-alley jobs, and to help them obtain suitable work. A program of follow-up work checks up on how well the children succeed in the jobs in which they have been placed.

The Juvenile Transfer Scheme

The junior instruction centers discussed in the preceding section are designed primarily to provide unemployed young people from fourteen to eighteen years of age with a constructive program for using leisure. The juvenile transfer scheme, on the other hand, was established actually to transfer boys and girls from an area where jobs were scarce to one where they were plentiful.

The needs of boys and girls living in industrial areas of Britain, such as South Wales, the northeastern coast, and parts of Scotland, where youth has very limited opportunities of employment, were the immediate cause for the establishment of the juvenile transfer scheme. Although these depressed areas contain less than half the juvenile population of the country, approximately 75 per cent of the boys and girls registered as unemployed in Great Britain are located in these areas. This situation is further intensified by the fact that until the end of 1937 the number of young people leaving school continued to be abnormally high, due to the post-war increase in the birth rate. In other parts of

[33] Bell, *op. cit.*, p. 74.

the country, notably in the Midlands and in and around London where there have been immediate opportunities for suitable employment for juveniles, trade and industry have been improving.

Only those boys and girls whose parents are willing to have them transferred, and who are themselves anxious to obtain suitable employment in a different part of the country, are accepted for transfer. Before a job is offered to a juvenile from the depressed areas, the wages and conditions of employment are thoroughly investigated, to ascertain as nearly as possible whether the transfer is a desirable one. In no case must the wages offered be less than the rate normally paid to local juveniles of corresponding age engaged on the same type of work in the new locale.

Arrangements are made by the Ministry of Labor to pay the full cost of travel to the new area in the cases of all transferred boys. The same provisions are made for girls brought in for industrial employment, although not for domestic. In the latter cases it is customary for the fare to be advanced either by the Ministry or by the employer.

Once a boy or girl has agreed to be transferred from a depressed area, every effort is made to encourage the young worker to settle down happily in the new district. Suitable lodgings are found, and arrangements made with the landlady. The boy or girl is met at the station on arrival and taken to his or her new home and if necessary shown how to reach the place of employment the following day. In case of illness, loss of employment, or part-time work, the transferred juvenile may receive from the Ministry of Labor a sum sufficient for the expenses he or she is temporarily unable to meet. The Ministry relies on voluntary agencies for help in insuring the successful settlement of the juveniles in the new area, and if wages are insufficient to meet the full cost of maintenance, as is sometimes the case at the start, the juvenile may receive a grant from the Ministry which, with the wages, will pay all the transferee's expenses and leave a small amount of "pocket money."

Since the inception of the transfer scheme, large numbers of boys and girls have been transferred to jobs in more prosperous parts of the country through arrangements made by the Ministry of Labor. From the end of July 1934 to February 15, 1936, 2,139 juveniles were transferred to the London County Council area. Of these, 998 were under sixteen. In addition, a considerable number of juveniles are known to have transferred on their own account. Of those under sixteen years of age who were transferred by the government, 276 (37 per cent) returned to their homes, usually because of homesickness.[34] The boys have been placed in a wide variety of industrial and commercial occupations. The majority of the girls have been placed in resident domestic employment in hotels and private houses, but a considerable number have also been transferred to industrial work, and the number of such jobs for girls is steadily increasing. Every effort is made to insure that all situations offer favorable conditions and prospects of permanent and progressive employment.

Privately Financed Projects

In addition to the government projects described above, a number of private organizations in England have set up various types of labor camps designed either for students or for the young unemployed, or for both.

The Springhead Ring

The Springhead Ring is a group of men and women, the greater number of whom have been engaged since 1922 in developing a cultural exchange between Britain, Germany, and the Scandinavian countries. The leaders were closely associated with the *Deutsche Freischar* in Germany, and helped that organization in the very early formative stages of the labor service, first among the students and then in the Silesian work camps for peasants, workmen, and students. The training of work camp leaders at Musikheim, Frankfurt-on-the-Oder, and the Boberhaus in Silesia, grew out of this Anglo-German collaboration. In England a center has been developed at Springhead, Fontmell Magna, in Dorset, a small estate of five hundred acres, with woods and farmlands, where there have been camps and schools since 1927.

Since 1933, when Springhead was dedicated, work camps and festival schools of ten days' or three weeks' duration have been instituted, to give men and women firsthand experience in community working,

[34] Minister of Labor in the House of Commons, March 10, 1936; Commons 309:1972.

thinking, and playing. At these camps the manual work is done in connection with agricultural and forestry activities on the estate, the aim being to make the center as nearly self-supporting as possible. The camp musicals and festivals are closely connected with such agricultural events as planting and harvesting, while lectures and discussions are focused on the history and modern needs of the region. Men from very different walks of life, but generally of student age, take part in these camps, which owe much to the example and inspiration of the German and Scandinavian folk schools and work camps.

In 1932 members of this group initiated a series of work camps for students and unemployed ironstone miners in Cleveland, Yorkshire, where small holdings had been started in three villages in cooperation with a local landowner. Five camps were held in this district between 1932 and 1934. Both in Wessex and in Yorkshire, education for regional reconstruction and responsibility is the intellectual theme in the camps. This educational idea can be developed completely only as longer courses of training become possible.[35]

Grith Fyrd Camps

The first Grith Fyrd camp was established late in 1932 by the Order of Woodcraft Chivalry. The name comes from the Saxon words *grith,* meaning peace, and *fyrd,* the name used by King Alfred for his citizen army. The organizing secretary for the camps is Guy Keeling. The guiding principles of this movement are: (1) to provide for small communities of young men of all classes a healthy outdoor environment in which they can make the best use of their leisure; (2) to give them, during periods of unemployment, an opportunity to live a full life; (3) to enable them to acquire or increase physical fitness and dexterity, mental alertness and self-confidence, and to apply these personal assets directly to the enlargement of their lives and the lives of others; (4) by acting in time to prevent the demoralization which so often accompanies long periods of unemployment.

The plan calls for year-round camps of no more than fifty men each, located in rural areas no farther than fifty miles from industrial centers.

[35] Rolf Gardiner, "Work Camps in Britain," p. 5; see also *Der Arbeitsdienst in der Welt,* S. 84-86.

The camps are self-maintaining in so far as possible, and do not compete with industry in the sale of goods or services. Their emphasis is on constructive and cooperative work for the benefit of the community, self-government, self-development, and the creation of an *esprit de corps.*

The first camp was opened at Godshill in the New Forest, and later another was started at Shining Cliff, Alderwasley, Derbyshire. During the summer and autumn of 1933 twenty-three men eighteen to twenty-five years of age attended.

Camp members who are unemployed pay 12 shillings 6 pence ($3.18) a week for their maintenance and receive 2 shillings (50 cents) pocket money. Men from other classes of society are encouraged to attend and they usually contribute 1 pound ($5.00) a week. Some additional money is needed to meet expenses, which amount to about 16 shillings 6 pence ($4.18) a man per week, and this is supplied by contributions.

The campers grow much of their own food, keep livestock, have built their dwellings, worksheds, and much rough furniture, and have thatched the roofs of the camp buildings with heather. In addition, they learn crafts, such as cobbling shoes and weaving, and are encouraged to take up hobbies. The course lasts eighteen months, the first six being given to productive work. During the second six months camping trips are added, and it was hoped that in the third six months many of the participants would volunteer their labor to help community work.[36]

These projects have attracted a good deal of notice since the opening of the first camp in 1932, but the plans have been handicapped by a program that is too ambitious and by a lack of leaders capable of carrying it out.[37]

Anglo-German Camps

Jochen Benemann, a member and leader of the Hitler Youth, conceived the idea of holding camps on the German model in which both German and English students, schoolboys, and workers could participate. The Hitler Youth encouraged Benemann in his project, and he

[36] *The Spectator,* CL (June 16, 1933), 866-67.

[37] *Der Arbeitsdienst in der Welt,* S. 84.

in turn has interested a number of Englishmen. His aim is to create a spirit of fellowship and good will between the youth of England and Germany, and to break down class consciousness in both countries. Arrangements are handled through the Anglo-German Academic Bureau.

Five of these camps are held each year in either England or Germany, one at Easter, two in the summer, one in autumn, and one in midwinter. The first camp was held near Hamburg from July 15 to August 15, 1934, and was attended by sixty persons. Because of private contributions, it is possible to keep the cost very low, and this enables workers to attend the camps.

The daily schedule is similar to that in a German labor service camp, but more freedom and variety are present than in camps made up entirely of Germans. At the first camp the youth spent their time widening a sports ground belonging to the Hitler Youth. At the second camp, held in October 1934 in Thuringia, the work consisted of repairing a footpath. At both these camps one week was devoted to a tour of German cities.[38]

Camps for School Boys

The second chapter discussed the student camps in England which began with the International Voluntary Service project at Brynmawr, Wales, in 1931, and which have been organized subsequently at Rhos in North Wales and Oakengates in Shropshire.

During the Easter holidays of 1932, the first work camp for secondary school boys was held at Brynmawr, and the students were billeted by twos in the homes of the villagers. In the summer of that year other student camps were held in South Wales and near Wrexham in North Wales. During the 1933 Easter holidays arrangements were made to put school boys to work helping unemployed men cultivate their land allotments. The boys live in men's homes as paying guests at 3 shillings 6 pence (93 cents) a day. In September 1933 the boys were sent to help on cooperative farms, rather than to assist individuals, and this has now become an accepted policy.

---

[38] *The Anglo-German Camps;* a collection of reports by Jochen Benemann.

In 1935 the first team of secondary school boys, entirely without staff leadership cut the initial sod on the cooperative farm at "Cleenton," South Lancashire. The first camp for secondary school girls was also held here, and the girls did work around the houses, chiefly color-washing of the homes. By 1936 there were more than seventy places in England, Scotland, and Wales, where groups of unemployed working on the land would welcome work camp teams. It would seem that the English working class prefers the leadership of educated men to that of members of their own group, and hence an opportunity exists for men just out of college to spend a year or two working on cooperative farms.[39]

In 1936 about 150 of these work camps were open, and in 1937,[40] about 280. A Central Clearing House at Woodbrooke Settlement, Birmingham, now forms a connecting link between the unemployed and student groups. In 1936 the first school liaison officer for work camps was appointed by a public school in the south of England. He had just completed his work at Cambridge, and had been closely connected with the work camp movement since 1932. He is given his room and board, without other pay, and is expected to devote his mornings to private coaching and demonstration work, with some teaching. In the afternoons and evenings he establishes contacts with the staff and with boys from other public and secondary schools within a radius of fifty miles, who might be interested in camps and likely to attend. He must also keep in touch with groups of unemployed men working cooperatively on the land, and try to bring other such groups into existence.

Conclusion

In England a few camps for students have been developed by private agencies, but the various camps and projects for the unemployed have been under the jurisdiction of the Ministry of Labor. As would be expected, the greatest emphasis has been on vocational training in order to prepare young men for jobs that actually existed or could be expected to be available in the immediate future. While the instruction centers

[39] J. S. Hoyland, *Digging for a New England* (London: Cape, 1936), pp. 157-58.

[40] Information supplied by J. S. Hoyland, June 24, 1937.

have not in recent years emphasized vocational training and the junior instruction centers have only more recently become specially interested in the vocational future of the participants, the government training centers and the juvenile transfer schemes have functioned primarily as institutions for the training of individuals for existing jobs. In England as in few other countries the camp officials feel that their responsibility for the participants continues until they are actually placed in jobs for which they have been trained.

Bibliography

F. BRITTEN AUSTIN, "Salvaging the Workless—Britain and Germany," *Saturday Evening Post,* CCVII, (August 11, 1934), 16, 76.

VALENTINE A. BELL. *Junior Instruction Centers and Their Future; A Report to the Carnegie United Kingdom Trust.* Edinburgh: Constable, 1934. 106 pp.

ARTHUR R. COBB, "Grith Fyrd Camps" (letter to the editor). *The Spectator,* CL (June 16, 1933), 866-67.

"Compulsory Camps for Young Unemployed Men," *The New Statesman and Nation,* XIV, 332 (New Series), (July 3, 1937), 7-9.

MAXINE DAVIS, *They Shall Not Want.* New York: Macmillan, 1937. 418 pp. Part IV, "Now in England. . . ."

H. C. EMMERSON and E. C. P. LASCELLES, *Guide to the Unemployment Insurance Acts,* 4th edition. London: Longmans, 1935.

ROLF GARDINER. "The Triple Function of Work Camps and Work Service in Europe," *North Sea and Baltic,* New Series, 2, (Harvest 1937), 17-32.

GREAT BRITAIN. Commissioner for the Special Areas (England and Wales). *First Report,* July 4, 1935. Cmd. 4957. London: H. M. Stationery Office, 1935. 106 pp.; *Second Report,* February 6, 1936. Cmd. 5090. London: H. M. Stationery Office, 1936. 120 pp.; *Third Report,* October 27, 1936. Cmd. 5303. London: H. M. Stationery Office, 1936. 210 pp.

——— Ministry of Labor. *Gazette.*

——— Ministry of Labor, Reports, 1925-1936.

——— Ministry of Labor. *Memorandum on the Establishment and Conduct of Courses of Instruction for Unemployed Boys and Girls. England and Wales* (ACM. 1). London: H. M. Stationery Office, 1934. 38 pp.

——— Royal Commission on Unemployment Insurance. *Final Report.* Cmd. 4185. London: H. M. Stationery Office, 1932. 529 pp. Chap. IX: "The Provision of Training, Occupation, and Instruction for Unemployed Workers," pp. 310-44.

FELIX GREENE, *Editor. Time to Spare; What Unemployment Means, by Eleven Unemployed.* London: Allen & Unwin, 1935. 188 pp.

A. C. C. HILL, JR. and ISADOR LUBIN. *The British Attack on Unemployment.* Washington: Brookings Institution, 1934. 325 pp.

JOHN S. HOYLAND. *Digging for a New England.* London: Cape, 1936. 224 pp.

D. GRAHAM HUTTON. "The Economic Progress of Britain," *Foreign Affairs,* XVI, 2 (January 1938), 279-93.

"Idle Hours," *Review of Reviews* (London), LXXXIV (December 1933), 19-21.

E. D. McCollum. "The Problem of the Depressed Areas in Great Britain," *International Labor Review,* XXX, 2 (August 1934), 133-57.

National Council of Social Service, Inc. *Unemployment and Community Service.* London, 1936. 99 pp.

"Recovery in the Special Areas," *The Economist,* CXXX, 4924 (January 8, 1938), 53-54.

Harry Roberts. "A Real Peace Movement," *The New Statesman and Nation,* VI, 132 (September 2, 1933), 259-60.

"The Situation in Great Britain; Camps for the Unemployed," *Industrial and Labor Information,* XLIII, 12 (September 19, 1932), 395-96.

"The Situation in Great Britain; Camps for the Unemployed." *Industrial and Labor Information,* XLVI, 13 (June 26, 1933), 433-34.

"Summer Camps for Unemployed Pronounced Success," *Christian Century,* LII (November 6, 1935), 1436.

F. Sykes. "Employment for Youth," *Spectator,* CLV (August 2, 1935), 179-80.

D. Christie Tait. "Unemployment of Young People in Great Britain," *International Labor Review,* XXXI, 2 (February 1935), 166-89.

"Unemployment in 1937," *The Statist,* CXXI, 3127 (January 29, 1938), 157-58.

"Young People in Depressed Areas," *The Times* [London] *Educational Supplement,* November 17, 1934, p. 389.

"Youth in Special Areas," *The Times* [London] *Educational Supplement,* November 21, 1936, p. 421.

The Scandinavian Countries

"If anywhere in modern life a balance has been struck, it seems to me to have been in the Scandinavian peninsula. . . ." There these small countries of Norway, Sweden, and Denmark "have achieved a measure of peace and decent living that will serve, and for a long time to come, perhaps, as a standard for larger nations."[1]

The interest of the United States in these countries has increased greatly during the last few years, due no doubt in part to such books as *Sweden: the Middle Way.* As this title indicates, the Scandinavian countries with their modified capitalistic systems are looked upon by writers in the United States as ideal democracies freed from many of the problems that have beset the other nations of the world during the depression and which suggest a middle course between the Scylla of fascism and the Charybdis of communism. Although they are insured to a certain extent against the shocks of economic crises, the world-wide collapse nevertheless did affect these nations.

Danish Camps

During the 1930-33 depression, unemployment reached acute proportions in all of the Scandinavian countries, especially in Denmark where, on January 31, 1933, nearly half of all trade union members were registered as wholly unemployed.[2] An inquiry undertaken by the Danish Statistical Office revealed that on June 30, 1934 out of a total of 56,000 young workers 8,400 between eighteen and twenty-one years of age were unemployed. Most of the unemployed were men. More than 3,000 had been unemployed at least 450 days during the two years covered by the inquiry, while the remainder had been unemployed about 350 days. Unemployment among the youth then had

---

[1] Marquis W. Childs, *Sweden: the Middle Way* (New Haven: Yale University Press, 1936), pp. xiv, xvi.

[2] C. J. Ratzlaff, *The Scandinavian Unemployment Relief Program* (Philadelphia: University of Pennsylvania Press, 1934), p. 11.

to a large extent been concentrated on a small number of persons who had been without work for a relatively long period.[3]

Work Camps Established

On May 20, 1933 an act was passed appropriating funds for work camps which were to provide work for these young unemployed persons and to rebuild their working capacity and energy, which deteriorated as a result of continued unemployment. In the summer of 1933 the first such camp was established.[4] In Denmark the work camps are for the most part open only during the winter months, for in summer there is sufficient employment to absorb almost all the young men who are out of work.

The Sjaeland Island Camp

With a Danish student as interpreter I visited one of these camps, sixty miles south of Copenhagen, in August 1936. A castle, built between 1593 and 1595, but uninhabited for forty or fifty years and fallen into a state of disrepair, was the site of the camp. At the time of my visit men were engaged in renovating the castle and grounds so that they could be used as a folk school.

After locating the director of the camp, we were conducted to the library, where he described to us the importance of the castle as a local landmark, and the plan of the local authorities to develop it into a folk school. The library where we sat contained about five hundred books and magazines and served also as a reading room. Most of the rooms we were shown had been redecorated by the workers and were furnished in good taste. One large room, used for festivals, plays, and large meetings, was equipped with a piano, chairs, and magazines. A smaller room adjoining it contained a collection of minerals from the near-by countryside. The beautiful hand-carved benches in this room had been made by the boys. In other rooms of the castle the men were at work installing electric lights, equipping

---

[3] International Labor Office, *Unemployment among Young Persons* (Supplementary report), p. 3.

[4] Memorandum prepared by Ministry of Social Welfare.

a dining room, building a dumb-waiter, making general repairs on the outer walls of the building and improving the grounds. A large vegetable garden, the products of which found their way to the camp table, was another work project.

Camp Organization and Finance

The establishment of the camp on Sjaeland Island, the largest of the Danish group, had been made possible through the cooperation of fourteen provincial towns, which united in agreement on the camp program and guaranteed to finance it. A similar procedure has been followed in setting up most of the camps in Denmark. While they are supported by government grants and controlled by the Ministry of Social Affairs, they are established and administered by communes, trade unions, and other suitable groups. In order to secure the government subsidy of 2.5 kroner (55 cents) a person a day, the camps must meet certain standards fixed by the Ministry. However, in order to receive the subsidy it is not necessary for young persons to be attached to a resident camp; in fact, young people employed under this plan often continue to live at home. In 1937 only five projects were operated in connection with camps.

The annual government appropriation for camps and other projects for unemployed youth may not exceed 4,000,000 kroner ($880,000),[5] and the full amount was expended for these activities each year from 1933 to 1935. While ordinarily the contribution of the central government to the camps may not exceed the above-mentioned 2.5 kroner per person, the Minister of Social Welfare may, when circumstances warrant it, grant an additional sum sufficient to cover the initial cost of organizing a camp, and may also set aside an appropriate amount for the traveling expenses of camp participants, as well as for special work clothes or equipment. Additional expenses, usually totaling about 1.25 kroner (28 cents) a person a day, are paid by the commune or other body organizing the camps. The communes also usually provide equipment. One-third of the sum granted by the state is to be refunded to it by the local communities, and payment is divided among them accord-

[5] On June 30, 1937 the exchange rate of the krone was 22 cents.

ing to their share in the state unemployment relief funds for the fiscal years 1936-37, 1937-38, and 1938-39.

If there is a camp in connection with a work project, the participants are supplied with board and lodgings and receive a remuneration in cash of from 50 to 75 öre (11 to 17 cents) a day for minor necessities. If, however, no camp is attached to the work project, the participants live in their usual lodgings, and receive 3 to 4 kroner (66 to 88 cents) a day in cash.

Camp Enrollees

In the camp we visited, the boys were from poor families and the majority were between eighteen and twenty-two years of age. Before coming to camp they had had very little training. Some of them had been delivery or office boys. Most of the young men in the camps had not gained sufficient skill in any trade to qualify for membership in a union, so had been employed in minor positions or been without any work, often for as long as two or three years.

One director described the typical camper as being about twenty-two years old, with an elementary school education. At the age of fourteen he had probably been an office boy and continued in that position until he was eighteen. Because of his lack of experience and ability, and the requirement that he follow union standards for work, he had not been as well qualified as others, and soon became unemployed. He may have returned to his home, and his parents, having become disgusted with him, turned him out. Having been entitled to relief while unemployed, he therefore registered for the 8 or 10 kroner per week ($1.76 to $2.20). He was informed of the camps when he registered, and either volunteered or was persuaded to enroll.

Another type of boy that comes to the camps is the one who does only seasonal work, and as a result is unemployed from two to five months during the year. He is not able to save any money while employed, so comes to the camps to live during off-seasons.

The usual effects of unemployment, demoralization and antisocial attitudes, were evident among these youth. It was not possible, of course, to make artisans out of all these young men in four months, but it was sometimes possible to help them to become proficient in a trade with which they were already somewhat familiar. Moreover, it was also possible to help them to better their social attitudes considerably.

The men who go into these camps are recruited through the employment offices, local social service agencies, and trade unions. The organizations sponsoring the camps receive the applications, and select the candidates who they believe will profit most from camp experience. The director of the projects in the Ministry of Social Affairs will, on request, forward to towns, communities, or organizations wishing to sponsor local projects, the needed information about unemployed persons who have expressed a desire to take part in such work.

Camp members are usually from eighteen to twenty-two years of age, but this age span is not always adhered to, since it is lawful to give employment to persons above or below these ages if the sponsors of the project guarantee that the work will in no way be impaired.

Although an enrollment period of four months has been established, the young men who enter the camps do not bind themselves to remain for any definite length of time, nor are they forced to stay in the camp for any set period. Whenever they find employment they may return to their homes. Neither do these men, by leaving camp, cut themselves off from again receiving unemployment relief. If after they have left they again become unemployed they may return to the camp. After they are prepared by camp experience for work, the organized labor exchanges try to find jobs for them, but in order not to interfere with regular trade union jobs, they try to make the placements through personal connections.

The number of employment days in connection with the work projects (camps as well as other activities) in 1933-34, 1934-35, and 1935-36 was about 110,000, 230,000, and 200,000 respectively.[6]

Camp Directors

The leaders of the camps are appointed by the communes, associations, or other bodies that sponsor the projects. Since no special training is given the leaders, an attempt is made to select men who are

[6] Memorandum prepared by Ministry of Social Welfare.

already fitted to administer the camps. The Ministry has not designated those who shall direct the educational activities, but the appointment of unemployed teachers has been recommended. At the camp we visited, the supervisors and personnel consisted of a director, two full-time teachers, and, in winter, two assistant teachers. The director of the camp emphasized that it was important for the teachers to have had practical experience in addition to teaching experience.

Camp Program

According to the provisions of the act regulating the camps, they are to provide a suitable proportion of physical work, sports, and education. The physical work is preferably to be of a productive nature, and must consist of work which would not otherwise be undertaken by the state or individual. The types of work mentioned in the act are forestry, agricultural and horticultural projects, regulation of watercourses, coast works, projects for the preservation of natural scenery, and the laying out of athletic fields and camp grounds.

The organized program for the camp members requires from six to eight hours a day. Two to four hours daily are taken up with physical work, and from three to four hours with education and sports.

A typical program in one of these camps is as follows:

7:00 A.M.	Reveille
7:30	Porridge and coffee
7:45– 8:00	Make beds and clean rooms
8:00–11:30	Work or study[7]
11:30–12:00	Wash and rest
12:00– 1:00 P.M.	Lunch
2:00	Afternoon cocoa
2:30– 5:30	Work or study[8]
5:30– 6:00	Sports
6:00	Dinner
6:30– 9:00	Games or educational activities, discussion groups, etc.
9:00	Evening coffee

[7] Usually the workers are divided into two groups; one goes to school while the other works. During the summer, however, owing to the small number of boys in the camp, there is only one group.

[8] The groups shift; the one that has been working goes to school, and vice versa.

Educational Program

Even though attendance at the camps is voluntary, and the educational program not compulsory, all volunteers must take part in some of the evening activities. The program is elastic and can be adapted or expanded according to the needs of the group, and may consist of reading, bookbinding, or any one of the different arts and crafts. During the summer months the youth read and discuss less than in the winter, but engage in more gardening and other out-of-door activities.

Since the Ministry of Social Affairs does not send out regulations governing the educational program, the organizations sponsoring the camps are free to develop the types of activity they feel will benefit the young men most. The broad objective of the educational program is to stimulate the participants and add to their general knowledge rather than to provide definite vocational training. It is necessary that the educational program be practical in nature, however, as well as politically neutral. No courses in military science are offered and no military discipline of any kind is used.

In the camp on Sjaeland Island the subjects taught were on the grammar school or high school level and resembled in many respects those of the folk high schools. The method of instruction was informal. Besides the instruction given on the job, there were courses in Danish, writing, geography, mathematics, arts and crafts, and history, and discussions of cooperatives and socialism. The young men were also organized into study groups.

When the camps were first set up, the behavior of the youth in some camps was not very praiseworthy, and as a result the projects were criticized by the press. With this reputation, it was therefore difficult at first for the camps to obtain the interest and cooperation of people in the near-by communities. Relations improved later, however, and are now on the whole quite friendly. Activities are often initiated by camp boys in which they ask people from outside to participate.

The youth have expressed some unwillingness to enter the camps, due in large part to the fact that after experiencing such a long period of unemployment they feel that there is no hope of getting work, and are willing to live on the dole.

The most constructive aspects of camps for the men seem to be the regularity of hours, good food, work of a worth-while character, and the educational and recreational program. The camps have become an important part of the general program to remedy the disastrous consequences of unemployment among young people.

Swedish Camps

On November 30, 1933, out of a total population of 6,211,566,[9] there were 170,203 unemployed workers registered with the Unemployment Committee in Sweden. About 57,000, or 33.7 per cent, of these persons were between sixteen and twenty-five years of age. In 1934 the Swedish Parliament appointed a committee of experts to study unemployment among young people, and on the basis of its report a law was passed providing for work centers and special "reserve works" for young people, mainly for men between eighteen and twenty-one years of age.[10]

In the same year a voluntary labor service for men [11] was established in Sweden by the National Unemployment Board, "to provide unemployed young persons with an occupation which will increase their ability and willingness to work and prepare them for subsequent employment." [12]

Camp Organization and Finance

Camps have been set up both by the board and by local committees. The organization of the camps run by the local committees is often turned over to a special committee, which includes representatives of the National Unemployment Board, local education authorities, youth organizations, and other interested groups. The camps are in no sense military training centers. They are distributed widely over the whole of Sweden, from the fifty-sixth parallel to the Arctic Circle.

The camps are financed by government subsidies to local authorities. These subsidies provide for (1) the salaries of camp leaders and in-

[9] Estimate of December 31, 1933, *World Almanac,* 1937, p. 699.

[10] International Labor Office, *op. cit.,* p. 14

[11] No camps have been established for women.

[12] International Labor Office, *op. cit.,* p. 116.

SWEDISH WORK CAMPS

ve:

uarters for campers

t:

amp workshop near Karlstad

w:

vedish unemployed in a camp near Stock-
n

NORWEGIAN WO
CAMPS

Above:

Workers in road-b
ing camp at Sognefjel

Left:

Work on the roa
Opdal

Below:

Area near Fantesci
net where a road is
constructed

structors, (2) pocket money for the workers, (3) transportation expenses, and (4) cost of work clothes. On the other hand, the organization undertaking the work bears the cost of all tools and, where necessary, the wages of foremen and other qualified persons needed to direct the work. If there are other expenditures they are borne by the local authorities. Voluntary donations are accepted for the support of unemployed workers not entitled to relief.[13]

The program was begun in 1934 with an initial appropriation of 5,500,000 kronor ($1,375,000).[14] The estimated cost of the year's program for assisting unemployed youth was 10,000,000 kronor (about $2,500,000), the 4,500,000 kronor over the original appropriation coming from the savings in cash benefits which would otherwise have been paid to the participants in the form of relief.

By March 15, 1934 local committees had set up twelve local work centers containing 482 workers, and the National Unemployment Board had opened eleven centers accommodating 817 workers. A bill of April 28, 1934 (adopted July 12, 1934) provided for the employment of 5,000 men in work centers. No camp was to contain more than fifty men.

Selection of the Men

Unemployed men receive information concerning the labor camps through employment exchanges. Monthly reports on the number and condition of the unemployed are sent into Stockholm from about a thousand communes, and on the basis of these reports the places in the camps are assigned.

In selecting the workers, priority is given to youth eighteen to twenty-one years of age who are entitled to unemployment relief. In exceptional cases persons sixteen and seventeen and twenty-two to twenty-five years of age are also admitted, but it is generally considered that those in the older age group can be taken care of on the usual work relief projects, and that boys under eighteen years find it less difficult to secure employment than do those above eighteen. Unemployed men not entitled to relief may also be admitted to the camps if funds for their maintenance are provided by individuals or by private organizations.

---

[13] *Ibid.*, p. 117.

[14] Based on 1934 average exchange value which was 25 cents.

In the Swedish camps the volunteers remain eight or nine months, and usually find jobs when they leave. If after leaving they again become unemployed, they may return to the camps.

Camp Leaders

The camp leaders are responsible for the educational programs and, if qualified, for the work projects. These leaders are selected from the heads of youth organizations, unemployed teachers, members of the forestry service, and agricultural employees. In order to qualify for the important positions in the camps, the candidates must have had considerable education as well as practical experience. The internal administration of the camps is autonomous so far as possible.

In 1935 there was one student camp for the training of leaders, its membership including both students and unemployed. The purpose of this camp was to train certain students who had completed their education, but had not secured positions, for work as teachers in the labor service.[15]

Housing and Care of the Men

The men are housed in reclaimed buildings and machine shops, and in a few instances in specially constructed barracks. In almost all cases the workers live in the camps day and night.

Workers in resident centers receive board and lodging, one-half krona (13 cents) for each day's work, and free transportation to and from the centers. Those in nonresident centers who are entitled to unemployment benefit continue to draw all or part of it. The men in both types of centers receive free work clothes. They are paid for their work and receive their money, averaging about ten kronor apiece, on Friday of each week.

There is no medical staff in the camps, but medical examinations are given by the district before the men come into the camps.

Camp Program

When the camps were first set up in Sweden, they were simply places where the unemployed could spend their time in a healthful environ-

[15] *Arbeitsdienst in der Welt,* S. 95.

ment and receive proper food and care. It became evident, however, that while the camps benefited the men for the time they remained there, many returned to their communities at the end of a camp period and fell back into practically the same condition as before. It was decided therefore to change the original idea of the camps and develop them as centers for the special training of young men for existing jobs. Most of the camps were then organized as training centers, and whereas at first the young men received little or no vocational training, now they are trained as machinists, carpenters, farmers, foresters, lumbermen, and the like. Usually the men are trained for jobs which are available in the vicinity of the camp. In most instances the young men are engaged in such activities as road building, forestry, drainage, and renovating old estates for folk schools during four hours each day.[16]

Camp Program

The campers also participate in educational and recreational activities for three or four hours each day. The educational program conducted in the camps is planned with the general aim of increasing the men's ability to work and preparing them for subsequent employment. The camp leader, university students in the camps, or instructors from near-by folk schools, carry out this program which consists of general education, vocational training, and physical exercises. In so far as possible the technical instruction is related to the work performed by the

---

[16] The 1935 report of the Stockholm Unemployment Committee listed the following projects:

The Birkagarden youth camp. In session from January 1 to March 31. Arranged in connection with the Birkagarden Institute. Work project consisted of carpentry and shoemaking. Accommodations for 24 pupils.

Tynningö youth camp. January 1 to June 8 at Norra Tynningö, at one of the summer homes belonging to the Sunnerdahlska Institute. Accommodations for not more than 24. Work project principally developing a garden belonging to the Institute and also building an outhouse.

Hässelby youth camp. January 1 to July 31 at Hässelby Farm with accommodations for not more than 40 men. Work project was the clearing and developing of a park near-by; also carpentry and odd jobs about the camp.

Angby youth camp. April 1 to December 31 at Stora Angby Farm for 22 to 26 men. Work project was building of a large sport cabin, also clearing of park grounds, and odd jobs such as painting and carpentry.

volunteers, while they are in camp and on the work projects. The cultural courses—civics, Swedish history and social problems—are often conducted when outdoor work is impossible, and during extremely cold weather, special attention is given to these studies.

The young men in the labor service are divided into two age groups—the sixteen to eighteen and the eighteen to twenty. The program for the younger group places greatest emphasis on general educational courses, whereas the training program for youth eighteen to twenty-eight years of age is planned primarily to assist these young men to learn some trade, so that when they leave camp they will be better prepared to find a job. In the older group more emphasis is placed on courses of a vocational nature than in the camps for younger boys. While the educational program in the camps is not strictly compulsory, the young men are expected to take part in all of the activities provided.

In a Swedish camp the participants rise at seven in the morning, eat breakfast at seven-thirty, work from eight until eleven, rest and have lunch between eleven and twelve, and work again from twelve until four. Then from four-thirty until six o'clock sports or swimming will occupy their time, and in the evening, reading, discussions, games, and the like. Lights are out at about ten o'clock. On Saturdays work hours are from eight until one o'clock. All boys must be in the camps by eleven at night except over the week end, when they may stay away over night.

I visited a center near Karlstad which was utilizing the abandoned buildings and equipment of an old iron mine to train young men to be machinists and carpenters. Since it was summer when I visited the camp, only twenty men were there, but during the winter about sixty are usually enrolled. Two of the old buildings have been rebuilt by the unemployed under the direction of foremen. One of these structures serves as a machine shop, where forty to forty-five young men learn to operate drills, saws, presses, and similar equipment. The other building, considerably smaller, is a woodworking shop which accommodates about twenty men. The articles made by the workers are not sold on the open market, but are the property of the boys themselves. The Karlstad camp has two full-time teachers of metal-work and one of woodwork. A few of the more experienced unemployed also serve as instructors. The course is planned to take two years, though some of the more skilled young men will be able to complete it in a shorter time. The men are not charged for this instruction, and receive fifty öre each day in addition to their food and clothing.

The workers are selected from the vicinity of the project. Most of them are between sixteen and twenty-one years of age, and have never worked before. After they have been in the camp two years, they are expected to attempt to find employment. If they are not successful, they may come back to the camp for additional training.

A camp visited near Stockholm was located on the grounds of a country estate of 150 hectares (375 acres), which had been given to the Humanistic Gymnasium. The young men were repairing and rebuilding this estate for use as a folk school for the people of that vicinity. The work consisted of cleaning and repairing the paths, planting trees and flowers, clearing out brush, building a wall in front of the house, erecting a Finnish bath house, leveling an athletic field, and making a road three-eighths of a mile long from the field to the house. Thirty-two boys ranging in age from seventeen to twenty years were in the camp. They worked daily from six to seven hours and had about three hours for recreation and education. The personnel consisted of a camp director and a woman who helped with the preparation of food, and instructed the boys in cooking and camp management.

One of the largest camps training men to become farmers is near Gothenburg in the western part of Sweden. At one time a very large cobblestone industry in this area employed many of the people of Gothenburg. Recently, however, there has been little demand for cobblestones, and the industry has almost gone out of existence. As a result many youth who ordinarily would have gone into the quarries have been unemployed. Since work is available in agriculture, camps have been established to train the men to become farmers' helpers. The Gothenburg camp has complete farming equipment, buildings, barns, herds of cows, sheep, and pigs. The men work and receive related instruction on this project from about six in the morning until six in the evening. This retraining process has enabled many of them to take the jobs available.

Since the camps in Sweden are closely related to the National Unemployment Board, the whole program is carefully worked out with employment in mind. The young men in the camps are subject to the same rules as men receiving unemployment benefit, and must accept any suitable work offered them by the employment exchanges. The camp leaders must communicate with the exchanges at least once a week in an endeavor to place the men in regular jobs.

Although the camps in Sweden have been very successful in training men for jobs, Swedish officials doubt that they will remain as a permanent factor in Swedish life, for eventually all of these young men will be absorbed in industry. The camps will probably exist only so long as young men are unemployed and in need of training experience.

Norwegian Camps

During the early part of 1933, Norwegian officials decided that neither the state nor the local authorities could finance a comprehensive program for unemployed young persons, and an organization was formed to develop work camps. The Minister of Social Welfare is chairman of the Central Committee for the Labor Army, and the Director of Employment Exchanges and Unemployment Insurance serves as the second member of the committee. Local committees were also set up in various municipalities. The first camps were established during the summer of 1933. They were voluntary in character and had no connection with the military organizations of the government.

Aims of the Camps

The general aims of the camp program in Norwary are: (1) to create work for as many young men between the ages of eighteen and twenty-four as possible; (2) to furnish access by road building to large uncultivated tracts of land in Norway, with the intention of stimulating new settlements and home building and thus providing permanent employment for several thousand persons; (3) to open the eyes of the people and of the government to the problem of unemployed youth.[17]

---

[17] *Arbeids-Fylkingen, 1933, 1934, 1935, 1936*, p. 1.

VEDISH WORK CAMPS

e:
hletic field being con-
ted by campers for folk
ol near Stockholm
:
vedish camp leader. In the
ground, bathhouse built by
lish campers
v:
d iron mine being used as
p site

NORWEGIAN WC
CAMPS

Above:

Campers at Sog
veien

Left:

Camp at Krossb
land

Below:

Road under cor
tion between Renneb
Opdal

Financial Support for the Camps

The Norwegian labor camps are supported in part by voluntary contributions from local groups and during the three years from 1933 to 1935, a total of 564,164 kroner (about $141,041) was collected by the Central Committee for their support. No new collections were undertaken in 1936. The state undertakes to repay one-third of the wages paid to voluntary workers. But this contribution of the state to the program cannot exceed 1.5 kroner (38 cents) a man for each day's work, which sum is equivalent to the contribution of the state to municipal relief programs.

Selection of Men

The young men who volunteer for the camps must be unemployed and have no prospect of employment. Only capable and industrious boys between the ages of eighteen and twenty-four years, in good health, and of good moral habits are considered. The number of young men in the camps has been very small. The average for each year from 1933 to 1936 was 350, and the total enrollment was 1,400. During the summer and fall of 1937, about 800 young men were in the camps.

Camp Directors

The work projects are under the leadership of four persons: (1) an engineer or other technical expert who acts as foreman, (2) an interested person from the locality, (3) a job foreman, and (4) one of the unemployed young men [18] participating in the project.

The work projects consist of clearing public lands, building public roads and bridges, making community gardens, and providing drainage. Between 1933 and 1936 about sixty kilometers of roads were built, affording access to about twenty thousand acres of land.

The educational program is not extensive or of primary importance. As far as circumstances permit, an attempt is made to teach the enrollees a trade.[19] Young men who in the opinion of the supervisor of a work

[18] *Rundskrivelse fra Socialdepartementet,* Oslo, 8 Mai 1937.
[19] *Ibid.*

project seem to be particularly capable are given preference in the assignment of scholarships at trade schools.

Camp Projects

Of the fourteen projects undertaken in 1937 one employed about 90 men, two employed 80 men, and the rest were using from 45 to 50 men each. The average enrollment of the camps was about 56. The men are quartered in the camps, usually country homes or inns, and live in them day and night.

The pay for ordinary enrollees, is about 2.5 kroner (63 cents) per day, but as soon as the workers have acquired some skill, the rate is increased to about 4.5 kroner ($1.13) a day, including lodging. Half the wages are paid during the course of the work, and the remainder upon completion of the project.

The youth pay for their board out of their wages, but receive free work clothes and shoes and half their traveling expenses. Each must provide his own toilet articles and eating utensils, but rents a mattress, pillow, two woolen blankets, and dishes, for 1 krone (25 cents) per week. The men are required to present a certificate of good health, signed by a doctor, when they enter the camp, but the expense of this is refunded up to 3 kroner (75 cents).

Attitude of Men toward the Camps

The participants seem to enjoy the work and "their contentment has grown with their earnings." [20] One youth who had had experience in the camps wrote as follows:

> I became acquainted with the Labor Army and life at Murudalen in 1933 and it was with pleasure that I went again this year. . . .
>
> The relation between the engineer and the inspector on one side and between the boss and the boys on the other is one of mutual respect.
>
> The work this year was of two kinds: bridge work and road work. We who worked on the road lived in cabins near the Volbu place and lived like princes. For 1.50 kroner a day—a third of what we earned—we had five meals a day, always excellently prepared and neatly served. There was always a princely amount of nourishing food on hand. We could have

[20] *Arbeids-Fylkingen*, 1933, p. 8.

"seconds" when we liked and cocoa made with milk. People from Volbu did the cooking, and we were all very appreciative of their generosity in giving us so much attention with no thought of gain for themselves. After a day of wielding a spade or hoe or axe in the burning mountain sun that seemed to scorch the skin, we were ready for the comforts of a pipe, a place to read the weekly paper, and a more or less musical phonograph. We hope that the government will make this a regular thing and yet we hope the Labor Army will continue also just as it is.[21]

Finnish Camps

On February 2, 1934 the Finnish government submitted to the Diet, the legislative body of the country, a proposal for the formation of camps for unemployed youth and young men. With this proposal the government presented a plan to introduce two different types of camps—a youth camp to be arranged for boys between the ages of sixteen and twenty years, and a labor camp for young men between the ages of twenty-one and twenty-five years. After the Diet had appropriated funds and authorized the use of relief funds in establishing the camps, the government, on July 4, 1935, approved the conditions and regulations for youth and labor camp activities proposed by the Ministry of Social Affairs, to which authority over the camps was given.

In 1936 there were four active camps: the youth camps at Latokartano, Liminka, and Perniö, and the labor camp at Vähäjoki. The youth camps at Perniö and at Latokartano were changed to government camps for alcoholics on January 1 and May 1, 1937 respectively. In 1935, 256 unemployed youth were in the camps.[22] In general the men at the labor camp have been unskilled workers who have had only seasonal or occasional jobs.

The labor camp performs special settlement and other work under the technical supervision of various government offices. When the work is completed, it is given a final inspection and then transferred to the government agency responsible for activities in the field of the project. Under skilled leadership the young men in the labor camp have built up and cleared new farms and performed drainage, forest,

[21] *Ibid.*, 1934, p. 9.

[22] International Labor Office, *Planning of Public Works in Relation to Employment*, 1937, p. 169.

and road work. In addition to the practical work, they have been given instruction in subjects pertaining to general education and the various trades.

A youth camp is an institution for vocational instruction of unemployed, penniless youth who have been sent to the camp by the employment boards of the communes (counties). The camps are located on estates and farms purchased by the government. Here the young men have been given, in accordance with the regulations of the individual camp, practical and theoretical instruction in unskilled and skilled labor, as well as in civics and other topics of general education. By means of physical and intellectual activity and directed recreation, it is hoped that enrollees will acquire the physical and moral stamina necessary to fulfill conscientiously the duties of citizenship, and also the ability and desire to work. No military instruction is given in these camps.

At the youth camps the principal work of the enrollees has been the performance of tasks connected with agriculture, forestry, dairying, and truck gardening. They have also been given in so far as possible skilled instruction in building, machine shop work, and other trades.

A youth camp enrollee receives free lodging, board, and work clothes, as well a wage of 2.5 to 4 marks (5 to 8 cents) per day, his earnings depending upon his diligence and skill. At the labor camp the wage is from 11 to 15 marks (22 to 30 cents) per day.

Both the communes and the central government contribute to the cost of the camps. The government's net expense per person is 6,860 marks ($137.20) annually. In 1935 the total expenses were 2,685,900 marks ($53,718).[23]

Camp Directors

Each camp is in charge of a director whose duties and rights are prescribed in the camp regulations. He is employed and discharged by the Ministry for Social Affairs on the recommendation of a camp committee, made up of five members appointed by the Ministry for

[23] On July 30, 1937, the exchange value of the Finnish mark was 2 cents. The average exchange value for 1935 was also 2 cents.

Social Affairs to supervise camp activities. The salaries of camp directors vary from 3,000 to 3,625 marks ($60.00 to $72.50) per month.

Eligibility for Camps

In the government decree concerning the camps, it is specified that any person sent to a camp shall be healthy and shall possess the physical and mental qualifications necessary to become an efficient worker and that the commune shall require the person to submit to a medical examination prior to his departure for camp. Hence the youth in the camp have in general been healthy, although frequently they have come to camp insufficiently nourished. This condition has, however, been rapidly overcome by the wholesome, plentiful food supplied them in the camps. In cases of serious illness the services of the communal district physician are secured, and on certain occasions he also makes a general inspection of the camps. Hospital care has been provided for those injured in accidents.

The enrollees remain at the camps for one year, and only in exceptional cases has this period been prolonged. The men live in the camps and, while ordinarily they work seven to eight hours, during rush seasons the working day has sometimes been extended to ten hours.

Future of the Scandinavian Camps

The labor services in the Scandinavian countries do not seem to be considered as permanent institutions, but as special projects for youth set up in a time of depression to provide work and decent living conditions for unemployed young men. The plans have been worked out by the government or voluntary organizations in close cooperation with the employment agencies of these countries and have tended to stimulate local initiative. With adequate and scientifically collected information concerning job opportunities available, it is possible to train the young men and place them in available jobs. Such programs have great advantages over those in camps in the United States, where as yet accurate information about job opportunities and occupational trends is not available and little is done to help enrollees find jobs when they leave camp and make satisfactory adjustment to them.

Bibliography

Denmark

DENMARK, SOCIALMINISTERIET. *Cirkulaere af 16. April 1934.* Copenhagen, 1934. 6 pp.
——— *Cirkulaere af 23., April 1935.* Copenhagen, 1935. 12 pp.

FREDERIC C. HOWE. *Denmark, the Cooperative Way.* New York: Coward-McCann, 1936. 216 pp.

GREAT BRITAIN. Department of Overseas Trade. *Report on Economic and Commercial Conditions in Denmark, August 1936.* London: H. M. Stationery Office, 1936. 78 pp.

LEAGUE OF NATIONS. Child Welfare Committee, 10th session, April 17, 1934. "Protection of Children and Young People from the Consequences of the Economic Depression and Unemployment; Memorandum Submitted by the Delegate of Denmark." C. P. E. 441. Geneva: Secretariat, 1934. 5 pp.

"Legislation Adopted in Denmark; Voluntary Labor Service," *Industrial and Labor Information,* XLVII, 4 (July 24, 1933), 165.

"Revision of Danish Unemployment Insurance Law, 1937," *Monthly Labor Review,* XLV, 2 (August 1937), 356-62.

Finland

GREAT BRITAIN. Department of Overseas Trade. *Economic Conditions in Finland, 1935.* London: H. M. Stationery Office, 1936. 68 pp.

LEO HARMAJA. "Economic Progress in Finland after the Great War Compared with Other Northern Countries," *Unitas,* August 1931, pp. 81-91.

"Unemployed Young Workers in Finland; Establishment of Labor Camps," *Industrial and Labor Information,* XLIX, 2 (January 8, 1934), 60.

Norway

Arbeids-Fylkingen, 1933, 1934, 1935, 1936. Avsluttende beretning. Oslo, n.d. 5 pp.

Arbeids-Fylkingen. Årsberetning for 1933. Oslo, n.d. 13 pp.

Arbeids-Fylkingens avsluttende år 1935. Årsberetning for 1934. Oslo, n.d. 10 pp.

GREAT BRITAIN. Department of Overseas Trade. *Report on Economic and Commercial Conditions in Norway, June 1936.* London: H. M. Stationery Office, 1936. 100 pp.

NORWAY, SOCIALDEPARTEMENTET. Saerskilte tiltak for arbeidsløs ungdom. Oslo, 8 mai 1937.

"Voluntary Labor Service in Norway," *Industrial and Labor Information,* XLVII, 11 (September 11, 1933), 368.

Sweden

"The Final Report of the Swedish Unemployment Enquiry," *International Labor Review,* XXXII, 1 (July 1935), 99-104.

GREAT BRITAIN. Department of Overseas Trade. *Report on Economic and Commercial Conditions in Sweden,* April, 1937. London: H. M. Stationery Office, 1937. 83 pp.

ALF JOHANSSON, "Unemployment in Sweden after the War," *International Labor Review,* XXVI, 5 (November 1932), 617-43.

BERTIL OHLIN, "Economic Recovery and Labor Market Problems in Sweden," *International Labor Review,* XXXI, 4 (April 1935), 498-511; 5 (May 1935), 670-99.

"The Problem of Unemployment in Sweden; Measures in Aid of Young Unemployed Workers," *Industrial and Labor Information,* L, 9 (May 28, 1934), 304-5.

C. J. RATZLAFF, *The Scandinavian Unemployment Relief Program.* Philadelphia: University of Pennsylvania Press, 1934. 221 pp.

STOCKHOLMS STADS STATISTIK, SPECIALUNDERSÖKNINGAR. *Arbetslöshetshjälpen i Stockholm, 1935.* Stockholm: Beckmans, 1935. p. 24.

"Unemployment among Young Workers in Sweden," *Industrial and Labor Information,* L, 5 (April 30, 1934), 163-64.

The Polish Labor Camps

FOLLOWING the World War, a Polish nation was reconstituted from territory and people which Austria, Prussia, and Russia had seized in 1772, 1793, and 1795 respectively. In 1918 the new Poland, occupying territory about the size of the state of Montana and containing 28,000,000 people, faced important problems of reorganization. The full effects of the century and a quarter of divided existence were felt when Poland undertook the task of re-establishing an independent, unified state. The backward and undeveloped condition of the country, together with numerous economic difficulties, were complicated by the effects of six years of war—four years in the World War and two years of fighting against the Bolshevist forces of Russia which for a short time overran two-thirds of Poland's territory. Poland's economic rehabilitation, difficult enough under the conditions outlined, was further handicapped by a period of inflation followed by a financial crisis in 1924. The Polish people had enjoyed barely three years of relative prosperity before the depression of 1929.

Polish youth, like those in other countries, suffered from these conditions and glutted the labor market. Poland has the highest absolute increase in population in Europe,[1] and it is estimated that 450,000 young workers enter the Polish labor market each year.[2] In 1934 there were approximately 400,000 either wholly or partially unemployed young people.[3]

Origin and Development of the Volunteer Labor Service

It was in 1932, the year the German government organized the *Freiwilliger Arbeitsdienst,* at a time when unemployment was steadily increasing, that a plan for voluntary labor service was introduced by

[1] Roman Dyboski, "Economic and Social Problems of Poland," *International Affairs,* XVI, 4 (July-August 1937), 587-88.

[2] Jan Rosner, "Productive Occupation for Unemployed Young Workers in Poland," *International Labor Review,* XXXI, 4 (April 1935), 514.

[3] *Ibid.,* p. 513.

Michal Grazynski, the governor of Polish Upper Silesia. The scheme proved so successful in operation that members of the Polish government became interested in the possibility of extending it to the whole of Poland. In the meantime the Rifle Club *(Schützerei),* a national patriotic organization, began to sponsor camps for the unemployed in other districts of Poland.

Late in 1933 a special committee met with the Minister of Social Welfare to consider ways of providing constructive activity for unemployed youth. The committee included representatives of the Ministry of Education and Religion, the Employment Fund, and of various welfare organizations. As a result of its deliberations the Association for the Assistance of Unemployed Young Persons (often referred to as the SOM) was formed on November 17, 1933 under the leadership of Stefan Hubicki, a former Minister of Social Welfare, who had been largely instrumental in calling the conference.

The task of the SOM was twofold: first, it was to provide for the occupation of unemployed youth in work camps, and for their moral, vocational, physical, and military training; and second, it was to educate the public concerning the needs of the young unemployed and to seek their cooperation in a program of practical assistance. The new association took over the labor camps which had been organized in Silesia and also those of the *Schützerei.* During the winter of 1933-34 seven work camps were in operation, and by the following year the camp program was in full swing.

From the beginning the Association for the Assistance of Unemployed Young Persons was thought of as a temporary organization which would develop camps to be administered eventually by the government, as it was evident that the unemployment problem was too large to be met by any private organization. In addition, some government officials were anxious to make a closer connection between the camps and the military training program of Poland. Therefore on December 1, 1935 the SOM turned its work over to the Employment Fund, a government agency in charge of relief work for the unemployed. Practically no change was made in the organization of the camps themselves, although administrative changes resulted in decentralization of control.

The control of the work camps by the Employment Fund, however, proved to be only another step in their development, for with added experience it was realized that the camps could not be efficiently handled in this way. Therefore on September 22, 1936 the Higher Command for Voluntary Labor Service was created and placed directly under the Minister of Defense. At this time Boguslaw Kung, a lieutenant colonel in active service, was appointed chief of the labor service by the Minister of Defense after consultation with the Minister of Social Welfare.

Under the Ministry of Defense was also established a Council of Labor Service, including representatives of the Ministries of Defense, Social Welfare, Interior, Agriculture and Agrarian Reform, Industry and Commerce, and Education and Religion. This council advises regarding the educational and training program in the camps, and it may invite others to take part in its discussions when the occasion calls for it.[4] The administrative staff, as well as the camp instructors, are chosen from among soldiers in active service, public officials, and employees of the state.

Financing the Camps

From 1933-36 the camps derived their income from two sources: from the Employment Fund which paid a subsidy of 2.5 zlotys (45 cents)[5] a day for each worker, and from funds supplied by the Ministry of Social Welfare, autonomous local authorities, or social institutions. Since that time the entire cost has been covered by the Employment Fund. The Ministry of Defense cooperates with the Fund in supplying materials and buildings.[6] Between April 1, 1935 and March 31, 1936 the amount actually spent for the labor service was 7,282,400 zlotys ($1,310,832).

In 1934 the cost of maintaining a worker was 2.7 zlotys (48 cents) a day, distributed as follows:[7]

---

[4] *Industrial and Labor Information,* IX, 3 (October 19, 1936), 83.

[5] The purchasing power of a zloty is about 70 cents in terms of our money; its exchange value on August 30, 1937 was 18 cents.

[6] Rosner, *op. cit.,* p. 524; see also *Industrial and Labor Information,* October 19, 1936, pp. 93-94.

[7] Rosner, *op. cit.,* p. 523.

Item	*Cost in Zlotys*
Board	.80
Money allowances (including higher payments to leaders)	.84
Outfit (clothing, boots, etc.)	.50
Cost of transport	.10
Cost of maintenance of outfit and equipment	.10
Training courses, publications, athletic equipment, subsidies to cooperative shops	.10
Health	.05
Bonuses	.03
Social insurance	.02
Miscellaneous	.11
Total	2.65

The per capita cost of the labor service has steadily decreased since 1934, amounting to 2.5 zlotys (44 cents) between April 1 and November 30, 1935 and 1.9 zlotys (33 cents) between December 1, 1935 and March 31, 1936.

The enrollees receive their food, clothing, and 30 to 40 groszys (6 to 8 cents) for each six-hour-day's work. In addition, 7.5 zlotys ($1.35) a month are credited to them in a savings account and turned over to them when they leave camp. In some camps bonuses are paid to groups and brigades that exceed the standard output.

Selection and Enrollment of Workers

Efforts to enroll workers in the camps were first concentrated on unemployed youth living in the cities. Field workers were sent out, and contacts were made through the public employment offices as well as through the Rifle Club and the Association of Working Youth. The largest number of recruits were secured by the employment offices, as is indicated in the table on page 210, covering the period between November 17, 1933 and November 30, 1935.[8]

Although need was perhaps more urgent among city young people, experience proved that they were not always adaptable to camp life,

[8] Stowarzyszenie Opieki nad niezatrudnioną Młodzieżą. *Sprawozdanie z Działalności Wokresie, od 17 Listopada 1933 R. do 30 Listopada, 1935 R.* (Warsaw, 1936 R.), p. 92, Table 14.

Referring Organization	*Men*	*Women*
Employment offices	22,664	757
Rifle Club	2,407	109
Association of Working Youth	1,761	83
Association of Boy Scouts	254	—
Others	498	351
Total	27,584	1,300

and the result was a rapid turnover of enrollees in the early months of camp development. On the other hand, it was found that country youth usually adapted themselves readily to the conditions in the camps. The selecting agents have profited by this early experience, and now select most of the recruits from peasant families or from those of rural and urban laborers. Very few young people from the intellectual class are enrolled in the camps.

Unlike that of Germany, the Polish labor service is voluntary. Enrollment is open to Polish citizens of either sex, eighteen to twenty years of age, who are in normal health, in search of employment, and have the consent of their parents or guardians. Employed persons may also be enrolled when they are needed for special work of the labor service. All members of the labor service are required to be persons of good morals and loyal to Poland.

Applicants for the camps must take an examination given by the recruiting committee. This committee consists of a representative of the commander of the district army corps, who acts as president, a representative of the general administrative district authority, an army physician (or any other physician who has a military degree) who is appointed by the corps commander, and, if women are concerned, a woman doctor. Another member of this committee may be the representative of the provincial bureau of the Employment Fund if this office wishes to send such a delegate.

The Minister of Defense decides how many persons can be admitted to the service and the conditions under which preference may be given to certain candidates. He also has the privilege of allowing persons from other age groups to enter for special reasons. He fixes the date of enrollment after consultation with the Minister of Social Welfare, and determines which youth organizations of educational character shall have preference in the selection of candidates. The Minister of Defense notifies the district army corps commanders of these decisions, and they then pass the information on to the local administrative officials. The local officials are responsible for publicizing this information, and any expenses incurred for this purpose are covered by the camp budget.

As soon as the lists of applicants are ready, the local administrators send them to the army corps commanders. Actual enrollment is carried out by the commander-in-chief of the labor service with the cooperation of army officers and local officials.

Until September 1936 enrollees were free to leave camp at any time after the completion of their ten-day probationary period, and the only restriction on the length of their stay in camp was their attainment of the upper age limit of twenty-three years. They now enroll for a period of two years, but are permitted to leave camp after having given four weeks' notice.

LENGTH OF STAY IN THE CAMPS, NOVEMBER 17, 1933 TO NOVEMBER 30, 1935 [a]

Length of Stay	Men Enrollees		Women Enrollees	
	Former	Active	Former	Active
Less than 1 month	2,266	1,414	44	35
1 to 3 months	7,787	5,427	275	114
4 to 6 months	2,544	1,686	91	81
7 to 9 months	302	1,346	140	136
10 to 12 months	1,298	996	163	48
1 to 1½ years	1,522	363	123	36
Longer than 1½ years	144	36	1	...
No information	167	286	2	11
Total	16,030	11,554	839	461

[a] Adapted from Stowarzyszenie Opieki nad niezatrudnioną Młodzieżą, *op. cit.*, p. 93, Table 15.

Number of Young People in Camps

In 1934 there were about sixty work camps (including two camps for instructors and six for girls) containing some 9,000 workers. In the summer of 1935 there were 20,000 enrolled. In both years a marked decrease occurred in the number of enrollees during the winter months, when the greater part of the work at the camps had to cease because of bad weather. Between November 17, 1933 and November 30, 1935, a total of 27,584 men and 1,300 women enrolled in the camps. From December 1935 to September 1936 the enrollment was 5,850. During 1936-37 about 120 brigades averaging a hundred persons each were organized, making a total of 12,000. The camps vary in size from those containing one hundred to those containing five hundred, depending upon the nature of the work projects and the housing facilities.

Camp Leadership

Each camp has a director, appointed formerly by the Association for the Assistance of Unemployed Young Persons and now by the Ministry of Defense. The policy is to select directors from among active members of the army or other government employees. Even during the first years of the camps a large number of the directors were military men, for it was difficult to find enough civilians with the necessary background and experience to manage them.

In addition to the director, the camp staff includes a bursar, instructors in physical training and civics, brigade and group leaders (recruited from among the workers), and when necessary technical instructors. The number of the personnel depends on the size of the camp. The Minister of Defense must secure the opinions of the Minister of Social Welfare and the Minister of Education and Religion as to the qualifications required of the instructing personnel of the camps. All camp leaders must be graduates of secondary schools and must have had experience in group leadership.

All candidates for leadership must participate in training courses. During the first year of the camp program approximately 350 group and brigade leaders were trained by the SOM, and the Employment

Fund trained an additional 292. Courses were also given by the Employment Fund for other members of the camp personnel as follows:[9]

Group	*Number Trained*	*Number of Courses Offered*
Substitute leaders	563	4
Educational instructors	64	1
Cooks	51	1
Warehouse attendants	70	1
Sanitary personnel	62	1
Total	810	8

The following regulations for the courses of instruction were issued by the SOM:

The candidate is placed on probation for two weeks, during which time he performs the same work as an ordinary voluntary worker; this serves to eliminate unsuitable candidates. He then enters on a six weeks' course during which he is employed on manual work for four hours a day and attends lectures and classes for another four hours. While doing their work the men receive detailed information concerning the organization of technical work, the productivity of labor, tools and technical instruments and their use, the duties of leaders, and the execution of the work assigned to voluntary workers.

The subjects dealt with during the four hours reserved for lectures and theoretical classes include education in civics. This forms the subject of three series of talks each occupying two hours weekly, the first dealing with the social, economic and cultural situation of Poland, the second with the essential factors in the progress of civilization and culture, and ways and means of mutual assistance, and the third with the future duties of the leaders at the voluntary labor centers.

The course as a whole comprises: (1) questions of industrial health and safety, sanitary questions, etc.; (2) the organization of the labor center, the duties and qualities of group leaders; (3) technical instruction (calculation of surfaces and dimensions, building materials, road building, land leveling, drainage, etc.); (4) educational and instructional work (libraries, reading, camp newspapers, artistic activities, etc.); (5) physical training.[10]

[9] Sprawozdanie z działalności Funduszu Pracy, za okres od 1 kwietnia 1935 R. do 31 Marca 1936 R. (Warsaw, 1937), p. 45.

[10] Association for the Assistance of Unemployed Young Persons; "Regulations for Courses of Instruction. Conditions for Acceptance and Continued Training of Candidates," quoted in *Unemployment among Young Persons,* p. 126, published by the International Labor Office.

At the end of this course an examination is given, and only those who successfully pass it are given positions as group or brigade leaders in the camps.

In addition to the training courses, library facilities are provided, which, together with frequent conferences, give staff members an opportunity to continue individual professional training.

Housing and Care of Enrollees

The camp buildings differ in the various centers and also according to the season. In some places wooden barracks, with dormitories, offices, kitchen, etc., have been built; in other places movable huts, tents, and barges have been used.

The daily food value of the ration is 4,000 calories per *Junak,* or enrollee. The amount of rations is 20 per cent larger than the army rations. Jan Rosner, of the International Labor Office staff, who visited the camps in 1934, reported that the food was as a rule well cooked and that there was always plenty of it. Each brigade appoints a representative to keep in touch with the cook and to see that the supplies are fresh and of good quality. This system of direct control by the persons concerned seems to bring very good results. Young people who enter a camp benefit in many ways, but probably the most important improvement is in their physical condition and this is due to the adequate diet.[11]

A medical examination is required of each candidate before admission to camp to determine his or her fitness for the work and to exclude those who have communicable diseases. The average level of health and physical development of the enrollees is good and few cases of illness or accident occur in the camps.[12] Every camp either has a doctor or a hospital attendant on the staff, or is permitted to obtain medical assistance from the nearest sickness insurance fund.

The standards of hygiene and safety defined for industries by social legislation are applicable to the camps. Since September 1936 free medical aid has been supplied in accordance with the provisions for

[11] Rosner, *op. cit.,* p. 522.

[12] *Ibid,* p. 523; see also Second International Work Camp Conference, 1937, *National Reports,* p. 5.

POLAND

ove:

Polish labor service men marching on rade

low and right:

Street scenes in Warsaw

the care of the army. In case of loss of working capacity, invalidism, or death, the same regulations apply to the workers as to men in the military services.

Relation of Camps to National Defense

From the beginning, the program of the camps has included a kind of preparatory military training consisting of such exercises as forming lines and columns and marching. According to Rosner, in 1936:

> No great importance can be attached to these exercises from the standpoint of military training. Their purpose is rather to introduce a measure of discipline among these children of the countryside and of the suburbs who have never had an opportunity of doing gymnastics as taught in the secondary schools or of performing open-air exercises as scouts. In practice, this kind of preparatory military training is given to all pupils in secondary schools, and the young people in labor camps are certainly not better trained from a military point of view than are the pupils in the secondary schools.[13]

Since the camps have been placed under the Minister of Defense, and have become more militarized, those who have served twelve months in them may secure a reduction in the length of their compulsory military service.

The Work Projects

According to the decree of September 1936, the labor service is an "honor service" for the nation. It consists of manual work designed to improve the national defense or the economic interests of the state. The Ministry of Defense draws up the work program in accordance with the plans of the authorities responsible for capital expenditures from public funds. The work in the past has consisted chiefly of river-control projects (78 per cent in 1934), the construction of railroad lines and roads, land improvement, and the building of holiday camps, athletic fields, and airports. At present the work projects are primarily of a type to improve national defense. In addition, a small percentage of the enrollees are occupied in workships, the products of which are used entirely within the labor service. The SOM has

[13] Rosner, *op. cit.*, p. 528.

estimated that up to April 15, 1935 goods and equipment valued at 1,530,000 zlotys ($275,400) were produced in its workshops. This work for the most part consisted of repairing camp equipment and tools.

The following table gives the number of groups working and the organization sponsoring the work projects for the period between September 1935 and December 1936:[14]

Sponsor	*Brigades*
Ministry of Communications	26
Ministry of Agriculture	5
Municipalities	3
Employment Fund workshops	9
Labor service	13
Total	56

The men cannot be required to do more than six hours of manual work a day, but this does not include time spent in military training, physical training, or orderly duties. The work week is thirty-six hours.

Projects have always been selected so as not to bring about competition with adult workers. Frequently the enrollees (*Junaks*) work on the same project with adult workers. This system has the advantage of keeping the young voluntary workers in touch with regular adult workers rather than in an artificial environment where work opportunities are devised for their special benefit. On the other hand, under this system it is difficult to determine whether or not enrollees are competing with adult workers who might be employed on the same job.[15] However, Poland, like Bulgaria, has vast areas, especially in the sections formerly belonging to Russia, that are in need of roads, railways, dykes, and other public works, before the land can be properly developed.

Educational Program

The educational program is intended to help develop a sense of citizenship and patriotism, to give the enrollees some vocational prepara-

[14] Sprawozdanie z Działalności Funduszu Pracy, p. 47.

[15] Rosner, *op. cit.*, p. 518.

tion, and to initiate them into collective activities by giving them experience in cooperative methods. It consists of physical training, preparatory military training, reading and writing (compulsory for illiterates), and such general educational courses as civics, history, economics, geography, and current political problems.

The Association for the Assistance of Unemployed Young Persons conducted an inquiry covering the period from January 1 to December 31, 1934 when 10,249 young persons of both sexes were in the camps. Of these enrollees 7.8 per cent were illiterate, 17.2 per cent had completed their primary education, 57.5 per cent had attended but had not completed the primary course, 8.7 per cent had attended a vocational school and completed the course and 8.8 per cent had not completed it, 5.8 per cent had attended secondary schools, and 0.4 per cent had pursued higher studies.[16] This shows that very few enrollees in the camps had the equivalent of a high school education or better. It is then obvious that the Polish camps do not provide an opportunity for the mingling of different classes and occupational groups as do the German camps.[17] Since social distinctions are more sharply defined in Poland than in western countries, the possibility of bringing students or professionals together with workers for discussion is considerably less.[18]

On the whole, educational activities are carried on more extensively during summer and winter, because of the heavy work program in spring and fall, when weather conditions are favorable to outdoor work. The rapid turnover of enrollees early in the development of the labor service was a great handicap to the orderly development of the educational program.

Educational methods used include discussions, lectures, meetings, celebration of national festivals, and wall newspapers *(gazettes murales)*. The labor service publishes a weekly, called *Junak,* for the enrollees, and the monthly *Labor Service Review* for the staff. Each camp has its own meeting hall, library, and sports grounds. Besides a central library the labor service has traveling libraries. Recreational

[16] "Measures against Unemployment in Poland," *Industrial and Labor Information,* LIV, 7 (May 13, 1935), 233.

[17] Rosner, *op. cit.,* p. 520.

[18] *Der Arbeitsdienst in der Welt,* S. 94.

activities include dramatics, singing, orchestra, camp papers, excursions, physical education, and moving pictures. Several camps have organized choirs, orchestras, and dramatic clubs.

Vocational Training

Among the 1934 enrollees covered by the inquiry made by the Association for the Assistance of Unemployed Young Persons, 26.3 per cent had never worked. Of these 21.6 per cent had had no education. Among those who had worked at something, 61.9 per cent had lost their jobs during 1933 and 1934. At first the association did not make vocational training a regular part of the program, although vocational courses were available at some camps, especially during the winter months.

In 1936 vocational courses were organized in hotel work, ship work, cement work, land improvement and regulation of waterways, domestic economy (women), sewing (women), mechanics and stonework.[19]

Also in 1936, 552 women and 361 men were trained in the workshops as carpenters, tailors, seamstresses, quarry workers, and farmers. Practical experience was provided for those taking courses. Scholarships were provided for 121 men and women who wanted to improve their vocational training or general education. Altogether 1,379 persons, or 24 per cent of the total enrollment in the camps, received complete or partial vocational training. Courses developed since 1936 have included, in addition to those listed above, aviation mechanics, auto mechanics, and navigation on inland waterways.

Cooperative Aspects of the Camps

One attempt to help the youth in the Polish labor service has involved the development of productive cooperative groups.[20] As in the case of the labor service itself, the initiative in experimenting with this idea came from Silesia, where a bakery and a farm were acquired to pro-

[19] *Sprawozdanie z Działalności Funduszu Pracy,* p. 46.

[20] Rosner, *op. cit.,* pp. 531-33; see also International Labor Office. *Unemployment among Young Persons,* p. 115; *"Measures against Unemployment in Poland,"* and *Industrial and Labor Information,* LIV, 7 (May 13, 1935), 234.

vide work for the unemployed, and also to produce goods which could be used in the labor service. The Association for the Assistance of Unemployed Young Persons had intended to transform the camps gradually into cooperative organizations, endowed in so far as possible with self-government. To this end it offered to make grants toward the establishment of cooperative societies in the camps and allowed credits up to 100 zlotys ($18.00) to finance shops set up for camp members. As a result, cooperative tailor, hairdressing, cobbler, and other similar shops were established, as well as camp canteens and mutual aid funds.

Between December 1935 and August 1936 fifty-four cooperatives were organized in the camps: forty-six retail stores, three hairdressing shops, one bookbindery, two vegetable gardens, one tailor shop, and one building enterprise. The cooperative method has been retained in the camps, but the administration and financing of the cooperatives have been placed under the supervision of trained workers.

The Association for Assistance to Unemployed Young Persons began in 1935 to make a serious attempt to introduce self-government into the camps. The experiment was begun in twenty groups, with the intention of extending it gradually into all the centers.

Attitudes Toward the Camps

The Polish camps have not been received with anything like the degree of popular approval given the camps in Germany and the United States. In fact the attitude of the men toward the camps has been rather negative.

When the camps were first begun the general public, and especially the population of the camp localities, frequently took a hostile or unfriendly attitude toward the enrollees, who seemed to be considered dangerous competitors for employment on public works. According to Jan Rosner,

> Occasionally there has even been serious trouble between the peasants and the employment centers. But in course of time relations have become normal and hostility has given way to neutrality, or even to cordiality. The disinterested way in which the young voluntary workers helped to rescue

the peasants and their belongings during the floods of August 1934, often behaving courageously, not to say heroically, contributed a great deal to this result.[21]

Summary

In 1932 a voluntary work service was organized in Polish Upper Silesia. The Association for the Assistance of Unemployed Young Persons was formed on November 17, 1933 under the leadership of Stefan Hubicki, a former Minister of Social Welfare, and took over the camps which had been organized in Silesia and other parts of Poland. Then on December 1, 1935 the Association for the Assistance of Unemployed Young Persons, which had carried the camps through the first stages, turned the work over to the Employment Fund, a government agency in charge of relief for the unemployed. The control of the camps by the Employment Fund, however, proved to be a transitional phase in their development. The Higher Command for Voluntary Labor Service was created and placed directly under the Minister of Defense, with a lieutenant colonel of the army as chief of the labor service. The labor camps for unemployed youth in Poland thus gradually came under the influence of the army and finally became a part of the military training program of the country.

From all indications, the labor service in Poland will continue indefinitely to prepare and train the young men for military service, to care for some of the unemployed youth, and to carry out public work projects.

Bibliography

"Centers for Young Unemployed Persons in Poland," *Industrial and Labor Information*, L, 6 (May 7, 1934), 206.

Dekret Prezydenta Rzeczypospolitej, z dnia 22 wrzesnia 1936 R. Ø słuzbie pracy młodziezy.

Roman Dyboski. "Economic and Social Problems of Poland," *International Affairs*, XVI, 4 (July-August, 1937), 579-600.

——— "Die endgültige Gestaltung Polens Arbeitsdienst," *Der Arbeitsmann*, III, 22, S. 15.

Funduszu Pracy. Sprawozdanie z Działalności, za okres od 1 Kwietnia, 1935 R. do 31 Marca 1936 R. Warsaw: Nakładem Funduszu Pracy, 1937. 96 pp.

[21] Rosner, *op. cit.*, pp. 526-27.

League of Nations. Child Welfare Committee, 10th session, April 12, 1934. "Protection of Children and Young People from the Consequences of the Economic Depression and Unemployment; Memorandum Submitted by the Polish Government with Supplementary Documentation." C.P.E. 449 and C.P.E. 449 Annex. Geneva: Secretariat, 1934, 11 pp.

————. "Measures against Unemployment in Poland," *Industrial and Labor Information,* LIV, 7 (May 13, 1935), 229-35.

————. "Measures against Unemployment in Poland; The Labor Service," *Industrial and Labor Information,* LX, 3 (October 19, 1936), 93-94.

Jan Rosner. "An Inquiry into the Life of Unemployed Workers in Poland," *International Labor Review,* XXVII, 3 (March 1933), 378-92.

————. "Productive Occupation for Unemployed Young Workers in Poland," *International Labor Review,* XXXI, 4 (April 1935), 512-38.

Rozporządzenie Ministrow, Spraw wojskowych i opieki społecznej, z dnia 10 lutego 1937.

"The Situation in Poland; Juvenile Unemployment," *Industrial and Labor Information,* XLIX, 11 (March 12, 1934), 368-69.

"The Situation in Poland; Labor Service for Young Unemployed Persons," *Industrial and Labor Information,* LXII, 10 (June 7, 1937), 425-26.

"The Situation in Poland; Organization of Young Unemployed Men," *Industrial and Labor Information,* XLIX, 2 (January 8, 1934), 57-58.

"The Situation in Poland; Unemployment among Young Persons," *Industrial and Labor Information,* LVII, 10 (March 9, 1936), 266-67.

Stowarzyszenie Opieki nad niezatrudnioną Młodzieżą (SOM). Sprawozdanie z działalności wokresie od 17 Listopada 1933 R. do 30 Listopada 1935 R. Warsaw: Nakładem Funduszu Pracy, 1936 R. 108 pp.

J. M. Zagórski. "Les camps de travail de la jeunesse," *Tribune of the Young Generation,* IV (August 1936), 25-27.

The Czechoslovakian Labor Service

In 1936 Czechoslovakia existed as a democracy among authoritarian or semiauthoritarian states. Her neighbors, Germany, Austria, Hungary, Poland, and Rumania, had all set up fascist or semifascist states. Even then it appeared to many observers that the next adventure of Germany would be expansion to the east at the expense of Czechoslovakia. Among 15,000,000 Czechs, Slovaks, Ruthenians, and Magyars, a German minority of 3,000,000 led by the Nazi leader Henlein agitated for autonomy, while the coordinated press of Hitler's Germany carried on tirades against Czechoslovakia alleging that the German minority was being mistreated and that this small country was under the influence, if not the domination, of Russia.

Arriving in Prague from Germany, during that summer of 1936, I had expected to find a feeling of tension and fear. On the contrary, I found a people going about their daily tasks quietly and resolutely, realistically aware of the danger of an attack, but occupied with the work of making the late President Masaryk's dreams for an ideal democracy become a reality.[1] Czechoslovakia, realizing that a generation of disillusioned, dissatisfied youth tends to bring about authoritarianism, had followed other democratic countries in developing labor camps and "labor battalions" to care for unemployed young men and women.

Origin of Camps

The Czech work camp movement had its origins in a project developed by the German *Hochschule* in Prague, where a group of young people built an athletic field for the school.[2] A number of towns and cities in northern Bohemia, the most important being Prague, then organized work camps and by 1932 approximately 10,000 young men and women from Prague were enrolled in work projects of both the resi-

[1] See Shepard Stone, "A Democracy Amid Dictatorships," *New York Times Magazine*, December 12, 1937, p. 8.

[2] *Der Arbeitsdienst in der Welt*, S. 106.

dential and nonresidential types. These young people did not enroll for any fixed period of time, and were permitted to leave upon a week's notice. Usually the camps did not contain less than twenty nor more than fifty men. Sometimes, however, as many as 500 to 600 young men were members of a single camp.

Camps under the Ministry of Social Welfare

As the unemployment problem among youth became more acute, the Council of Ministers proposed a national system of labor camps. Following negotiations with workers' organizations and other groups which would be affected by the camps, in May 1934 the Council of Ministers decided to develop a labor service.[3]

The Ministry of Social Welfare was given responsibility for the general management of the camps as well as for the selection and carrying out of the work projects. Socialist youth organizations were instrumental in establishing at Terezin the first camp. The aims of the Czechoslovakian work camp program were: (1) to relieve unemployment; (2) to provide education for unemployed youth; and (3) to train men in communal work.

The work projects for the camps consisted of building tourist roads, building and repairing railways, regulating streams, repairing swimming pools, playgrounds, and athletic fields, tree-planting and general forestry work, and the cleaning and classification of books and newspapers. Proud of her democracy, Czechoslovakia made these voluntary camps as far as possible self-governing. "All questions relating to cultural matters, physical training, or general education are settled by chosen representatives of the members of the camps, who form an 'autonomous council.' "[4]

The state subsidy for the camps came from the productive work relief funds and amounted to 36 koruny ($1.25) a person per week, of which an amount up to 1.2 koruny (4 cents) could be applied toward wages.[5] This subsidy was supplemented by the public entrepreneur employing the labor service, bringing the amount up to the pre-

[3] International Labor Office, *Unemployment among Young Persons,* p. 100.
[4] *Ibid.*
[5] On July 30, 1937 the exchange value of the koruna was 3.48 cents.

vailing wage per man. This wage, however, was not paid to the workers in cash, because the costs of maintenance, food, equipment, and insurance were first taken out of the total, the remainder then being divided among the men. The Ministry of Social Welfare supplied additional funds for the educational supervision of the camps.

City Camps or Labor Battalions

During the same month that the Council of Ministers decided to establish a camp system (May 1934), the municipal council of Prague adopted the idea of "labor teams," or "labor battalions," in addition to the camps that had been organized for several years. The labor teams or battalions were to be composed of unmarried young men from eighteen to twenty-four years of age, and in exceptional cases for those under that age if they had completed their apprenticeship.

The managing and disciplinary board of the labor battalions included representatives from the physical training clubs, chief among these being the Sokol, instituted in 1862 primarily to develop the Bohemians physically, morally, and spiritually for life as a strong, independent race.[6] Since the establishment of the Czechoslovakian state on October 28, 1918, the Sokol has devoted itself to what might be called patriotic athletics. Other organizations sponsoring the labor battalions were the DTJ, or the Laborers' Physical Culture Union (mainly Social Democratic), the Straiv Svobody (mainly from the Center party), and the Eagle Club, whose members were Catholics.

Brno, Prague, and other large cities in Czechoslovakia had camps of this type, which were operated the year around. Besides camps for the unemployed workers, there were camps for students, and recreation camps for workers and members of different organizations.

These camps were nonmilitary in nature—set up to give physical help to unemployed young men, to raise their morale, and to provide educational opportunities. They were closely linked with the unemployment service, and since all the members of the camps were registered in the unemployment bureaus, frequently young men were transferred from the camps to jobs. Few of the workers who went into the camps had

[6] L. J. Fisher, "The Bohemian Sokols," in *Bohemia* (Votja Benes and J. J. Zmrhal, editors). Chicago: Bohemian National Alliance, 1917, pp. 51-59.

had work experience, and many of them had never held a permanent job.

Before sending a boy into one of the labor camps, a study was made of his background and experience in order to discover, first, whether or not he deserved this public assistance, and second, whether or not he would benefit from the camp experience.

Members of the labor teams were given their board six days of the week, provided with work clothes and shoes, and paid 35 koruny per week. They were also insured against accidents and were entitled to medical attendance. They worked forty hours a week, were expected to take part in cultural and recreational activities,[7] and were usually offered general education courses, discussions, sports, and physical exercises.

Each camp was administered by two directors, one who was responsible for the educational program and general administration of the camp, the other who acted as camp foreman in charge of the work projects (under the supervision of a city official). In general, the directors were young men.

A trip to one of the camps at Strava, run by the city of Prague, took us across the historic old King Charles Bridge and up the steep Petrin Hill overlooking Prague, where stands the St. Vitus Cathedral and the President's Palace. Driving still higher we came to a large sports field, where the great athletic festivals for which Czechoslovakia is well known are held. Under the grandstands in the dressing rooms were located the headquarters of the group of about eighty men who were engaged in developing the field, as well as the parks and roads in the surrounding areas.

As we entered the offices of the camp about noon four of the boys carrying large trays were leaving the kitchen with food for the workers. The portions were generous and the food looked appetizing.

After meeting the camp director and inspecting the offices and supply rooms we walked to the southern end of the field where the majority of the young men were working on a road and sidewalks. These youth, short and wiry, deeply tanned, wearing a variety of work

[7] International Labor Office, *op. cit.,* p. 101.

BOR CAMPS IN CZECHOSLO-
/AKIA BEFORE ITS ABSORP-
TION BY GERMANY

ve:

zech unemployed doing landscape
·k at Strava

ht:

'he old Town Bridge Tower,
gue

ow:

abor camp leaders, Czechoslovakia

LABOR CAMPS IN CZECHO-
VAKIA BEFORE ITS ABSO
TION BY GERMANY

Above:
Czech girls' camp.

Left:
Headquarters of a labor
near Prague

Below:
Czech unemployed taking
out to workers near Prague

clothes, were filling small two-wheel wagons with dirt and rock and then hauling them to a low place in the road and dumping them. As we started toward another group of workers doing some landscaping along the road a strong wind raised clouds of dust so that they were obliterated. In the west we could see flashes of lightning against the black wall of clouds that was rapidly approaching. After a quick glance at the landscaping we ran for the sheds where the tools were stored and as the rain began to fall the young workers from the road came dashing up pulling their small two-wheel wagons filled with tools.

While waiting for the rain to stop we inspected the sheds and the benches and tools used in making the wagons, chairs, and other equipment for the camp. Much of this equipment was made by the enrollees, who showed with considerable pride the small wagons used in hauling dirt and the benches, tables, and chairs which they had made. Members of the camps also did all the repairing of equipment, and in their leisure made pieces of furniture for their homes.

At the Strava camp a typical day's program for the worker was as follows:

7:00 A.M.	Breakfast
7:30–10:00	Work
10:00–10:15	Second breakfast
10:15–12:00	Work
12:00	Lunch
1:00– 3:00 P.M.	Work
3:00– 3:15	Rest period
3:15– 5:00	Work
5:00	Return to shed with tools
6:00	Dinner

The city of Prague had rented a house with a beautiful garden which was used for the educational classes of the camps in that vicinity. One day each week the men went to this center, instead of to the work project, to study and receive instruction. They were given great freedom in the selection of their courses.

Four hours of recreation and education courses a week were required of each enrollee. Frequently, however, the young men spent a longer time studying or engaging in sports. The educational program was conducted every day during the late afternoons and evenings. Sometimes groups alternated at playing and studying. The youth at Strava were especially interested in languages, but also took courses in stenography, geography, and philosophy.

Sudeten German Labor Service[8]

A centrally directed labor service, patterned as closely as circumstances permitted after that of the "Fatherland," existed among the German minority in Czechoslovakia, even before the taking of the Sudetenland by Germany. The service had its origin in two small and short-lived camps held in 1933. Government opposition halted its growth for a time, but after 1935 the labor service experienced uninterrupted development. Two organizations cooperated in organizing and administering the service—the League of Germans *(Bund der Deutschen)*, which carried the chief administrative responsibility, and the German Athletic Union *(Deutscher Turnverband)*, which directed the cultural program and had charge of the training of camp leaders. The leaders were nominated by the two organizations jointly and were responsible to both of them. The nominations were submitted to local camp committees for approval.

The camps which were all "closed," that is, "resident," had increased in number yearly; in 1935 there were twenty-one; in 1936, twenty-nine, and in 1937, forty-three. About 1,000 young men participated in the work each year.

The Sudeten German labor service received no subsidy from the government of Czechoslovakia except where work camps were held by district governments having access to emergency funds. In 1936, 50 per cent of the cost of the camps was provided by the *Bund der Deutschen,* 20 per cent by the district or national government, and 30 per cent by contributions from other German organizations.

The average daily cost of supporting a man in a work camp was 15 koruny (about 52 cents). This sum did not include rent or maintenance of buildings, cultural events (moving pictures, concerts, etc.), or tools

[8] See Second International Work Camp Conference, (1937), *National Reports;* and *Der Oesterreichische Arbeitsdienst,* IV, 2 (February 1938) 6.

and materials, all of which were usually provided either by the organization for whom the work was done or by private individuals.

Camp enrollees were young men between the ages of eighteen and twenty-five, who were recruited through the various German organizations cooperating with the labor service. The largest number of enrollees were unemployed who had registered with the employment office of the *Bund der Deutschen.* They received 16 koruny (about 56 cents) a week for pocket money. A man usually stayed in camp until he could find a job or until the work project had been completed. Where unemployment was especially widespread, however, the men worked in shifts, from six to eight weeks.

Selecting work projects was the responsibility of the Work Camp Department of the *Bund der Deutschen.* This group sent agents into the districts and cantons to study local possibilities. These agents were allowed to submit proposals and budgets to the central office. When a project was approved, a sum up to one-third of the cost of the camp, exclusive of the cost of materials, was set aside for the execution of the plan.

In order to be approved, a project had to have not only sound financial backing, but had also to meet the familiar requirements that it be "extra" work[9] of public benefit, requiring a preponderance of unskilled workers. The following types of projects were given consideration: building cross-country roads, laying out parks, village greens, athletic fields and playgrounds, constructing swimming pools, making ponds for fire-fighting purposes, improving land, regulating streams, and constructing youth hostels.

The camp leader, an unemployed young man who had participated in an eight-weeks training camp, was responsible for the execution of all phases of the camp program. He was assisted by a group leader, who also had been trained for his work. A group of local representatives of interested organizations acted as a liaison committee between the camp and the central office. On this committee were a technical adviser and an economic director who supervised these aspects of the camp activities.

The camps were usually held in summer. The work week averaged forty hours, and free time in the afternoons and evenings was devoted

[9] That is, work not in competition with ordinary labor.

to such educational and recreational pursuits as physical culture, folk singing and dancing, lectures on historical and social subjects, the reading aloud of German literature, amateur theatricals, and so on. The labor service contributed to the cultural life of the community by occasionally giving programs to which the public was invited.

The Sudeten Germans had accepted the Nazi attitude toward labor service and regarded it as an essential instrument by which the younger generation could be educated for participation in national life. Its educational aims, as formulated by the *Bund der Deutschen,* were as follows:

1. The education of youth to a new sense of responsibility in regard to work for the good of the community.
2. The education of youth to a spirit of comradeship, subordination, and to a new community spirit which bridges the gap between one class and another and thereby contributes to social peace among the Sudeten German minority.
3. The education of youth to a new social attitude, which consciously ingrafts the individual in the community and regards all action from the point of view of the community.

Conclusion

Although by the summer of 1938 the camps in Czechoslovakia had not been developed to the extent that they had in many other countries, they played an important part in the program for the care and training of Czechoslovakian youth. True to the traditions of democracy, the camps in Czechoslovakia emphasized the educational and recreational programs, and usually provided a special time and place for their conduct. The youth were also given sound citizenship training through the self-government program within the camps. While the camps did not seem to be considered a permanent institution in Czechoslovakia, they would undoubtedly have been continued so long as there were large numbers of unemployed youth in that country.

The labor service of the German minority along the borders of western Czechoslovakia had been modeled, in so far as was possible, after the labor service of Nazi Germany. When the Sudetenland was incorporated in Germany proper the labor service of this minority was taken into the Reich labor service. The final orientation and reorganization of the labor service since Czechoslovakia was broken up during March 1939, are still in doubt. However, since Moravia and Bohemia have been taken over by Germany, it is very possible that the entire labor service will be patterned after that of Nazi Germany, and thereby lose its democratic qualities.

Bibliography

"Camps for Young Unemployed Workers in Czechoslovakia," *Industrial and Labor Information,* L, 10 (June 4, 1934), 342-43.

"Employment Centers for Young Men in Czechoslovakia," *Industrial and Labor Information,* LVI, 5 (November 4, 1935), 180.

L. J. Fisher, "The Bohemian Sokols," in *Bohemia; A Brief Evaluation of Bohemia's Contribution to Civilization* (Vojta Benes and J. J. Zmrhal, editors). Chicago: Bohemian National Alliance, 1917, pp. 51-59.

League of Nations, Child Welfare Committee. *Campaign against Unemployment among Young People; Note Prepared by the Information Center.* C.100.M.41. 1936. IV. (C.P.E.-C.I., 4). Geneva: Secretariat, 1936. 3 pp.

"Measures against Unemployment in Czechoslovakia," *Industrial and Labor Information,* LV, 3 (July 15, 1935), 98-99.

"Young Unemployed Workers in Czechoslovakia," *Industrial and Labor Information,* L, 6 (May 7, 1934), 205-6.

Work Camps in the Netherlands

CAMPS for the unemployed were first organized in the Netherlands by the Workers Youth Center of Amsterdam during 1932. At the end of this year the total of the registered unemployed had reached 350,770.[1] In 1933, with unemployment still growing, Catholic and other religious groups took up the work camp idea, and began to develop short-term camps. The primary emphasis in these camps was on improving the morale of the enrollees, rather than providing them with work. The first year each camp lasted only a week, but in 1934 their duration was extended to two weeks. With the encouragement of the government, the first large long-term labor camp was held in May 1935.

The camps in the Netherlands were established and had their early development under the aegis of private organizations. Of these the National Roman Catholic Commission for the Care of Young Unemployed, the Center for the Care of Unemployed (a Protestant organization), the Modern Center for the Care of the Unemployed (a Social Democratic organization), and the Federation of Labor Camps (a nonpartisan, lay organization) have continued to organize work camps.

A large proportion of the young men who go into these camps are members of the organizations sponsoring the movement, and they learn about the camps from fellow members. Youth who are not members of these organizations hear of camps through the churches, and to some extent through the newspapers. The Protestant organization makes an annual drive for subscriptions, and in 1936 sponsored a radio program on which the Minister of Social Welfare spoke. Other men hear of the camps through having ex-campers among their associates.

The three general aims of the camps have been to keep unemployed youth fit for labor, to release them, at least for awhile, from what is often a depressing environment, and to get them again accustomed to regular work, order, and system.[2]

---

[1] *Europa,* I, 497.

[2] This statement of aims was drawn up by officials of the Dutch Ministry of Social Welfare and is part of their reply to a questionnaire on the camps.

Administration and Financing of the Camps

Since 1935 the government has coordinated all unemployment measures, including the camp program, and the four organizations mentioned above now receive government subsidies for camps. All the camps are supervised by the Ministry of Social Welfare.

Prior to May 1935 the National Crisis Committee, which had state funds at its disposal, subsidized the camps to the amount of 6 guilders ($3.31) a man per week (six days), provided the cost for a man per week was at least 10 guilders ($5.52). The remaining 4 guilders ($2.21) were contributed by the organization maintaining the camp.[3]

The government now subsidizes the camps to the extent of about 75 per cent of their total cost, the remaining 25 per cent being raised by the organizations operating the camps. The 1937 appropriation amounted to 500,000 guilders ($275,000). The government contributes .72 guilders (40 cents) a man per day plus 75 per cent of his railway fare for two trips to and from the camp, or .78 guilders (43 cents), which includes a bounty for the use of bicycle. The workers receive 1.75 guilders (96 cents) pocket money each week. In addition, the government contributes .54 guilders (30 cents) a man per week for the cost of lodging and .18 guilders (10 cents) per capita for maintenance of the equipment. The short-term camps receive a subsidy of one guilder a man per day, including Sunday.

The following table indicates the amounts which have been spent by the government and by private organizations for the work camps:[4]

Year	*Cost to Organizations, in Guilders*	*State Subsidy, in Guilders*	
1932	18,500		
1933	62,000		
1934	98,000		
1935	85,000	125,000.00	
1936	180,000	381,291.40	
Total	443,500	506,291.40	
Grand Total			g. 949,791.40 ($522,385.27)

[3] On August 30, 1937 the exchange value of the guilder was 55 cents.

[4] See Second International Work Camp Conference, "National Report from the Netherlands," p. 5.

Private organizations have estimated the cost per capita for a six-day week at 6.25 guilders ($3.44), not including the cost of housing and the maintenance of equipment. The cost, however, undoubtedly varies among the different camps. The salary of the camp leaders is fixed by the organizations, and as a rule amounts to 100 to 125 guilders a month ($55.15 to $68.94), with free board and lodging.

The following data for the camps are for the year 1936:[5]

Sponsoring Organizations	*Number of Camps*	*Short-term*	*Long-term*	*Number Enrolled*	*Number of Man Days*
Modern Center for the Care of the Unemployed	30	11	19	1,410	45,794
Center for the Care of Unemployed (Protestant)	69	19	50	5,633	175,491
Roman Catholic Commission for the Care of Young Unemployed	108	81	27	5,771	128,272
Federation of Labor Camps	19	13	6	1,146	29,221
Total	226	124	102	13,960	378,778

Selection and Enrollment of the Men

The organizations which maintain the camps select the participants from applicants for the work service. The Protestant Center for the Care of Unemployed has about three hundred local committees that receive applications. The central office of this organization examines the records and qualifications of the candidates and sends back to the local committee the names of those men whom it accepts. A quota is assigned to each local committee and the committee may make substitutions in case any applicants withdraw. The list of acceptances is then sent back to the central office, which forwards it to the camp leader. The Catholic organization seems to have no elaborate selection system and its candidates are recommended by local groups or by priests.

The Protestant group accepts for the camps only unmarried, unemployed youth from Christian homes. Since freethinkers contribute to

[5] *Ibid.*, pp. 6-7.

NETHERLANDS

ınd right:

ses constructed by campers at
veen, Friesland

loor theatre constructed with sod
:mployed Dutch youth

NETHERLANDS

Above:

Protestant labor camp "Ouverberg" near Rumpen

Right:

Liberal Protestant labor camp "De Kuil," Beekbergen

Below:

Dormitory of the boys labor camp "Het Putven" at Chaam

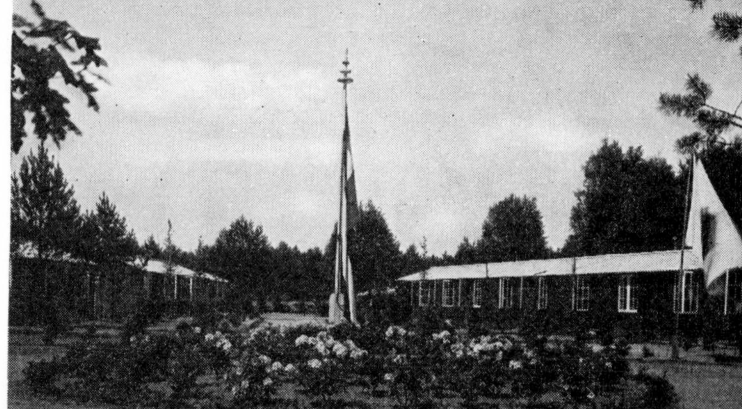

this organization, a separate camp is maintained for them. The participants must be between the ages of seventeen and twenty-five, in good health, and willing to obey camp regulations, including attendance at religious services. If the campers do not own bicycles, these are furnished them while in camp. It is not necessary that camp members belong to any particular Protestant youth organizations. Qualifications for participation in the Catholic camps are similar to those required for the Protestant groups.

The enrollment period of the camps varies from eight to nine weeks. Usually about a hundred men are enrolled in each camp, though a few camps have smaller groups. The average number of youth enrolled during one period is 1,800. The camps of the Protestant organization have five nine-week periods yearly. The Catholic enrollees are required to live two weeks at a "short camp" before having six weeks at a "long camp."

The general practice in the Netherlands is for the campers to remain in the camps night and day, but they are permitted to leave over week ends.

Camp Leadership

A camp leader appointed by the supporting organization directs each camp. In the Roman Catholic groups the leaders are generally friars who have had some pedagogical experience. These camps usually also have two or three assistant leaders.

In the Protestant camps, in addition to the camp leader, there are group leaders in charge of from eight to twelve boys each, and two camp mothers, who do the sewing and cooking. The group leaders are usually unemployed men between twenty-five and thirty years of age, who are hired to live with the boys and to maintain discipline. They also act as foremen of the projects. No special training is given the camp leaders before they go into the camps. Usually, however, group leaders are promoted to positions of camp leaders, which insures the camps having experienced directors.

Health Aspects of the Program

As in other countries, a medical examination is required before a man is admitted to a camp in the Netherlands. Some camps have a resident physician; others call in a local physician when he is needed. Most of the camps have small infirmaries to care for youth who become ill or receive minor injuries. The enrollees are insured against accidents during the time they are working in a camp, and the premium is paid by the government and the organization which sponsors the camp. Camp life undoubtedly results in a general improvement in the health of the workers. According to one doctor, the men gain about 3.9 kilograms (about nine pounds) weight while in camp.

Work Projects and Educational Program

The type of work done in the camps varies greatly, but forestry is most common. In some places the work consists of improving and building homes for young men, making athletic fields, and providing similar educational and recreational facilities. Other projects take the form of clearing, leveling, and preparing land for cultivation, making bicycle and foot trails, and carrying out drainage projects. The youth work seven hours on five days and five hours on Saturday, making a forty-hour week.

As the camps are promoted and administered by private organizations, the educational program depends on the sponsoring group for inspiration and orientation. While programs vary considerably according to local needs and available facilities, the general purpose seems to be to increase knowledge, and to reawaken interest. This is done largely by informal discussions on social, economic, and religious subjects.

It is considered undesirable to establish regular courses or formal classes, and any suggestion of the traditional school is avoided. Informal discussions, field trips, and excursions are encouraged, as are handicrafts and a variety of different hobbies. Talks are sometimes given by labor union officials to explain the organization and purposes of the labor movement. Discussions of technical subjects, such as drainage and bridge-building, are sometimes illustrated by lantern slides or moving pictures. Certain general courses are offered, among them first aid. Besides these activities, which occupy two or three hours in the evening, afternoon excursions are occasionally conducted by the camp leader or his assistant.

Conclusion

The educational results of the camps may be said to consist of a revived interest on the part of the campers in a variety of subjects, but especially in religious, social, and economic problems. The communal experience also increases their interest in, and understanding of, the purposes of the youth organizations. It has resulted frequently in their becoming leaders of some youth group and playing an important part in the development of effective youth organizations.

All participants must be registered with one of the Labor Intermediary Offices, and the camp directors endeavor to have the men work at their own trades in so far as this is possible. While vocational training is not offered in the camps, such training is sometimes available outside the camps on a voluntary basis.

After leaving the camps, the youth often go to the central workshops for vocational training.[6] In an attempt to reach and assist all young people who are eligible for aid, the municipalities are trying the efficacy of having a special bureau for registry of both employed and unemployed young men between the ages of fourteen and twenty-one inclusive. All employed young men so registered receive a booklet in which the employer records the period during which the holder has been in his service. The young men are asked to keep in touch with the bureau constantly. When they are unemployed, their attention is called to the possibilities that are open to them, including enrollment in the labor camps.

The men participating usually appreciate the work camp program, and the general public is very sympathetic toward the camps. Concrete evidence of this is shown in the generous gifts of money collected for the camps by the private sponsoring organizations. Such collections amount to about 25 per cent of the total budget.

---

[6] During the last half of 1936 there were about twenty-five of these central workshops in as many districts. In them unemployed young men are taught trades under conditions resembling regular factory work. They receive one guilder a week. Between February and December 1936 the average number of participants in the central workshops was 1,839. (See Second International Work Camp Conference, "The Struggle against the Unemployment of Young Persons in Holland," p. 3.)

Bibliography

HOMER BRETT. "Measures to Provide Employment for Young Workers in the Netherlands," *Monthly Labor Review,* XLIV, 3 (March 1937), 580-81.

D. G. DRAAYER. "Der Kampf gegen die Arbeitslosigkeit der Jugendlichen in Holland." *International Education Review,* VI, 4-5 (1937), 292-301.

NATIONALE R. K. COMMISSIE VOOR JEUGDWERKLOOZEN. Congres op 21 October 1935. *Jeugdwerkloosheidsproblem.* 150 pp.

——— *Conclusies die in Bespreking gebracht worden op het congress.* 12 pp.

——— *Rapport van het nijmeegsch congres in zake het jeugdwerkloozenvraagstuk.* 'S-Hertogenbosch, 1936. 39 pp.

——— *Katholicke Jeugdwerkloozenzorg; rapport naar aanleiding van de enquête in zake het vraagstuk der jeugdwerkloosheid.* 'S-Bosch, 1933. 64 pp.

——— *Ons Kampen Internaatswerk in 1933.* 'S-Bosch, 1934. 32 pp.

——— *Jaarverslag, 1935.* 'S-Bosch, 1935. 32 pp.

——— *Werklooze Jeugd.* 1936. 174 pp.

——— *Jaaroverzicht,* 1936. 36 pp.

LANDELŸKE COMMISSIE TER BESTRIJDING VAN DE GEVOLGEN DER JEUGDWERKLOOSHEID. *Zorg voor werklooze Jeugd; Rapporten enwenken.* Amsterdam: Plantage Franschelaan, 1932. 39 pp.

Centrale voor Werkloozenzorg. Raad en Daad, I, 3 (Februari, 1936), 12-28.

Labor Service for Women

WHILE work camps for men have developed and expanded during the past decade, and have come to be thought of as a permanent institution for the training of male youth, camps for women, whenever organized, have for the most part been limited in scope and short-lived. As we saw in the second chapter, student and pacifist camps, from their beginning, have given young women an opportunity to join with young men in voluntary labor service by preparing meals, mending and washing clothes, and sometimes doing the lighter kinds of work on the projects. It has been acknowledged that in these instances women have made a genuine contribution to the work and morale of the camps. Nevertheless, although life in a work camp ordinarily includes activities for which women are adaptable, the work projects usually chosen for such camps are of a type requiring muscular strength that women do not possess.

We have seen in the preceding chapters that youth agencies and governments for the most part were not interested in labor service until the idea was forced upon them as one means of taking care of unemployed youth. In general, unemployment has affected young persons of the two sexes in about equal proportions,[1] yet in thinking of the unemployed, we usually visualize dilapidated looking men "pounding the pavement" in search of jobs, slumping in a bread line, or "riding freight" to another part of the country in the hope of finding work. Women as unemployed are less well known to us. Also, in utilizing labor service as a relief project much less has been done directly for women than for men.

In this connection, Mrs. Franklin D. Roosevelt said in New York in 1933:

> The government . . . has been tremendously unfair to women, in a way, because most of the re-employment relief measures have been directed toward the men. Times were never worse for women . . . we have concentrated

[1] International Labor Office, *Unemployment among Young Persons,* p. 17.

so much on families and men . . . but women have complained much less and been pretty meek.[2]

Women in the Bulgarian Labor Service

As a matter of fact, the first opportunity for participation in a state labor service had no connection with unemployment. It came to the women of Bulgaria which, as the first state to introduce a compulsory labor service, was also the first to extend the program to include women. However, since the women's labor service functioned for only four months in Bulgaria, it has had little influence except, perhaps, as an idea.

The law inaugurating the Bulgarian labor service was planned to apply to all citizens regardless of sex, and about five months after the revised form of the law had been adopted,[3] regulations governing compulsory labor service for women were published (March 8, 1922).[4]

The aims of labor service for women were similar to those of the service for men and were directed toward

a) Awakening in them, irrespective of their social status or financial position, a love of work in the service of the community and of manual labor;
b) Instructing them in rational methods of work in the branches of economic activity mentioned in section 5 of the present regulations;
c) Organizing and utilizing their labor power in the interests of production and the welfare of the country.[5]

Unmarried young women between the ages of sixteen and thirty years were made liable for four months of service. It was expected that they would eat and sleep at home, and Moslem women were to be permitted to work at home. No maintenance allowance was to be paid the workers during their service. They were to work eight hours a day, and night work (defined as that done between eight o'clock at night and six o'clock in the morning) was specifically prohibited.

---

[2] *New York Times*, November 9, 1933, p. 23.

[3] Max Lazard, *Compulsory Labor Service in Bulgaria* (Geneva: International Labor Office, 1922), pp. 34-35.

[4] Regulations for the Rendering of Compulsory Labor Service for Young Women, March 8, 1922; quoted in full in Lazard, *Compulsory Labor Service in Bulgaria*, pp. 145-55.

[5] *Ibid.*, Sec. 4.

As in the case of Bulgarian men, it was possible for young women to purchase exemption from the service. Provision was also made for temporary exemptions in special circumstances and for permanent exemption for those who were mentally or physically disabled or who were the breadwinners of their families.

The young Bulgarian women might be employed in the following types of work:

a. Cooking, washing, ironing, and general training in household duties;
b. Training in social, domestic and personal hygiene, in sick nursing, and in the campaign against infectious disease;
c. Sewing, knitting, weaving, embroidery, the making of national embroidery and lace, hatmaking, the making of artificial flowers, children's toys and baskets, bookbinding;
d. Typewriting, bookkeeping, telegraph and telephone service, general training in electrotechnics;
e. Cultivation of orchards and kitchen gardens; care of flower gardens for the embellishment of public open spaces;
f. Preserving of different kinds of food (vegetables, fruit, Italian pastes, milk products, etc.);
g. Raising of silkworms and bees, breeding of cattle and poultry;
h. Afforestation and vine culture.[6]

Administration of the women's service was carried on through the central office and the district councils which had been set up by legislation. Special advisory councils upon which public officials and leading women were represented planned the work. The actual development of plans was left to the local governments except that directions of a general nature were provided.

These Bulgarian regulations were put into force in 1922, when it was decided to limit the first call for service to girls from the middle-class families of Sofia. From the 3,000 available workers who were registered, 300 were sent out as office workers among the various ministries. Max Lazard, of the International Labor Office, reported that the women he observed took their work very seriously.[7] In spite of their own good will, however, the work was not very productive, and provision was not made for the utilization of the other 35,000 women available for service. In

[6] *Ibid.*, Sec. 5.
[7] Lazard, *op. cit.*, p. 95.

addition to practical administrative difficulties, there arose the problem of operating cost, and of native customs opposed to the principle of such service for women. For these reasons the compulsory labor service for women in Bulgaria was suspended on June 15, 1923, and has not been resumed.

Women in the German Labor Service

In Germany, work camps for women have been developed on a more extensive scale than in any other country. During 1937 about 20,000 young women were enrolled in the camps. A deputation of these daughters of the soil attended both the 1937 and the 1938 Nazi gatherings at Nüremberg. In 1937 they took part for the first time in the demonstrations with their brothers in the German labor service. The 600 girls eighteen years of age and above who were selected from women's labor camps

> . . . wore heavy shoes with gray socks folded over the tops, earth-colored skirts and white blouses open at the throat. They were hatless, and their hair, blond, brown and black, was neatly coiled at the nape of the neck. They did not parade, but at a given moment they filed out six abreast in two columns, one on each side of the reviewing stand, and formed circles about each of two flagpoles, on which they raised their own flags.[8]

According to a recent statement as reported in the *New York Times* Germany plans eventually to enroll for labor service about 400,000 women.[9]

We have already seen that before the advent of Hitler, in the privately organized camps, young women participated in the labor service, sometimes in the same camps with the men. It was hoped that the voluntary labor service established in July 1931 by the German Republic would help not only the unemployed men, but also the unemployed women, who in 1932 numbered about 400,000.[10] The first women's camp was opened February 1, 1932, and by the end of that year there were 242 camps, with about 10,000 enrollees.[11] Some of the private women's organizations also gave active support to the camp program.

---

[8] Frederick T. Birchall, *New York Times,* September 9, 1937, p. 4.

[9] *New York Times,* January 3, 1939, p. 3.

[10] Margarete Ehlert, "Der freiwillige Arbeitsdienst der weiblichen Jugend," *Reichsarbeitsblatt,* XII, 33 (25. November 1932), Teil II, S. 480.

[11] C. W. Gray, "Labor Service Camps for Women in Germany," *Monthly Labor Review,* XXXVIII, 5 (May 1934), 1079-81.

ʀK CAMPS FOR WOMEN

and below:

A resident center girls in
sippi

ticipants in a Nazi girls

WORK CAMPS FOR WO

Left and above:

Work and play in
girls camps

Below:

Negro girls ironing i
NYA resident center, M
sippi

The principles in accordance with which the women's camps were operated were similar to those for the men. Camp life was built around a work project, and educational activities were not unlike those in the men's camps. However, it was not as easy to find suitable work for the women as for the men, especially work that was economical and did not compete with that of ordinary laborers. Among the tasks assigned to the women were the following: cooking for the men's camps or for needy families, making and repairing clothing for men's camps, gardening and agricultural work, some types of forestry and soil culture, sewing, and various types of social service, for example, helping poor rural and urban mothers with housework and the care of their children. The women's camps were both "closed," or resident, and "open," or "half-open," in which case the girls slept at home and worked and ate in the camp.

One of the most important needs of the women's camps, as of the men's, was for the right type of leadership. It was necessary to have leaders who were experienced in the practical work done in the camps so that they could properly direct the work projects. It was equally necessary that leaders have strong personalities and qualities of leadership. Previous experience in work with girls and women was a desirable requisite. Where possible, leaders with such experience—most of them social workers, teachers, and pastors' wives—were selected. Even those with backgrounds of this type were required to take a training course of from eight to fourteen days.[12]

These pre-Hitler camps for women were successful in providing the limited number of participants with excellent experience, but the labor service for women did not appeal to the imagination of the German people as did that activity for the men. The relief aspect of the camps remained paramount for some time, even under the Nazi government, and their administration was not transferred to the Ministry of the Interior until June 1935. In the meantime, under the Ministry of Labor, they were administered by the Reich Institution for Employment Exchanges and Unemployment Insurance, which

[12] Proclamation of the Federal Commissioner for Voluntary Labor Service for Young Women, quoted in Gertrud Bäumer, *Der freiwillige Arbeitsdienst der Frauen; Grundlagen, Sinn, Praxis und künftige Bedeutung* (Leipzig: Voigtländer, 1933), S. 8-11.

regarded the object of the labor service "chiefly as a means of directing girls from the towns toward employment in the country or in domestic service, and to increase their chances of finding work after they have been through their half year."[13] Under National Socialist direction, however, the educational or propaganda value of the program, as distinguished from the vocational, has been increasingly stressed.

On April 1, 1936 the women's labor service became an integral part of the Reich labor service. In theory labor service is compulsory for German youth of both sexes; in practice it has been compulsory for all young men and those young women who plan to matriculate at a university, although the officials in charge of the service have never lost sight of the goal of universal National Socialist labor service for all young women.[14]

The delay in making the women's service compulsory is due to several reasons. First, it was not so well developed as the men's service in 1935, and an automatic change in its character was impossible. Also, there would have been a large expense involved in extending the service to 600,000 girls a year, and the government considered the development of the men's service more urgent.[15]

The intention of the German government to make the women's labor service compulsory seems borne out by the decree issued by Field Marshal Goering on February 21, 1938, announcing the formal introduction of one year of service in household or farm work for all working girls under the age of twenty-five. Unless a girl has first performed this service, she will not be able to secure a job in private or public enterprises. For practical reasons, office employees and girls working in the textile and tobacco industries were exempted from the application of the decree. The official statement declared:

> If German male youth is willing to serve the Fatherland with spade and arms for two and one-half years, feminine youth will not want to stay behind, but will joyfully do its duty where the Fatherland demands.[16]

---

[13] Helmut Tormin, "Die Zukunft des Frauenarbeitsdienstes," *Soziale Praxis*, September 5, 1935; see also *Industrial and Labor Information*, LVI, 1 (October 7, 1935), 15.

[14] Hanna Röbke, "Unser Ziel: die Arbeitsdienstpflicht," *Der Arbeitsmann*, III, 2 (9. Januar 1937), 4.

[15] *Ibid.*

[16] *New York Times*, February 22, 1938, p. 1; see also Konstantin Hierl, "Ziel und Aufgabe bleiben," *Der Arbeitsmann*, IV, 9 (26. Februar 1938), 1.

The women's labor service under the Hitler regime began by enrolling 10,000 young women every six months for service in about 300 camps. On July 1, 1937 the enrollment was increased to 20,000, and on January 1, 1938, to 25,000.[17]

In 1935 Reich labor leader Hierl appointed an active Nazi party member, Gertrud Scholtz-Klink, to the leadership of the women's labor service. Frau Scholtz-Klink is also the director of the German women's work *(Deutsche Frauenwerk)* through which all the activities of German women are coordinated.

The importance of the women's labor service camps as National Socialist training centers was recognized from the first. Their most important aim is "the molding of the German women into real German women of today." And what is the German woman of today expected to be like?

> She must be able to deny herself luxury and enjoyment; she must be able to work, mentally and physically; she must be mentally and physically healthy, and she must be able to form the life we are forced to live into a beautiful life; she must be acquainted with the needs and dangers that threaten the life of our people. She must gladly do all that is needed of her. In short she must be able to think politically, not party-politically, not in the sense of political struggles with other nations, but in such a manner that she feels, thinks, and sacrifices in common with the whole people.[18]

Through the press and radio programs, and by publications distributed from the central office, young German women between seventeen and twenty-five years of age are encouraged to enroll in the labor service for six months. They are not accepted for enrollment, however, until they have established their Aryan origin and have passed an official medical examination.

For purposes of administering the women's labor service, Germany is divided into thirteen districts. Each district headquarters has a district leader and has charge of the following: service and organization, registration, instruction and recreation programs, physical train-

[17] Information supplied by the office of the *Frauenarbeitsdienst.*

[18] Gertrud Scholtz-Klink, "The German Women's Labor Service," a speech delivered to the International Congress for Domestic Service at Berlin, August 1934, p. 3.

ing, administration, and health service.[19] Each camp is under the direction of a leader, and each leader has three assistants.

Emphasis is now being placed on the possibilities of leadership in the women's labor service as a career, and a careful preliminary training program is being conducted. Women camp leaders are expected to be familiar with economic, household, and social problems and to have had practical experience as well as academic training. They must, of course, be National Socialist in thought, feeling, will, and methods.[20]

Only those who have already spent six months working in the labor service are eligible for leadership training. This period of service must be followed by six months as an "Eldest Comrade" *(Kameradschaftsälteste)*. If ability for leadership has been demonstrated during these periods, there follows a two-year furlough from the service for practical work elsewhere. One year of this period must be spent in a rural college for women (*Landfrauenschule*), one-half year in social work, and the remainder in hospital work. Work as a public health nurse, kindergarten teacher, youth leader, technical teacher, child's nurse—all count toward this required practical experience. During this period quarterly reports on progress must be made to the district office *(Bezirksführung)* with which the candidate is connected.

At the end of these two years, six months must be spent at one of the four district schools (*Bezirkschulen*). A typical daily schedule in a training school for women camp leaders follows:

5:55 A.M.	Arise
6:00 – 6:15	Setting-up exercises
6:15 – 7:00	Washing, bedmaking, dressing
7:00	Flag salute
7:05 – 7:20	Breakfast
7:20 – 8:00	Singing
8:10 – 9:10	Gymnastics and group work
9:30 – 9:45	Second breakfast
9:45 – 12:45 P.M.	Practical work
12:55 – 1:20	Midday meal
1:30 – 2:30	Rest in bed

[19] *Jahrbuch des Reichsarbeitsdienstes,* 1936, S. 31.

[20] "Die Lagerführerin im Deutschen Frauenarbeitsdienst," *Deutscher Arbeitsdienst,* V, 25 (23. Juni 1935), 844.

2:45 – 4:25	Reading time and sports
4:30 – 4:45	Tea
4:45 – 6:00	Classroom instruction
6:30 – 7:00	Evening meal
8:00 – 9:00	Recreation
9:30	Flag salute

Upon the successful completion of all this training, the candidate is eligible for appointment as a camp leader. If she gives continued proof of her ability, she may be promoted to higher positions after having taken additional courses at the Reich school for women leaders *(Reichsführerinnenschule)*.[21]

In compensation for their work, camp leaders receive free board and lodging, clothing, and, according to their education and length of service, 100 to 150 reichmarks ($40 to $60) a month. Assistant leaders receive 50 to 120 reichmarks ($20 to $48). In each camp there are about forty women, including the leader, her three assistants, and three Eldest Comrades. Usually the camps are in rented houses, and of course all of them are now residential. As pocket money the girls receive 20 pfennigs (about 8 cents) daily.

Camp members do all the household work required for the maintenance of the camps. In addition they spend seven hours a day outside of the camp on their work projects, which include aiding rural settlers and farmers by helping with the housework, caring for their children, and sometimes working in the gardens or fields; assisting poor city families by doing housework, nursing the sick and disabled, and caring for the children; and operating kindergartens. Many of these projects are done in cooperation with the National Socialist Welfare Organization, the official social service agency. Of the 382 camps in operation during April 1935, 80 per cent were doing settlement and farm aid work in the country, 15 per cent were doing social service in the cities, and 5 per cent were engaged in agricultural development.[22]

The educational program in the camps, to which about an hour and a half is devoted each day, is intended to prepare the women intellectually, as the work program prepares them physically, to assume the role of obedient, hardworking wives and mothers, who will give their

[21] *Der Arbeitsmann,* III, 10 (6. März 1937), 11.

[22] *Deutscher Arbeitsdienst,* V, 23 (9. Juni 1935), 772.

unquestioning loyalty to the dictates of the Nazi state and who will rear their children in the same faith. The chief importance of women in the development of the National Socialist state lies in their ability to produce children, their willingness to inculcate Nazi doctrines into infant minds, and their economic function as consumers.

The camps give four hours each week to instruction, chiefly of a political nature, and about three hours to gymnastics. The latter period includes twenty minutes of setting-up exercises daily, and a general sports hour once or twice a week. Sports are intended only as a means to build health and provide relaxation after working hours.[23] The girls are under daily medical supervision.

The recreational program includes singing, folk dancing, dramatics, and such handicrafts as weaving and decoration. Community evenings are planned with and for their neighbors, the villagers or peasants.

The following is a sample daily schedule in a women's camp:

5:30 A.M.	Arise
5:35–6:00	Setting-up exercises
6:00–6:45	Bathing, dressing, bedmaking
6:45	Flag salute
6:50–7:30	Breakfast, singing
7:30–3:00 P.M.	Work, with one-half hour free at noon
3:00–4:30	Rest
4:30–5:00	Tea
5:00–6:00	Instruction and sports
6:30–7:00	Evening meal
7:30–9:00	Recreation
9:00	Flag salute
9:30	Lights out

Although all of the camp members are registered in the state employment offices, no specific vocational training is provided in the camps. Apparently, no particular interest is taken in the vocational and employment problems of the labor service members. When the six months of the service have been satisfactorily completed, each enrollee receives a labor pass which entitles her to preferential treatment by the public employment offices.

Rigid discipline is maintained in the women's camps. The leader of

[23] "Sport der Arbeitsmaiden," *Der Arbeitsmann,* II, 30 (25. Juli 1936), 13.

the camps has said: "We do not march as men in the labor service, but we do everything regularly and jointly in accordance with the will of the leader. We rise and retire at the same time. We obey unconditionally. Service and sacrifice are performed without any fuss." [24]

All members of the women's labor service are subject to punishments for acts which injure the honor of the group and public esteem for the labor service, or the comradeship within the service, or which imperil or offend against discipline and order in the labor service. In less serious offenses a reproof, admonition, or reprimand suffices. A few fines are permissible. The most severe punishment is discharge from the service.[25]

To meet the requirements of Hitler's four-year plan women have been encouraged to volunteer for work in the rural service *(Landhilfe)*. After thirteen weeks in the labor service they transfer to the rural service, but must serve in it for at least twenty-six weeks if they are to receive a labor pass. A work certificate from the rural service gives them special advantages if they return to the labor service. Girls above sixteen years of age who volunteered for at least nine months' work in the rural service before November 1, 1938, were not required to enroll in the labor service when it became compulsory.[26]

Among the advantageous results attributed to the work of the women's labor service, Frau Scholtz-Klink believes that the greatest "is the palpable experience of responsibility." She adds to this a new respect for work and valuation of leisure, an increasing respect for simple people on the basis of their social value, and the benefit to the individual girl of sharing life with a group of her contemporaries.[27]

Undoubtedly the labor service for women in Germany does bring girls from the higher economic levels into close touch with the poor of both rural and urban areas. It provides prospective students with an opportunity to obtain practical experience before entering the academic walls. It builds up the young women campers physically. But, like the service for men, it propagandizes them in National Socialist doctrine with all of its fantastic myths of Nordic supremacy, communistic buga-

[24] Scholtz-Klink, *op. cit.*, p. 5.

[25] *Reichsgesetzblatt*, I (1937), 756 ff.

[26] *Deutscher Arbeitsdienst*, V, 19 (12. Mai 1935), 616; see also *Der Arbeitsmann*, I, 15 (10. April 1935), 4.

[27] Scholtz-Klink, *op. cit.*, pp. 4-5.

boos, German preëminence, and the godlike character of Hitler and his satellites. Unofficial reports indicate that there is considerable opposition to the labor service for women in Germany. Refugees from Germany allege that girls returning to their homes from the service are frequently pregnant. The young women on the whole are not enthusiastic about the camp idea, and their parents are reluctant to let them go into the labor service when there are so many rumors, if not facts, concerning morals in the camps.

British Projects for Unemployed Women

No government-sponsored work camp program for young women exists in Great Britain. The only form of labor service open to them is that provided in student camps under private auspices. However, the government has to a limited extent aided unemployed young women to equip themselves to earn their livings, chiefly through home training centers and individual vocational training schemes. In addition the junior instruction centers are open without charge to unemployed girls between the ages of fourteen and eighteen years. The latter do not offer job training, but the other government projects mentioned are definitely vocational.

A survey made in 1920 revealed that the only occupation for women in which a definite shortage of trained workers existed was domestic service. Consequently the central committee proceeded to establish centers to provide training in homecrafts. The courses were thirteen weeks in length; and at least twenty-five, and not more than thirty, hours a week were devoted to instruction in various phases of household work. Also included in the weekly schedule were general education courses, three hours; physical training, one hour; and group singing, one hour.

These courses were open to women between the ages of sixteen and thirty-five years who were unemployed and who were willing to promise to enter domestic service at the end of the course. The women were paid not more than one pound a week as a maintenance allowance, from which they contributed a small amount for their lunches and three shillings a week toward the cost of their outfits. They did not receive unemployment benefit during the training period.

Candidates for the courses were selected by the women's subcommit-

WOMEN IN CAMPS

ove and below:

Girls in NYA resident centers. king furniture models in New mpshire. A typewriting class in ston

ht:

Pre-Hitler Austrian girls sewing m

WOMEN IN CAMPS

Left and above:
Girls in Nazi camps

Below:
Saluting the flag in an N
resident center, Alabama

tees of the employment exchanges or by the juvenile advisory committees. Success in selection was gained through experience. During the first two years of the work the committee found that in spite of the care taken in selecting candidates, there was a considerable turnover in enrollment. On the basis of this experience they concluded that it was false to assume that every able-bodied woman could do domestic work. From 60 to 70 per cent of the women had been factory workers, some of whom found that the variety of duties involved in domestic work was a strain on them, and that they were not sufficiently resourceful to succeed at it.

At the same time that the homecraft centers were established, a homemakers scheme was started, to which unemployed women from eighteen to forty years of age were admitted. These centers differed from the homecraft centers in that they were designed merely to maintain the morale of women who would probably return to their former occupations, by interesting them in their own household problems. The women were not, therefore, required to pledge themselves to go into domestic service, although about one-fourth of them did so. In 1924, because the complaint had arisen that women were receiving inadequate recognition in the spending of relief funds, the two types of courses were merged. At this time the name of the scheme was changed to Home Training Courses, and the work is still known by this name.

During the 1929 depression a demand arose for the admission of girls under sixteen years of age to training given in the centers. This was of course caused by widespread unemployment among girls who had left school at fourteen. In 1929, therefore, a limited number of girls over fifteen were admitted to some of the centers for a course of seventeen, instead of the usual thirteen weeks. At first it was not easy to place such young girls, but as experience was gained in handling them and as mistresses became accustomed to the idea, the difficulty disappeared.

Between 1927 and 1930 one or two centers were maintained where women were trained for household work in Australia and Canada. This work was discontinued in 1930 because the demand from overseas ceased at that time. Since 1934 the committee has also provided short courses for hotel workers, and has had great success in placing those who have completed such courses. The positions obtained are usually for summer work, but a fair proportion of the women later accept permanent domestic employment.

HOME TRAINING COURSES

Year	Number Completing Training			Per Cent Placed in Domestic Employment
	Women	Girls	Total	
1921–24	....	....	23,058	....
1925	....	....	6,575	....
1926	....	....	5,400	66.5
1927	....	....	2,826	66.0
1928	....	....	3,506	....
1929	2,770	1,519	4,289	78.0
1930	2,014	1,928	3,942	89.0
1931	2,979	2,661	5,640	76.0
1932	2,429	2,706	5,135	80.0
1933	2,112	2,570	4,682	83.0
1934	1,355	2,723	4,078	82.0
1935	1,516	2,894	4,410	79.0
1936	1,024	2,262	3,286	96.0
1937	904	2,503	3,407	79.0
Total	17,103	21,730	80,234	

INDIVIDUAL TRAINING SCHEMES

Year	Number of Grants Made
1924–26 [a]	477
1930	216
1931	165
1932	21 (mostly to women above thirty-five years of age)
1933	72 (all but 16 for training as cooks)
1934	79 (all but 18 for training as cooks)
1935	99
1936	169
Total	1,298

[a] Giving grants for assistance was discontinued in June 1926, but was resumed in 1930.

Work Camps for Women in the Netherlands

Successful experience with work camps for unemployed men in Holland resulted in the formation of similar camps to meet the spiritual and material needs of women and girls who were suffering from the effects of unemployment. In 1933 the Catholics began to admit women to their short-term camps. Since 1935 various other private organizations, such as religious groups, the Young Women's Christian Association, and the Socialistic Women's movement, have been encouraged by government subsidy to organize work camps for women.

These camps are under the supervision of the Department of Social Affairs, which has issued uniform regulations for them. Seventy-five per cent of the total cost of the camps is provided by the government, leaving the sponsoring organizations only 25 per cent of the budget to raise among themselves. The camps cost 5 guilders ($2.75) a person per day.

Unemployed young women hear of the camps through the sponsoring organizations, youth organizations, trade unions, and the press. To enter a camp a young woman must be in good health, and eligible for relief. She is required to furnish a reference, usually from her pastor, as to her moral conduct, and she must agree to try to secure work in the field in which she is to be given training. Members of the organizations sponsoring the camps receive preference in the selection of enrollees. The young women, who are between sixteen and thirty years of age, enroll for a period of three months. The first two weeks are considered a trial period, but if a girl stays the full two weeks and subsequently leaves camp without consent before the end of her enrollment period, she is required to pay a fine of .25 guilders (about 14 cents).

The work camps are directed by women, many of whom are from the domestic science departments of the schools. They receive from 15 to 40 guilders ($8.25 to $22.00) a month in addition to their room and board. The camps are housed on former country estates, farms, and the like, and there are usually from forty to eighty young women in each. They are paid 8 to 10 guilders ($4.40 to $5.50) a month, and their transportation to and from camp. Out of this money they must buy their dresses and aprons at the end of the course.

Six to eight hours a day are spent learning housework, cooking, and sewing. Three hours a day are given up to an educational program which is intended: (1) to improve the morale of the young women and orient them in the present-day world; (2) to strengthen their religious faith (especially in camps conducted by church groups); and (3) to teach them that housework and housekeeping is not unpleasant work and can result in much personal satisfaction. Selected teachers conduct courses in social ethics, housekeeping, laundry, dietetics, hygiene, and etiquette. Practice is provided in cooking, cleaning, laundry, sewing, cutting, and alteration of garments. The camps are organized also for recreational games and singing. By dividing the girls into groups of twelve and letting each group select a representative who assists the camp leader, a degree of self-government is achieved.

About 60 per cent of the girls in the camps have not been previously employed, and the program is definitely planned to train them for work as housemaids, parlormaids, cooks, and children's nurses. All of the young women are registered in the employment offices, and a special effort is made by organizations and by the government to help them to find jobs and to adjust to their work. During the first year of the Protestant camp program about 60 per cent of the camp members were placed in jobs.

It is reported that girls who have had camp experience are improved in appearance, bearing, and health, and get along well with others.

Women in the Polish Labor Service

Labor service for young women in Poland is organized along the same lines as that for the young men and is administered by the same central office.[28] It is open to girls between sixteen and twenty years of age, who sew and knit clothes for the men's camps and, in the rural areas, work on farms and in gardens.

The training program for the girls is designed to enable them to earn their living after they leave camp. Each girl is free to choose the type of training she wants, but full training in some one subject is obligatory. In preparing the girls for professional work, different camps

[28] For the training given Polish men, see International Labor Office, *Unemployment among Young Persons*, pp. 113-14.

specialize in the following fields: sewing, domestic economy, domestic nursing, gardening, clerical training, and work for cooperative institutions. All the girls are trained in housework, and special attention is paid to hygiene, and the rational organization of a household. The housework in the camps is carried on entirely by the girls themselves.

Earnest consideration is also given to the practical training of girls in cooperative work. All camps have cooperative stores for food products, stationery, and toilet articles. Some of the camps organize labor cooperatives in sewing, hairdressing, bookbinding, etc.

Two types of camps are used for girls — "closed" camps, provided with dormitories, and "open" camps without sleeping accommodations. In August 1936, there were only 700 women enrolled in the Polish labor service. It was recognized at the time that this was a small number, but the service was only beginning. In the summer of 1937 there were seven camps. Two of these provided training in farming and gardening and had workshops; one was specially designed for rural work; the remaining four gave workshop training.

Jan Rosner, in the course of his observations of Polish camps for the International Labor Office, visited one for girls at Raszyn near Warsaw, and was very favorably impressed. The girls lived in a house with modern conveniences, under conditions definitely better than those in the Polish men's camps at that time. The house was a model of cleanliness, and the atmosphere particularly impressive. Although discipline was strict, the relations between the girls and their director and leaders, all of them women, were more friendly than was usual in the men's camps between the campers and their directors. In short, in the women's camps cooperation took the place of subordination, and the result was a homelike and contented atmosphere seldom found in the young men's camps.[29]

Women in the Austrian Labor Service

Women's camps were established in Austria in August 1933 to meet the essential relief needs of unemployed women for food, shelter, and clothing, and in some degree to satisfy important educational and social

[29] "Productive Occupation for Unemployed Young Workers in Poland," *International Labor Review*, XXXI, 4 (April 1935), 529-30.

needs. The first model camp was established at Gugging, near Vienna,[30] as an experiment. Changing official attitudes toward the labor service in Austria were reflected in the women's labor service in changing emphasis in the aims of the program. The camps continued to function as part of a relief program, but the importance of the work projects was minimized, and the chief aim became to restore women to the home and to teach them to perform joyfully all their womanly tasks.[31]

Various social welfare groups, such as the National Association for the Protection of Maternity and Youth at Work, were instrumental in developing the first women's camps. Later their activities were coordinated by the Women's Council of the Fatherland Front *(Frauenreferat der Vaterländischen Front)*, of which Princess von Starhemberg was the leader, in cooperation with the Ministry of Social Administration. The president of the board of examiners for the camps was a civil servant from the Ministry of Social Administration.

One Austrian camp for women that was visited by the writer was housed in a large building which had formerly been a private residence. The twenty-eight young women in the camp were spending their time repairing clothes for the men in work camps. Most of the girls came from the near-by village and had been selected by a local committee familiar with their problems, but some were from as far away as Vienna. Nearly all enrollees were daughters of poor peasants and workers.

A typical day's schedule was to rise at six o'clock, work from eight to twelve, rest from twelve to two, work from two to five, and then have study courses or recreation from five to eight in the evening. From eight until ten their time was their own. The household work was done, with the aid of one professional cook, by groups of five or six girls who, for two weeks at a time, assumed almost full responsibility for camp maintenance. The women seemed to be enthusiastic about the camp life, if one could judge by the singing, laughter, and gay conversation which were audible.

---

[30] "Relief Works in Austria: Voluntary Labor Camps for Girls," *Industrial and Labor Information*, XLVIII, 12 (December 18, 1933), 368.

[31] Ruth von Hout, "Zielsetzung des weiblichen Arbeitsdienstes," *Der Oesterreichische Arbeitsdienst*, I, 5 (Oktober-November 1935), 9-10.

These camps were financed out of relief funds assigned to the Ministry of Social Administration, and the government subsidy almost entirely covered their expenses, which amounted to about 2 or 2.2 schillings a day (38 to 41 cents). In 1937 the appropriation for the women's camps was 800,000 schillings (about $149,600).

Women were recruited for the labor service by the employment offices, relief and publicity agencies, and the Women's Council of the Fatherland Front. Their enrollment was entirely voluntary, but in order to participate in the camps they were required to be Austrian citizens, needy, in good health, and willing to work. Each enrollee was given a health examination before admission to camp and was insured against illness, thus entitling her to free medical treatment. The enrollment period was forty weeks, although enrollees were allowed to remain longer.

The majority of the women in the camps were between sixteen and twenty-five years of age. Older women were permitted to enroll in the camps if they were receiving, or had received, unemployment benefit. Enrollees received from 20 to 50 groschen (4 to 9 cents) a day as pocket money. During 1936 and 1937, 1,500 women were enrolled in the labor service.

The camps were directed by women who had attended a school for camp leaders and who had passed an examination. The leaders received salaries varying from 50 to 100 schillings ($9.35 to $18.70) a month.

The camps were housed in vacant public buildings such as schools, and usually contained from twenty-five to thirty-five young women, depending upon the accommodations available. Both "open" (nonresidential) and "closed" (residential) camps were used for women.

The work projects consisted of sewing and mending old clothes for the Winter Help or Relief *(Winterhilfe)*, mending and washing clothes and uniforms for the men's camps, working in the kitchen garden that was attached to almost every camp, and performing various types of social service, such as helping mothers, caring for children and the sick, and working in maternity and welfare institutions.[32] Enrollees were occupied at these projects eight hours a day, forty-two hours a week.

[32] League of Nations, Assembly, 16th Ordinary Session, *Fifth Committee*, September 1935, p. 24.

In every camp an educational program was organized, having the following aims: (1) to establish or re-establish courage and self-confidence in young women who had come to adult life during the period of extreme economic depression; (2) to reorient those who had been out of school a number of years and who were faced with a new set of problems and interests; (3) to teach young women housework; and (4) to help them to be patriotic. Camp leaders and trained teachers conducted classes by the discussion method in home economics, German, religion, and health. Supplementary workshop activities were provided, and the recreational program included gymnastics, exercises, sports, and folk songs. Two hours a day were devoted to educational work, with additional time given to recreational activities. All camp members were required to participate in the entire program.

Noticeable changes took place in the appearance and bearing of the young women while they were in camp. Their general health improved, they learned to organize their time, and to get along with others. All of them were taught housework, and an effort was made to improve their employability by raising their morale and bettering their social attitudes. The enrollees were registered in the employment offices and, although 50 per cent of them had never been employed before entering the labor service, many of them did secure positions afterwards.

The women's camps in Austria, like those for men, have now been incorporated in the German labor service. The camp program for Austrian women in the future will be, therefore, essentially the same as that for the German women described earlier in this chapter.

Conclusion

Since labor camps for women have not been developed on as great a scale as men's camps, it is difficult to evaluate their achievement. Leaders of women's camps seem to be in general agreement that camp experience improves the appearance, health, and employability of young women, and that it teaches them how to get along with other people. On the whole, however, work camps for women have not been so successful as have the camps for men, but neither have they received the sustained public support and interest that the men's work camps have.

The relative failure of the women's camps has been due (1) to the difficulty of finding satisfactory work projects; (2) to the young women's lack of interest in the camp; (3) to the failure to provide the camps with well qualified leaders; and (4) to the insufficient appropriations for their maintenance. When funds for relief projects were limited, preference was almost always given to projects for men.

Bibliography

General

HENRI FUSS. "Unemployment and Employment among Women," *International Labor Review*, XXXI, 4 (April 1935), 463-97.

LEAGUE OF NATIONS. Child Welfare Committee, 10th session, April 17, 1934.

"Protection of Children and Young People from the Consequences of the Economic Depression and Unemployment; Information Supplied by Various International Organizations of Women." C.P.E. 440. Geneva: Secretariat, 1934. 20 pp.

Austria

"Relief Works in Austria; Voluntary Labor Camps for Girls," *Industrial and Labor Information*, XLVIII, 12 (December 18, 1933), 368.

"Voluntary Labor Camps for Girls in Austria," *Industrial and Labor Information*, LXII, 7 (May 17, 1937), 257-58.

RUTH VON HOUT. "Zielsetzung des weiblichen Arbeitsdienstes," *Der Oesterreichische Arbeitsdienst*, I, 5 (Oktober-November 1935), 9-10.

Germany

GERTRUD BÄUMER. *Der freiwillige Arbeitsdienst der Frauen; Grundlagen, Sinn, Praxis und künftige Bedeutung*. Leipzig: Voigtländer, 1933. 35 S.

BEINTKER. *Der deutsche Arbeitsdienst in Frage und Antwort*. Leipzig: Armanen-Verlag, 1934. S. 22.

ROBERT A. BRADY. *The Spirit and Structure of German Fascism*. New York: Viking, 1937. Chap. VI, "Women, the Cradle, and the Plow."

FRITZ EDEL. *German Labor Service*, Berlin: Terramare, 1937, pp. 26-30.

ELIZABETH L. FACKT. "The German Frauenwerk," *Journal of the American Association of University Women*, XXX, 3 (April 1937), 135-41.

"German Women's Labor Service," *Industrial and Labor Information*, LVI, 1 (October 7, 1935), 13-15.

Das Gesicht des Arbeitsdienstes für die weibliche Jugend. Berlin: Müller, n.d. 28 S.

C. W. GRAY. "Labor Service Camps for Women in Germany," *Monthly Labor Review*, XXXVIII, 5 (May 1934), 1079-81.

HERMANN KRETZSCHMANN and FRITZ EDEL. *Der Arbeitsdienst in Wort und Bild*. Berlin: Deutscher Verlag für Politik und Wirtschaft, 1936, S. 59-62.

"Die Lagerführerin im Deutschen Frauenarbeitsdienst," *Deutscher Arbeitsdienst,* V, 25 (23. Juni 1935), 844.

REICHSLEITUNG DES REICHSARBEITSDIENSTES. Amt Pressechef beim Reichsarbeitsführer. *Die Arbeitsmaid.* Berlin: Allstein, n.d. 51 S.

HANNA RÖBKE. "Arbeitsdienst für die weibliche Jugend," *Jahrbuch des Reichsarbeitsdienstes* 1936, S. 46-48.

——— "Die Erziehung im Arbeitsdienst für die weibliche Jugend," *International Education Review,* VI, 4-5 (1937), 284-88.

GERTRUD SCHOLTZ-KLINK. *The German Women's Labor Service,* n.d. 6 pp.

"Sport der Arbeitsmaiden," *Der Arbeitsmann,* II, 30 (25. Juli 1936), 13.

Great Britain

CENTRAL COMMITTEE ON WOMEN'S TRAINING AND EMPLOYMENT. *Second Interim Report for the Period Ending December 31, 1922.* London: H. M. Stationery Office, 1923. 42 pp.

MADELINE ROOFF. *Youth and Leisure; a Survey of Girls' Organizations in England and Wales.* Edinburgh: Constable, 1935. 264 pp.

Poland

"Polnische Mädel arbeiten," *Tribune of the Young Generation,* IV (August 1936), 27-28.

Camps in Other Countries

As has been indicated earlier in this book, labor camps of one type or another are found in nearly thirty different countries of the world. While space will not permit consideration of all of these systems of camps in detail, a few paragraphs about some of them may be enlightening.

Belgium

"In Belgium the government leaves the initiative in matters connected with the general and vocational education of young unemployed persons to the local authorities, to occupational organizations, and to organizations set up to promote the welfare of the younger generation, while giving every encouragement to such schemes."[1] For the most part, these schemes deal with the organization of general and vocational courses for the young unemployed.

Since 1933 the government has required that juveniles between fifteen and eighteen years of age who wish to receive *unemployment* benefits must prove that they have actually been employed for not less than six months, that they have followed for at least two years a full-time course in an industrial, vocational, or general education center established or approved by the government, or that they have worked under an approved contract of apprenticeship. Even to receive *relief* benefits, persons under twenty-one years of age *may* be required to follow available vocational courses.

Some private organizations, by 1933, had already set up work centers or camps for young unemployed persons, offering both vocational and cultural instruction. At a congress held in Antwerp in September 1934 the Christian Employers Association recommended the establishment of a labor service for unemployed youth sixteen to twenty-four years of age, and in 1935 the Young Catholic Workers' Association reported to the Fifth Committee of the League of Nations Assembly that it had

[1] International Labor Service, *Unemployment among Young Persons,* p. 68.

formed camps to which unemployed youth were periodically admitted and that these young people were able to train for some occupation and follow suitable courses and lessons.

On September 30, 1935, a Royal Order was issued empowering the Minister of Labor and Social Welfare to grant subsidies from public funds to organize voluntary labor centers for youth. The receipt of this subsidy was contingent on previous approval of the plan for a camp by the National Employment and Unemployment Office. The subsidies for these centers have continued to be granted, and, in 1936, 1,000,000 francs ($168,000) of the budget were earmarked for labor centers. The Minister of Labor and Social Welfare has the power to fix the amount of subsidy to be paid each center. In order that the largest possible number may have the advantage of experience in the center, enrollees are required to stay at least fifteen days, but cannot stay longer than thirty days. Proof is required of the eligibility of persons so aided. One camp is reserved for unemployed young women.

The purpose of these centers, according to the decree, is to enable youth to restore their physical and moral health and to avert idleness and discouragement. A Ministerial Order of May 23, 1936 established a four- to six-hour work day at the centers, and required that at least one hour a day be devoted to physical exercise and two to education.

Hungary[2]

The best developed work service in Hungary is that of the Hungarian Students Union. This Union held its first camp in the summer of 1933. The organization at first operated under financial handicaps, but by 1936 it was receiving the assistance of both the national and the local governments. In 1935 fifty students and sixty professional workers attended a camp and cooperated on a project for the improvement of dikes. In 1936 there were five camps in all, including one camp for leaders. For a two-week period the prospective leaders received both practical and theoretical training, including instruction in camp discipline, patriotic subjects, and sports. Projects for the men included work on roads and highways, and the building and repairing of dikes.

[2] *Arbeitsdienst in der Welt,* S. 107-8; see also *Der Arbeitsmann,* 18 (1. Mai 1937), S. 7, and *Planning of Public Works in Relation to Employment,* p. 181.

ORK PROJECTS IN
FERENT COUNTRIES

:

ilding low-cost houses
Vienna

:

mmunity center built
YA boys in Mississippi

:

CC workers making
shingles, Morristown,
.

WORK PROJECTS IN DIFFEREN
COUNTRIES

Above:

A pre-Hitler project near the
Canal

Left:

Friends service camp project D
Cooperative Farm, Mississippi

Below:

CCC enrollees building drains

The women's camps helped peasant families with their work in house, garden, and field. The camp period was divided into three-week terms, beginning on June 20 and closing on September 20. The mornings were devoted to work, while afternoons were given over to recreation and patriotic instruction. Foreign students were permitted to attend these camps, just as Hungarian students were privileged to attend work camps in other countries.

A few voluntary camps for the unemployed have been in operation since 1935 for groups of from ten to fifty persons, who undertake work needed in their localities. The workers continue to live at home and are paid from 8 to 20 pengös ($1.36 to $3.40) a week.

Besides providing work camps for unemployed youth, Budapest and other cities have also provided nonmanual work for intellectuals. In 1934 approximately a thousand intellectuals were cared for in this way at a cost of about 1,000,000 pengös ($170,000). With the approval of the Ministry of Education, the National Committee of Unemployed Graduates attempts to increase the demand for nonmanual and professional workers through the radio and the press.[3]

Estonia[4]

In May 1935 the Estonian Ministry of Agriculture opened an experimental camp for young unemployed persons, in the neighborhood of Tallinn, the capital city. The camp accommodated about a hundred young people between the ages of seventeen and twenty-five who were employed at agricultural and land settlement work. Lectures and recreational activities were part of the camp program. Strict discipline was maintained.

The workers were paid the prevailing wage rate. Twenty-five per cent of the pay of unmarried workers and 15 per cent of that of married workers were deposited in savings accounts to be given them when they left camp. Food was prepared for the workers by the Tallinn branch of the Y.M.C.A., which received a subsidy of sixty cents per person for the purpose.

[3] *Ibid.*

[4] *Industrial and Labor Information,* IV, 3 (July 15, 1935), 104; see also *Planning of Public Works in Relation to Employment,* p. 169.

Free City of Danzig [5]

The government-sponsored labor service in the Free City of Danzig has developed similarly to that in Germany. Voluntary labor service came into existence April 1, 1932, and was converted into a compulsory service on June 19, 1934, more than a year before the Nazi government in Germany took similar action, and while the Danzig Nazis still had only a bare majority of votes in the Volkstag.

The order which created this compulsory service aimed (1) to carry out public works of national economic and cultural importance; (2) to turn out young citizens conscious of their duties towards the state; (3) to mold the young into a social unit by enabling them to serve the state side by side; and (4) to help win respect for manual labor in every class of the population.

All citizens between the ages of seventeen and twenty-five years are required to spend one year in the labor service. Exceptions, however, are made for certain classes of youth—those who are physically unfit for manual labor, those who are the breadwinners of families, and those who are in school. Besides board and lodging, work clothes, tools, and a small daily allowance, the men receive free medical care when they are ill and compensation insurance in case of accidents.

In Danzig the service is administered by the Senate, a body which combines legislative and executive functions. The policy here, too, is that the labor service must not compete with free labor or result in the dismissal of regularly employed workers.

Latvia [6]

In 1935 the Minister of Social Welfare decided to establish labor centers for young unemployed students and university men. These centers, known as labor clubs, are composed of groups of from ten to fifteen students and graduates registered at employment exchanges. Clubs choose their instructors from among graduates of agricultural colleges, students of agriculture, and persons with practical knowledge,

[5] International Labor Service, *op. cit.*, pp. 101-2; see also *Industrial and Labor Information*, XLV, 13 (March 27, 1933), 377; *ibid.*, LI, 4 (July 23, 1934), 152-93; and *Planning of Public Works in Relation to Employment*, p. 169.

[6] *Planning of Public Works in Relation to Employment*, pp. 181-82.

and members employ their work time improving the appearance of roads and public buildings by planting trees, farm work, and various types of agricultural work. The cost of administering the labor clubs is borne by the Ministry of Social Welfare, and each club member receives a monthly allowance of 60 lats ($19.80) from the Unemployment Fund, while the instructor receives 100 lats ($33.00). Institutions or individuals for whom the work is done provide the members with free lodging, and farmers are required to supply cooking utensils and firewood. Members are entitled to the same medical care as state employees.

Luxemburg

A Grand-ducal Order of March 14, 1936 set forth measures for organizing vocational training and land settlement centers for young unemployed persons in Luxemburg, based on the recommendations adopted by the International Labor Conference in 1935.

The state has established centers for young unemployed persons at its own expense and also has carried half the expense incurred by local authorities in establishing such centers. The object has been to train prospective employees for manual occupations and also for land settlement.[7]

The program of vocational training in the centers includes apprenticeship in an industrial, handicraft, or agricultural occupation, and supplementary instruction in such subjects as bookkeeping, technology, elementary principles of hygiene and safety, and social insurance.

The work projects of the centers have been centered on the reclamation and development of lands belonging to the community. These reclaimed lands are then leased for long periods to workers who have assisted in their development or to their families.

Unemployed persons admitted to these centers must not be more than twenty-four years old if they intend to take up agriculture. If their vocational preference is along another line, however, they cannot be admitted until they are twenty-one years or older. The centers cannot employ the participants more than forty hours a week. During their leisure time they are free to engage in physical training and sports or to visit industrial plants and factories.

---

[7] *Ibid.*, p. 171.

Room and board for the youth on these projects are provided in hostels at the expense of the state. Young persons receiving such maintenance, if they are also entitled to unemployment benefit, receive as a cash payment only 50 per cent of the total amount contributed for the plan, which is the amount paid by the local authorities. The allowance to an individual ordinarily consists of a basic sum of 12 francs a work day, plus 1.5 francs each work day for an unemployed dependent, and a supplementary amount for every hour of work actually performed, the rate being fixed by the Director of Labor and Social Welfare.

State and local authorities may pay to young persons not entitled to unemployment allowances, or to their parents, a sum not to exceed the normal amount of unemployment allowance for every day spent in a center. Equipment and transportation may be provided by centers.[8]

Rumania[9]

The *Official Monitor* of March 24, 1937, published the Law for the Organization of Work of Public Utility, which launched the Rumanian Labor Service, and workers were soon enrolled. The Rumanian labor service seeks "to work for the development of cohesion of the different social classes by means of the education of youth through fundamental, well-ordered work on projects useful to the country." For this reason the Rumanian government requires labor service of all Rumanian youth as part of their premilitary training.

Camps and work projects may be organized either by the state or by public organizations under state authorization, and this authorization may be given by the Council of Ministers on the recommendation of the Minister of Labor. The Ministry of Labor not only arranges for the state labor service and supervises camps and work projects of other organizations but also undertakes to assist with the training programs. The labor service office accepts or rejects plans and budgets submitted for projects, but the technical leadership is supplied by the organization for which the work is to be done. Persons or organiza-

---

[8] *Industrial and Labor Information,* LVIII, 4 (April 27, 1936), 98-99.

[9] Müller-Brandenburg in *Der Arbeitsmann* (15 Mai 1937), S. 7.

VORK PROJECTS IN DIFFERENT COUNTRIES

e:

vaging stones from an old coke oven, ds service camp

t:

C boys constructing farm building at Wal-Arkansas

v:

hletic field in the dunes of the Isle of Sylt by a pre-Hitler German labor camp

WORK PROJECTS IN
FERENT COUNTRI

Left:

CCC enrollees at w

Lower left:

Members of a pre-I
work camp harvesting
toes

Below:

Nazi labor service
pulling out stumps

tions who seek to use labor service on their projects without permission of the state are severely punished.

Camp leaders are selected from among reserve officers and individuals receiving military training so as to give them practical experience in handling and instructing men. The leader of the labor service, or the general inspector of public utility work, is under the supervision of the Minister of Labor but is generally an army man.

Work on the projects has included: road and railroad building, dam building, irrigation and drainage, sanitation work, insect and plant disease control, afforestation, soil cultivation, building of athletic fields, building of shelters for the use of the army, the premilitary training groups, and the labor service, and archaeological excavations.

Workmen are usually employed near their homes. If employed at a greater distance, however, the men are housed in public or private buildings, buildings belonging to premilitary training service, or in barracks. Those who desert or who are disobedient are punished in accordance with premilitary training rules.

Union of South Africa [10]

On May 1, 1933 the Department of Defense organized a special service battalion in which unemployed youth between seventeen and twenty-two years of age might enlist. The purpose of the Department is three-fold: (1) to provide a means of temporary employment for the better educated young men who would otherwise be out of work; (2) to sustain the morale of the younger generation and by means of military discipline to create more self-reliant citizens; and (3) ultimately to find suitable and more permanent means of employment after a period of military training. The plan provides for the military and physical training of 1,990 youth. A limited number of the same group are also given vocational training with the hope that they can be placed in permanent employment after nine to twelve months in the service.

The battalion was organized as a unit of the permanent defense forces and serves as a reserve from which such government departments as defense, police, prisons, etc., may draw suitable recruits.

---

[10] *Industrial and Labor Information,* L, 2 (April 9, 1934), 54-55; LXIII, 1 (July 5, 1937), 29.

In addition to being clothed, housed, and fed, the members of the battalion receive a minimum daily pay of 1 shilling (25 cents). The staff of the battalion consists of trained officials from the Department of Defense.

Canada

In the autumn of 1932 more than 70,000 single homeless men in Canada were unemployed and had no prospects of employment. An Order in Council of October 8, 1932 provided for the care of 2,000 of these men until March 21, 1933.[11] Labor camps were set up by the Department of National Defense in cooperation with the Department of Labor, and since these were successful, others were established. A total of 35,000 men were provided for in this way between November 1, 1933 and March 31, 1934.

Most of the supervisory and administrative staff for these camps were selected from married men with dependents, who had the necessary qualifications and were in need of relief. Military personnel were in charge of only a few of the camps. The projects were open to all homeless single men in need of relief who were free from communicable disease and physically fit for manual labor. As would be expected many of the enrollees were under twenty-five years of age.

The work projects included the development of landing fields for the Trans-Canadian Airway, building municipal airports, forestry work, highway construction, and the restoration of historic buildings. During the winter when road work was impossible, simply constructed buildings were begun. All work was selected so that its execution did not deprive anyone of work under normal conditions.

Men were encouraged to work at their own trades, and young men were given an opportunity to work as tradesmen's helpers. Return to normal employment was aided by the camp authorities and free transportation was given to men who secured jobs. As a result men were constantly leaving the camps to go back to private jobs in industry. Men were also permitted to engage in seasonal employment and were taken back into the camp at its termination if they desired.[12]

---

[11] International Labor Service, *op. cit.*, pp. 95-100.

[12] *Ibid.*, p. 100.

The men who enrolled were given free transportation to the camps, where they were housed in barracks or tents. The food supplied the campers was the standard army ration. Each worker was given an outfit of clothing and a supply of smoking tobacco. He was also entitled to twenty cents for each day of actual work. The health of the participants was given special attention, and qualified doctors were available at any time to provide medical care.

Camp facilities provided for such educational and recreational activities as outdoor sports, indoor games, reading, and listening to the radio. Instruction in elementary subjects was given in the evenings for those who wished it, and in certain camps vocational courses were also available.

On February 15, 1934, 108 schemes were in active operation, two had been completed, and thirteen closed down for the winter. At that date the authorized enrolled strength was 24,697, but the actual strength was only 19,725.[13] On July 1, 1936 these relief camps for single homeless men were closed by the government, but arrangements were made for the men to be employed on railway work.[14] At the present time, camps and other projects for youth are being studied by Canadian officials and private organizations[15] and it is possible that some type of camp program will again be developed during 1939.

New Zealand

Several relief work projects employing men between the ages of twenty and twenty-five years have been instituted by the Unemployment Board in New Zealand. Most of these provide partial employment for a large number of men in the chief centers of population. A considerable number of men (most of them unmarried) have also been placed in camps established in cooperation with the Public Works Department. They are doing such work as constructing and repairing roads and highways, improving land, and planting trees.

[13] *The Labor Gazette,* March 1934, pp. 228-30; see also International Labor Service, *op. cit.,* 1935, pp. 99-100.

[14] *Planning of Public Works in Relation to Employment,* p. 168.

[15] *Ibid.,* p. 171.

Australia

The state of Victoria in Australia has a Youths' and Forests' Conservation Plan for which funds have been made available both by the Commonwealth and by the state government. The plan provides for the employment in forest camps of a thousand young men between the ages of sixteen and twenty years for enrollment periods of six months. The young men work thirty-six hours a week and receive a pound ($4.96) a week in wages, out of which they pay for their food and clothing. Under expert supervision they receive practical training in forestry work, road making, and bridge building. Living conditions in the camps are satisfactory, but are not so comfortable that they will keep youth from seeking private employment.[16]

In Tasmania the Forestry Department has been operating several camps for young men under the ages of twenty-one, nineteen, and eighteen years respectively. The boys are paid wages at rates graduated according to their age. The average number of men in each of the camps has been seventy. While there is rather strict camp discipline, no military training is permitted and much of the job training is given informally. The aim of the program is to give employment and also to train the young men for useful citizenship by developing habits of self-help, self-reliance, and cooperation.[17]

Japan [18]

In Japan various forms of labor service exist sponsored by both public and private organizations, and both rural and urban units of government have experimented with work camps as a means of helping unemployed young people. Since 1936 the urban camps have been subsidized by the central government and uniform standards have been established for them.

In 1936 there were thirteen of these camps with 422 participants enrolled for a period of six months, and plans for 1937 called for

---

[16] *Industrial and Labor Information,* LVIII, 4 (April 27, 1936), 93; LXII, 12 (June 21, 1937), 528-29.

[17] *Ibid.,* LXII, 12 (June 21, 1937), 528-29.

[18] Second International Work Camp Conference, *Training Camps in Japan;* see also "Conditions in Japan," *Industrial and Labor Information,* LIX, 5 (August 3, 1936) 162-63.

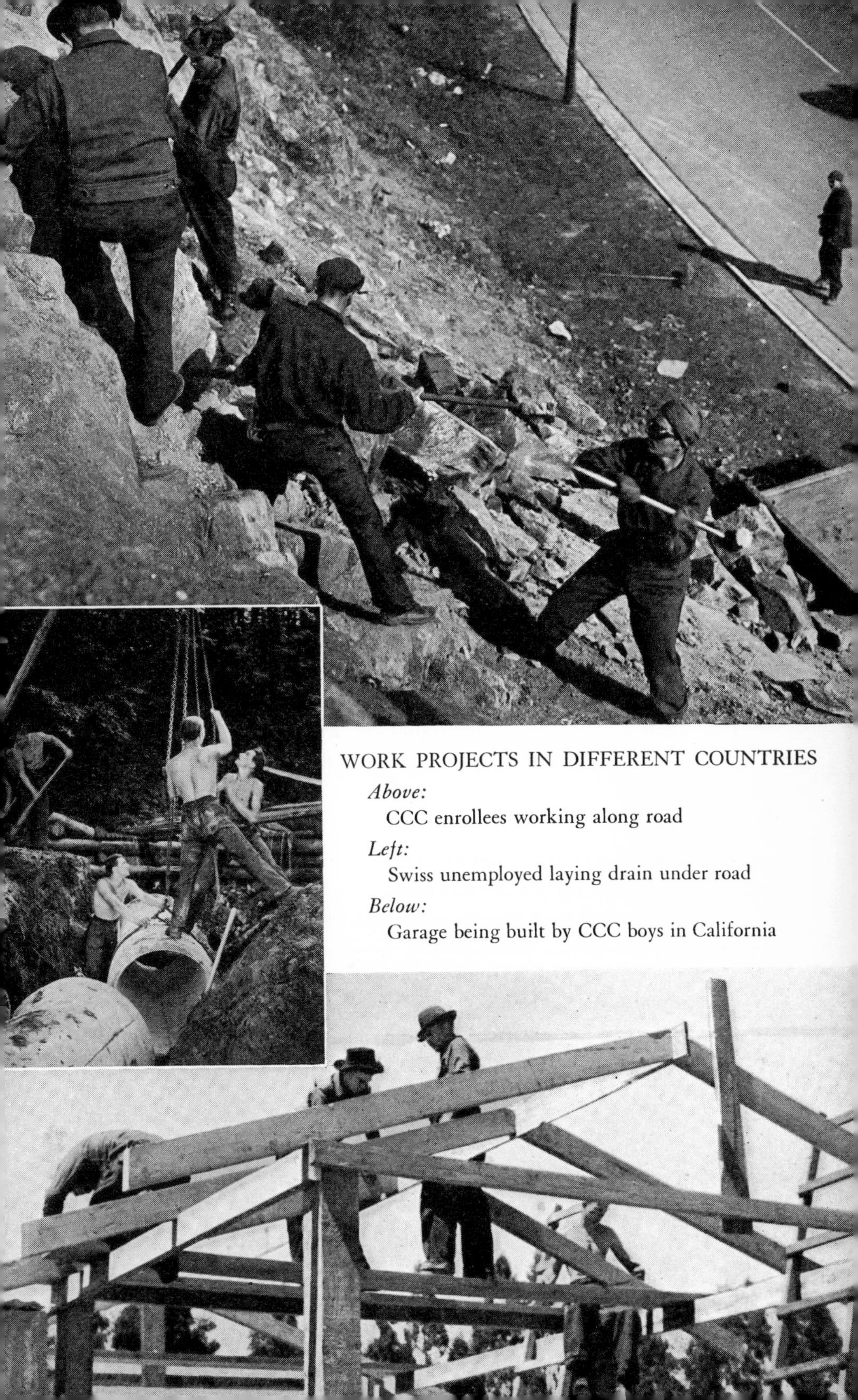

WORK PROJECTS IN DIFFERENT COUNTRIES

Above:
CCC enrollees working along road

Left:
Swiss unemployed laying drain under road

Below:
Garage being built by CCC boys in California

WORK PROJECTS IN DIFFERENT COUNTRIES

Upper right and middle:

Before and after the drainage work of Nazi campers in southern Bavaria, Germany

Below:

CCC enrollees clearing debris at Grand Teton National Park

1,000 enrollees. The camps are administered by the governments of prefectures and cities, or by agencies designated by them. The state subsidy covers the cost of the work projects, the salaries of the staff, the rent of the camps, the initial cost, and half of the running expenses.

Most of the enrollees are single men under thirty-five years of age. They must be chosen from among the registered unemployed, be of good moral habits, have sufficient physical stamina to endure hard work, and be free from contagious diseases. Enrollees are required to pay for their own food and half the cost of their simple uniforms. In order to encourage habits of thrift and to provide the enrollees with a cash reserve when they leave the camps, about 40 per cent of their earnings are put into a savings fund.

The chief aim of the camps is to strengthen the morale of the participants, many of whom have been unemployed for a number of years, and to provide both vocational and character training. There is one teacher for every twenty to thirty men. The men work eight and one-half hours a day, and each evening an hour is set aside for lectures on ethics and civics or for recreation.

A camp at Kobe takes care of unemployed intellectual workers, and one in Tokyo trains men for farm work in Manchukuo. The other camps train manual workers. After the completion of an enrollment period the men are aided in securing jobs.

A German visitor to Japan during 1938 reported that the prefect of Miyazaki, which is an agricultural district, has started on his own initiative a labor service which is financed from provincial funds. Recruits between the ages of thirteen and twenty are secured from out-of-school youth by schools and youth organizations. During 1938 there were about 400 work sites with about 90,000 young people employed, for the most part, in their own neighborhoods. The work projects included erecting barriers to prevent the movements of dunes, cultivating land for tea planting, weeding, and laying out playgrounds. The workers received no compensation for their efforts, but were provided with food and clothing. The boys and girls worked in separate groups under the leadership of young teachers. The German observer pointed out that, as is true of the *Reichsarbeitsdienst,* the economic value of the work accomplished is secondary in importance to the major goal of educating the younger generation.[19]

In addition to these government experiments with labor service there exists in Japan a religious group called *Itto-en,* meaning Brotherhood of the One Light, whose members devote their lives to a "sacred labor service" and by giving up their worldly possessions, identify themselves with the servant class in the performance of menial labor. With the members of this brotherhood, work is a form, indeed almost the chief form, of religious expression. Members of the cult are sent out from the organization headquarters upon request to perform such tasks as sweeping and cleaning, to act as manservant, maidservant, or nurse, or to perform skilled work, such as teaching and translating. They receive only food and transportation for their services, but the brotherhood guards them against exploitation and supplies them with the minimum necessities of life.

The *Itto-en* maintains factories, farms, shops, and inns in which members work side by side with ordinary workmen receiving wages. It also runs a school for young people between the ages of twelve and twenty-four. The relief work performed by this order during the 1923 earthquake in Japan was similar in kind and spirit to that which the International Voluntary Service has performed in other parts of the world.[20]

Bibliography

Australia

"The Situation in Australia; Juvenile Unemployment," *Industrial and Labor Information,* LVIII, 4 (April 27, 1936), 93.

"The Situation in Australia; Unemployment among Young Persons Recommendation," *Industrial and Labor Information,* LXII, 12 (June 21, 1937), 528-29.

Belgium

"Conditions in Belgium; Employment Centers for Young Persons," *Industrial and Labor Information,* LIX, 5 (August 3, 1936), 159.

"Employment Centers for Young Workers in Belgium," *Industrial and Labor Information,* LVI, 6 (November 11, 1935), 220-21.

"The Situation in Belgium; Employment Centers for Young Persons," *Industrial and Labor Information,* LVIII, 7 (May 18, 1936), 190.

[19] *Der Arbeitsmann,* F. 19 (7. Mai 1938), S. 11.

[20] Information supplied by Miss Teresina Rowell, former resident of an Itto-en community.

"The Situation in Belgium; Proposals of Christian Employers," *Industrial and Labor Information*, LII, 3 (October 15, 1934), 87.

Canada

D. M. SUTHERLAND. "Unemployment Relief Camps in Canada," *The Labor Gazette*, March 1934, pp. 228-30.

Danzig

"Compulsory Labor Service in Danzig," *Industrial and Labor Information*, LI, 4 (July 23, 1934), 152-53.

"Voluntary Labor Service in Danzig," *Industrial and Labor Information*, XLV, 13 (March 27, 1933), 377.

Estonia

"A Camp for Young Unemployed Persons in Estonia," *Industrial and Labor Information*, LV, 3 (July 15, 1935), 104.

France

EDWIN A. PLITT. "French Labor Camps for the Unemployed," *Monthly Labor Review*, XL (May 1935), 1184.

"Measures against Unemployment in France; Centers for Young Unemployed Persons," *Industrial and Labor Information*, LVI, 5 (November 4, 1935), 178-79.

Japan

"Conditions in Japan; Training Camps for the Unemployed," *Industrial and Labor Information*, LIX, 5 (August 3, 1936), 162-63.

Luxemburg

"Centers for Young Unemployed Persons in Luxemburg," *Industrial and Labor Information*, LVIII, 4 (April 27, 1936), 98-99.

Rumania

Der Arbeitsmann, III, 2 (9. Januar 1937), S. 15; III, 20 (15. Mai 1937), S. 7.

Union of South Africa

"The Situation in South Africa; the Special Service Battalion," *Industrial and Labor Information*, L, 2 (April 1934), 54-55.

"Unemployment among Young Persons in South Africa," *Industrial and Labor Information*, LXIII, 1 (July 5, 1937), 29.

Summary and Conclusion

THE CAMPS of the Civilian Conservation Corps and the resident centers of the National Youth Administration have developed in the United States as a new type of institution to provide training and educational opportunities for youth, bridge the gap between the leaving of school and permanent employment, and provide food and shelter for youth from the lower economic levels. In deciding whether or not these institutions should become a permanent part of American life it was suggested in the first chapter of this book that something might be learned from the experiences of other countries with labor camps, especially where these projects have become permanent institutions. For instance, the camps of the International Voluntary Service developed under the leadership of Pierre Ceresole have been in existence for about eighteen years. They show that many youth can be appealed to for constructive service to their country in time of peace as well as of war; and that this appeal can be based not only on love of one's country but also on respect for humanity as a whole, and belief in a world community that knows neither frontiers nor barriers of race or religion. Without flags, marching, martial music, and other emotional appeals that accompany military service, young men and young women will voluntarily undergo toil and hardships similar to those experienced by soldiers in military service in time of peace and war, in order to demonstrate their desire for friendly relations with other countries of the world.

These camps of the International Voluntary Service are a "moral equivalent of war" in the sense that William James used the term; that is, an opportunity for young men and young women to work for an ideal which is supernational and at the same time satisfy their natural desire for adventure, dangerous living, and the surmounting of obstacles. Instead of slaughtering individuals they can battle fires, avalanches, floods, and other forces of nature. These camps of the International Voluntary Service have not enrolled a large number of young men and women, but they are significant because in a time of intense nationalism they have provided an opportunity at least for a few people, who in no sense have lost their natural love for their native land, to devote themselves to the ideal of a world community.

The Bulgarian labor service, which was established in 1920 and, so far as is known, is the oldest compulsory labor service in existence, demonstrates that an institution of this type can provide worthwhile experience for youth while carrying on work projects in a country over a long period of years. The Bulgarian service also shows how an economically backward country can greatly improve its trails, roads, and railroads, by using the labor of the young men who would otherwise be unemployed.

The National Union of Swiss Students has planned and administered, since 1925, the most extensive system of camps for students existing today. These projects show that camps are an excellent method of providing students with opportunities to become acquainted with conditions in economically backward areas and thus to supplement academic work at colleges and universities by practical experience in the summer. At the same time, these camps, by permitting students from other countries to enroll, provide a practical way of bringing together young people of different nationalities. The results of these projects are somewhat similar to those of the International Voluntary Service, although they have not been motivated by a pacifist ideology.

The camps for unemployed, which were first organized and subsidized by the Swiss government in 1933, demonstrate how a democratic country can utilize private organizations for the development of labor camps and yet stimulate and preserve local initiative. The Swiss camps also suggest the possibilities of adapting the camp program to the individual needs and interests of the volunteers. Unlike Germany, where youth spend several months in labor camps of about the same type, Switzerland provides specialized programs of training and education to prepare the young men for jobs known to be available.

The camps in Germany before Hitler came into power, while well organized and efficiently administered, show clearly that caring for youth in camps for a period of time is not a complete solution of the youth problem. Young people must be provided with something more than the temporary type of employment found in a camp, however fine the experience offered may be at the time. While German young people were becoming depressed and demoralized because they had neither work nor a satisfying place in society, the politically divided

Reichstag debated, split into numerous factions, temporized, and was unable to take definite steps to help all the youth. As a result, even the youth who benefited from camp experience while they were there tended, after returning to their home communities, to follow extremists who promised better conditions.

The camps in Germany before Hitler also demonstrate that it is possible to utilize the time spent in labor service as an orientation period, when young people who are thinking of going on to colleges or universities when there is already a surplus of "intellectuals" may be directed into other types of training programs for other fields of activity. Nevertheless, these pre-Hitler camps clearly show that, however successful projects of this type may be, they do not solve the problem, if, after leaving the camps, the young people return to the same communities and again are unemployed.

The labor service in Germany under National Socialism strikingly demonstrates that, however democratic in their origin camps may be, they can be taken over and immediately transformed into effective propaganda institutions for the extremes of authoritarianism. The youth in camps are isolated from families, schools, churches—from any traditional influences. Then, too, many who go into the camps for unemployed are discontented, dissatisfied, or thwarted. Since many of them are without specific interests and goals, or have been prevented by circumstances from achieving any they might have had, they tend to welcome leadership that supplies, or promises to supply, these lacks for them.

The German camps under Hitler also demonstrate that while in other countries it is possible for such camps to provide democratic education, those in Germany are organized to prepare young men and young women for an authoritarian regime by minimizing the importance of the individual in the development of a mass program of regimentation.

While not agreeing with the aims or approving of the results of the system of camps in Germany, it must be admitted that they have developed a comprehensive selection and training program for the personnel in charge of the labor service. If camps are to be efficiently administered, and are to contribute materially to the training and educational experience of the enrollees, the personnel must

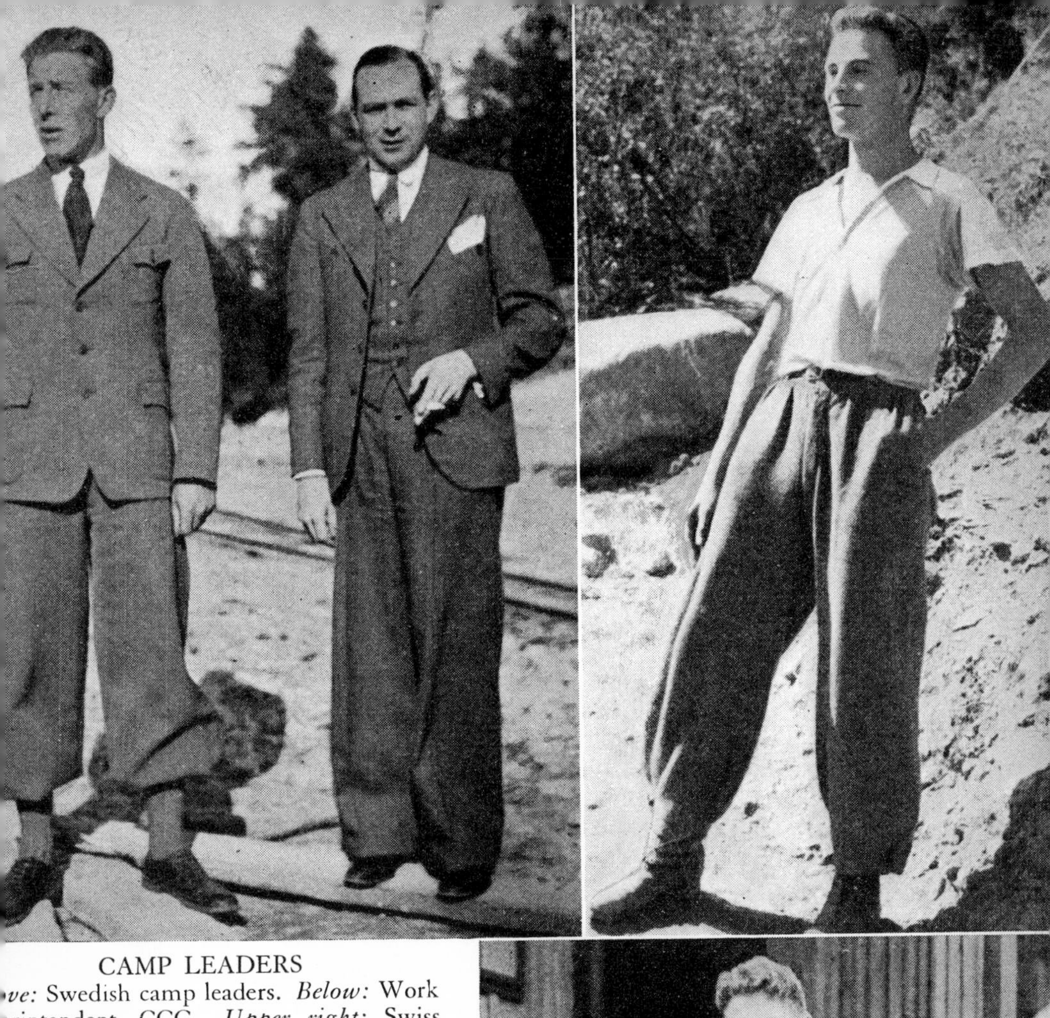

CAMP LEADERS

ve: Swedish camp leaders. *Below:* Work
erintendent, CCC. *Upper right:* Swiss
lent camp leader. *Right:* Pre-Hitler Aus-
n camp leader

CAMP LEADER

Left:

Robert Fechner, rector of CCC (with a Colorado commander. *Abou* Negro supervisor, N *Below:* Nazi labor ice leader Konst Hierl talks to an rollee

be carefully selected, specially trained, and given some degree of security in their work. The National Socialist labor camps also demonstrate the advantages of concentrating administrative responsibility in the central and district headquarters as well as in the camps themselves.

The results of the system of camps in Austria, which has now been coordinated with the National Socialist Labor Service, will soon be like those of the National Socialist camps. Before her conquest by Germany, however, Austria's system of camps had demonstrated that it is possible to build low-cost houses or operate government monopolies with the assistance of unemployed youth. While this is not to be recommended if it competes with private labor, it does demonstrate that unemployed youth can be used to assist skilled workers on construction and operation projects.

The English projects show that in a country where an adequate system has been developed for the collection and dissemination, at periodic intervals, of information on vocational opportunities and trends, it is possible to develop various types of projects and camps to train and prepare men and women for jobs that actually exist, and then to place them in work for which they have been trained. The British experience with young unemployed also demonstrates that for a government to meet adequately the individual needs of youth, a variety of projects and schemes is necessary.

The results of the systems of camps in the Scandinavian countries are similar in many respects to those in England and Switzerland. These camps show that where complete information on job opportunities and trends in occupations is available, it is possible to develop a system of camps that train men for specific jobs. The work projects of these camps also demonstrate that folk schools, recreation centers, and similar projects can be developed with unemployed youth and, judging from available evidence, need not compete with regular labor.

A study of the labor service in Poland shows how a project started for the relief of unemployed youth, largely at the suggestion of a former Minister of Social Welfare, can by gradual steps come under the influence of army officers and finally be made a part of the military training program of the country.

The camps in Czechoslovakia before the Munich Pact proved that it is possible to provide practical training for citizenship in a democratic state through a system of camps, by permitting the participants in the camps to have a large measure of self-government. By actually experiencing in their own organizations some of the responsibilities of a self-governing community, youth learn how to become responsible citizens in a democratic state. One of the strongest arguments against military control of the camps, if they are to train the young people for life in a democratic community, is that military officers usually forbid, as "subversive to command," organization of the participants for self-government or self-expression. While this type of restriction, as imposed by military officers, may be necessary in strictly military organizations, it can scarcely be justified in civilian camps in time of peace. There are, of course, notable instances where military officers have permitted the young men to take considerable responsibility for the formulation and enforcement of rules of conduct for camp members, as in the instance of the organization of the Junior Safety Council in the CCC camps, and as a result morale is better and the enrollees gain infinitely more from their experience.

The experiences with camps in the Netherlands, like those in Switzerland and Czechoslovakia, show that it is possible for private organizations (in this instance religious ones) to take considerable responsibility for the labor camps. The Netherlands camps also demonstrate that it is possible to provide leisure programs that consider social, economic, and religious problems. The most important results of the camps in the Netherlands are said to be an increased knowledge of and respect for the Christian religion, and greater awareness of the problems of society.

Labor camps do not appeal to young women as much as they do to young men, and it is difficult to find work projects and qualified leaders for women's camps. On the whole, camps for women have not been so successful as have those for men. This has been due to insufficient funds, a feeling that first consideration should be given to the projects for men, and the fact that camp programs are not as well adapted to young women as to young men.

CAMP LEADERS

ve:

're-Hitler camp
der, Northern Ger-
ny

ht:

Camp commander
l his assistant, CCC,
ssachusetts

w:

're-Hitler Austrian
men camp leaders

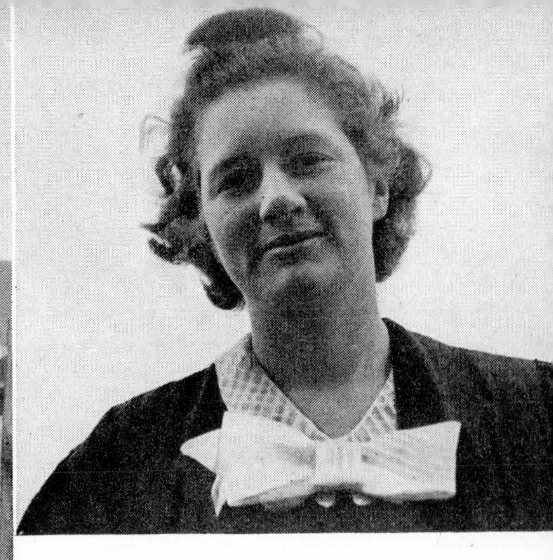

CAMP LEADERS

Above:

Supervisor of a girls resident cer in the United States National Youth A ministration

Left:

Pre-Hitler Austrian district leader

Below:

Supervisor of a boys NYA resident c ter, United States

Camps in Authoritarian and Democratic Countries

The camps for unemployed may be roughly classified as those organized in authoritarian and semiauthoritarian countries, which tend to be highly centralized, and those organized in democratic countries, which tend to be decentralized.

Compulsion

In authoritarian countries such as Germany and Bulgaria, the labor camps are compulsory for all young men and for some young women. On the other hand, the camps in the democracies, for example Switzerland and the Scandinavian countries, are voluntary. In the latter countries all young men and women are not forced to go into the camps, for it is felt that all will not benefit from exactly the same type of experience. Instead, it is maintained that each individual should be given careful consideration, and a plan worked out for him in accordance with his interests, needs, and experience.

Education

In the authoritarian states the camps are usually used to further the definite nationalistic aims which characterize these regimes. The full force of the propaganda machines is therefore loosed on the young men and young women while they are participating in the camp program. In the democratic countries, the educational program tends to reflect the interests of the various organizations responsible for the camps or the various points of view that exist in the country as a whole.

Permanency

The authoritarian countries having camp systems tend to consider these as a permanent and distinct part of their government program, whereas most of the democratic countries look upon the camps as agencies planned and established in a time of emergency to provide satisfactory work, living conditions, and educational experience for a generation of youth who might otherwise suffer the demoralizing experience of long months, or even years, of unemployment. There is a tendency on the part of democratic countries to feel that, if the camps are to be made permanent, they should be coordinated with the established educational and employment agencies, and thus become an integrated part of a wide and varied training program for youth.

Personnel

In both the authoritarian and democratic countries where the camps are permanent it has been possible to develop a selection and training procedure that provides well-qualified individuals for the work. Of course, in the selection of these individuals in authoritarian countries their political loyalities and allegiances are usually of paramount importance. Moreover, to achieve the aims of camps in authoritarian countries, the personnel is in general more efficient than that in the camps in democratic countries, where the positions on the camp staffs are often looked upon as stopgaps for the unemployed, to be abandoned as soon as more permanent jobs are available elsewhere.

Militarism

The authoritarian countries tend to consider their camps as premilitary or military training centers. The atmosphere of the camps and their programs are similar in many respects to those of army camps. The democracies, however, usually keep their labor services civilian in character and atmosphere, and separate and differentiate them from the military organizations by administering them through departments of social welfare or labor.

Centralization

In authoritarian states there is the tendency to centralize authority and to make the systems of camps dependent almost entirely on one central government headquarters. The subordinate officials are responsible to the central office and are given detailed and usually rigid instructions concerning how the camps are to be conducted. In the democratic countries the authority for the camps is decentralized and an attempt is made to provide labor service for unemployed youth by utilizing such organizations as already exist. Frequently the private organizations have first developed the camps with their own funds. Then, as the numbers of unemployed have increased, the central government has assisted them with substantial grants, but has left to the private organizations a large part of the responsibility for the development and administration of the camp program.

Work Projects

In the authoritarian states the work projects are frequently intended to increase the military efficiency of the country. The projects therefore undertake to provide additional farm land to make the country self-sufficient, in so far as food products are concerned, to harvest crops, or to construct roads, trails, and fortifications which can be used in time of war. In democratic countries the work projects generally provide vocational training opportunities for the participants, and include the building of schools, athletic fields, recreational centers, ski and hiking trails, and the conservation of natural resources.

Conclusion

Labor camps have been in existence since 1920. They now seem to be a permanent part of the world program for the care and training of youth. The labor camps developed after the depression that provided simply work, food, clothing, and shelter justified their existence only so long as there were unemployed youth and worthwhile public works projects which did not interfere with ordinary labor. As the immediate emergency passed and the camps developed, however, those which provided basic human needs and also performed valuable work, placed greater and greater emphasis on the training aspects of the camps. As the educational values of the camps have increased they have tended to become more permanent.

In the United States it seems to be generally admitted that the work done by the CCC enrollees could be performed by contract labor at about two-thirds the present cost. It would seem then that, so far as the United States is concerned and also many of the other democratic countries, the camps cannot be justified alone on the basis of the work performed. To be justified the camp experience must also contribute considerably to the preparation of the young man or young woman for the life which he or she must lead after leaving the camp. While the camps should continue to emphasize productive work under conditions similar to those in private industry, "in planning for the future of these camps it is imperative that their objectives be made ever more clear as primarily educational—the development of American youth—and secondarily, the conservation of our natural resources." [1]

The labor camp, which is becoming a permanent institution in many countries, combines work and education and bridges the gap between the time youth leave school and the time they are able to find relatively permanent employment. Functioning in this way, the labor camp is probably best adapted to the young man of limited social and economic background who has not adjusted well to the established school system.

Thus far the labor camps in the United States, as well as in many of the foreign countries, have been continued as independent agencies. As a new social institution the camps should be given ample opportunity to develop methods and techniques without the standardizing influence of established training and educational institutions. Nevertheless, if the camps are to be established on a permanent basis, they should be carefully integrated with educational, vocational, employment, and adjustment activities of institutions already in existence.

[1] Report of the Committee on Education at Fifty-fifth Annual Convention of the American Federation of Labor, Atlantic City, 1935, p. 488.

Acknowledgment for Illustrations

The author is indebted to Dr. Richard Gothe for editing and placing the photographs in this book. While some of the illustrations are not of the highest quality they are a type of documentation that it was felt should be included. Credit for the photographs should be given as follows:

Page

iv—Polish Labor Service
xv—Kenneth Holland
xvi—*Upper left,* Kenneth Holland; *upper right,* National Socialist Labor Service; *left,* American Friends Service Committee; *below,* Kenneth Holland
xvii—Kenneth Holland
xviii—*Left,* Charles Whitaker; *above,* Kenneth Holland; *below,* Polish Labor Service
xix—*Above,* Kenneth Holland; *right,* Kenneth Holland; *below,* United States Army Signal Corps
5—*Above,* Kenneth Holland; *right,* Kenneth Holland; *below,* Charles Whitaker
6—*Above,* Kenneth Holland; *left,* Kenneth Holland; *below,* Swiss Center for Voluntary Work Service
11—*Above,* Ministry of Social Affairs, Netherlands; *right,* Kenneth Holland; *below,* Kenneth Holland
12—*Above,* Austrian Labor Service; *left,* Kenneth Holland; *below,* Kenneth Holland
15—*Above,* Ministry of Labor, Great Britain; *right,* Richard Gothe; *below,* National Socialist Labor Service
16—*Above,* Kenneth Holland; *left,* Civilian Conservation Corps; *below,* G. F. Jewett
25—*Above,* and *below,* International Student Service; *right,* American Friends Service Committee
26—*Left,* and *below,* American Friends Service Committee
35—*Above,* Kenneth Holland; *upper right* and *right,* Kenneth Holland; *below,* American Friends Service Committee
45—Bulgarian Labor Service
46—Bulgarian Labor Service
53—Kenneth Holland
54—Kenneth Holland
59—*Above,* Swiss Center for Voluntary Work Service; *right,* Kenneth Holland; *below,* Swiss Center for Voluntary Work Service
60—Swiss Center for Voluntary Work Service
73—*Above,* Richard Gothe; *upper right,* Kenneth Holland; *right,* Richard Gothe
74—Richard Gothe
79—Richard Gothe
80—Richard Gothe
85—*Above,* Richard Gothe; *right,* Kenneth Holland; *below,* Richard Gothe
86—*Above,* Richard Gothe; *left,* Kenneth Holland; *below,* Richard Gothe
99—*Above,* Kenneth Holland; *right,* National Socialist Labor Service; *below,* National Socialist Labor Service

100—*Left,* National Socialist Labor Service; *above,* Kenneth Holland; *below,* National Socialist Labor Service
109—*Above,* Charles Whitaker; *right,* Charles Whitaker; *below,* National Socialist Labor Service
110—*Above,* Charles Whitaker; *left,* Charles Whitaker; *below,* National Socialist Labor Service
123—*Above,* Charles Whitaker; *right,* National Socialist Labor Service; *below,* Charles Whitaker
124—*Left,* National Socialist Labor Service; *above,* Kenneth Holland; *below,* National Socialist Labor Service
133—*Above,* Austrian Labor Service; *right,* Kenneth Holland; *below,* Austrian Labor Service
134—*Above,* Austrian Labor Service; *left,* Kenneth Holland; *below,* Kenneth Holland
141—*Above,* Kenneth Holland; *right,* Austrian Labor Service; *below,* Kenneth Holland
142—*Above,* Austrian Labor Service; *left,* Austrian Labor Service; *below,* Kenneth Holland
157—*Above* and *below,* Ministry of Labor, Great Britain; *right,* Charles Whitaker
158—*Above,* Ministry of Labor, Great Britain; *left,* Charles Whitaker; *below,* Charles Whitaker
169—*Above,* Ministry of Labor, Great Britain; *right,* Charles Whitaker; *below,* Charles Whitaker
170—*Above,* Ministry of Labor, Great Britain; *left,* Charles Whitaker; *below,* Charles Whitaker
189—Kenneth Holland
190—Norwegian Legation, Washington, D. C.
197—Kenneth Holland
198—Norwegian Legation, Washington, D. C.
215—*Above,* Polish Labor Service; *below* and *right,* Kenneth Holland
227—Kenneth Holland
228—*Above,* Czechoslovakian Legation, Washington, D. C.; *left,* Kenneth Holland; *below,* Kenneth Holland
237—Kenneth Holland
238—Ministry of Social Affairs, Netherlands
247—*Above* and *below,* Richard Gothe; *right,* National Socialist Labor Service
248—*Left* and *above,* National Socialist Labor Service; *below,* Richard Gothe
257—*Above* and *below,* Richard Gothe; *right,* Kenneth Holland
258—*Left* and *above,* National Socialist Labor Service; *below,* Richard Gothe
271—*Above,* Kenneth Holland; *right,* Richard Gothe; *below,* Civilian Conservation Corps
272—*Above,* Richard Gothe; *left,* American Friends Service Committee; *below,* Civilian Conservation Corps
277—*Above,* American Friends Service Committee; *right,* Civilian Conservation Corps; *below,* Richard Gothe
278—*Left,* Civilian Conservation Corps; *lower left,* Richard Gothe; *below,* National Socialist Labor Service
283—*Above,* Civilian Conservation Corps; left, Swiss Center for Voluntary Work Service; *below,* Kenneth Holland

284—*Upper right* and *middle,* Kenneth Holland; *below,* Civilian Conservation Corps
291—Kenneth Holland
292—*Left,* Civilian Conservation Corps; *above,* Richard Gothe; *below,* National Socialist Labor Service
295—*Above,* Richard Gothe; *right,* Kenneth Holland; *below,* Kenneth Holland
296—*Above,* Richard Gothe; *left,* Kenneth Holland; *below,* Richard Gothe
Outside cover—U. S. Army Signal Corps